Nominated for 3 EISNER AWARDS including
Best New Series and Best Ongoing Series

"For fans of literature (from classics to contemporary) this series is worth a read. . . .
The Unwritten is **a roller-coaster ride through a library, weaving famous authors and characters into a tale of mystery** that is at once oddly familiar yet highly original."–
USA TODAY

"*The Unwritten* makes a leap from being just a promising new Vertigo title to being on track to become the best ongoing Vertigo book since *Sandman*. And given that Vertigo has delivered the likes of *100 Bullets*, *Y: The Last Man* and *Fables*... that's saying something."
–THE A.V. CLUB

the Unwritten
THE UNWRITTEN FABLES

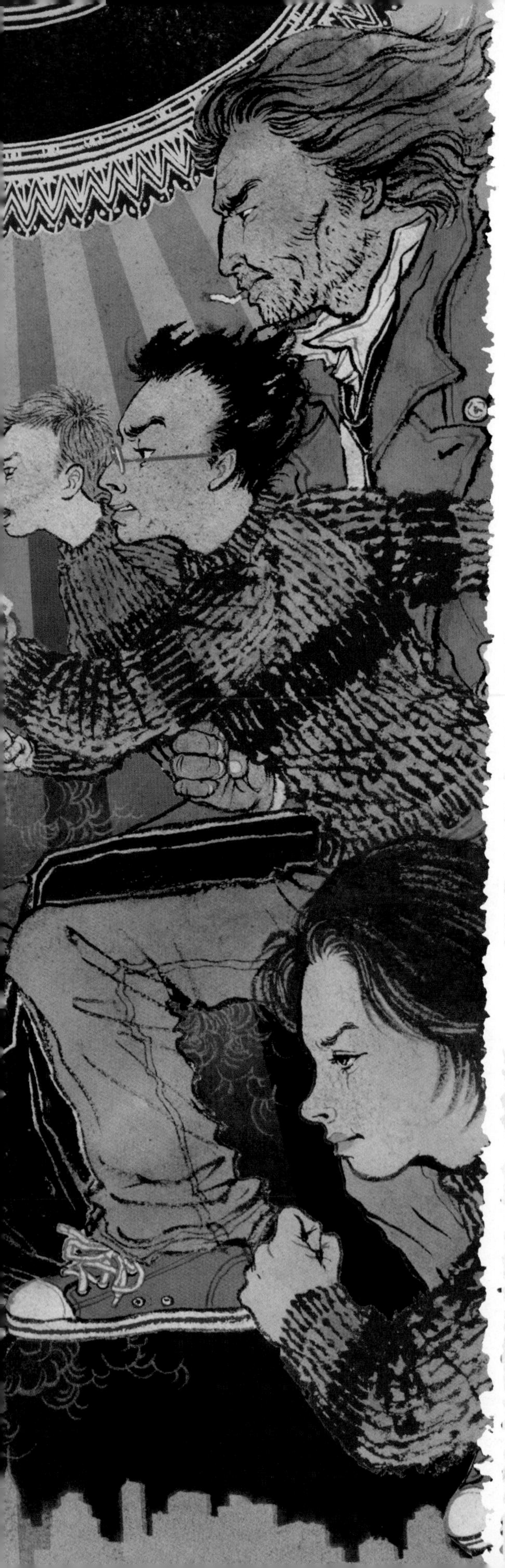

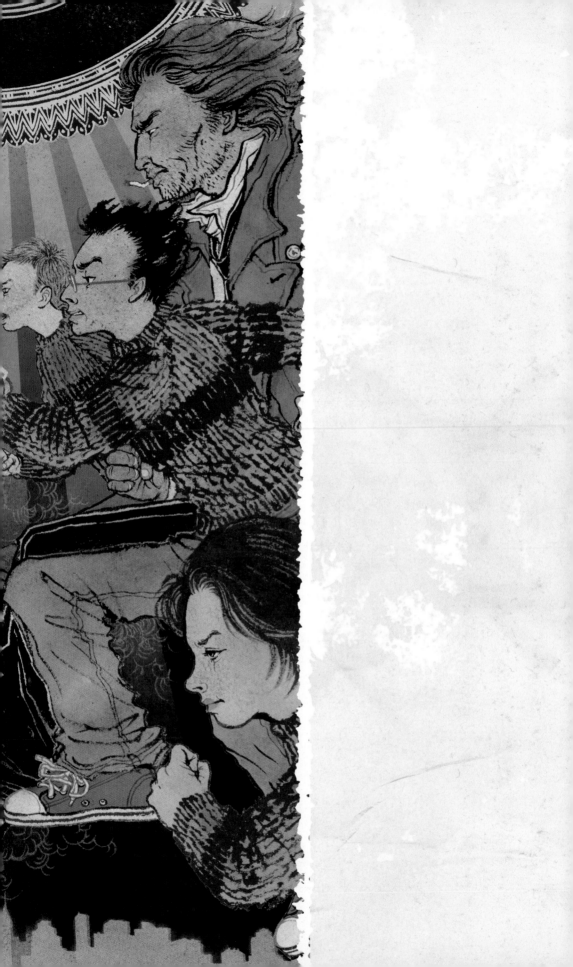

the Unwritten

THE UNWRITTEN FABLES

Mike Carey Bill Willingham Writers
Peter Gross Mark Buckingham Artists
Steve Leialoha – issue #50 Inaki Miranda – issue #50, #52
Russ Braun – #51 Dean Ormston – #52, #53, #54 Finishes
Chris Chuckry Colorist Todd Klein Letterer
Yuko Shimizu Cover Artist
THE UNWRITTEN created by Pete Gross and Mike Carey FABLES created by Bill Willingham

Greg Lockard Editor – Original Series
Rowena Yow Editor
Robbin Brosterman Design Director – Books
Louis Prandi Publication Design

Shelly Bond Executive Editor – Vertigo
Hank Kanalz Senior VP – Vertigo & Integrated Publishing

Diane Nelson President
Dan DiDio and Jim Lee Co-Publishers
Geoff Johns Chief Creative Officer
Amit Desai Senior VP – Marketing & Franchise Management
Amy Genkins Senior VP – Business & Legal Affairs
Nairi Gardiner Senior VP – Finance
Jeff Boison VP – Publishing Planning
Mark Chiarello VP – Art Direction & Design
John Cunningham VP – Marketing
Terri Cunningham VP – Editorial Administration
Larry Ganem VP – Talent Relations & Services
Alison Gill Senior VP – Manufacturing & Operations
Jay Kogan VP – Business & Legal Affairs, Publishing
Jack Mahan VP – Business Affairs, Talent
Nick Napolitano VP – Manufacturing Administration
Sue Pohja VP – Book Sales
Fred Ruiz VP – Manufacturing Operations
Courtney Simmons Senior VP – Publicity
Bob Wayne Senior VP – Sales

Library of Congress Cataloging-in-Publication Data

Carey, Mike, 1959- author.
  The Unwritten. Volume 9, The Unwritten Fables / Mike Carey ;
illustrated by Peter Gross and Mark Buckingham.
    pages cm
  ISBN 978-1-4012-4694-5 (paperback)
  1. Graphic novels. I. Gross, Peter, 1958- illustrator. II. Buckingham,
Mark, illustrator. III. Title. IV. Title: Unwritten Fables.
  PN6727.C377U588 2014
  741.5'973 – dc23

THE STORY THUS FAR

Tom Taylor doesn't know which way up his world is. Immortalized as Tommy Taylor, the boy-wizard hero of his father's best-selling novels, he always tried to distance himself from his fictional counterpart – until he met some of the other characters from the books and began to suspect (or maybe to fear) that he might actually **be** Tommy.

Seeking to uncover the secrets of his own origins and nature, Tom clashed with a mysterious cabal whose leader, Pullman, also straddles the line between fiction and reality. Pullman claims to be Cain, the first person whose life was ever destroyed by a story – a story that has made him immortal, very much against his will.

But not all fictional characters become real boys, and not all real people get dragged into fiction. The interface is a creature called Leviathan, which feeds on story and lives symbiotically with humanity.

And Pullman has managed to give Leviathan a mortal wound. Which is bad news for everyone. So Tom is looking for a way to save Leviathan from death and restore normal service to the human collective unconscious.

But his quest has been hijacked by somebody else's quest, as he now finds himself face-to-face with a coven of powerful witches and wizards. Not ones his father wrote, but those from much older stories. In fact, from Fables.

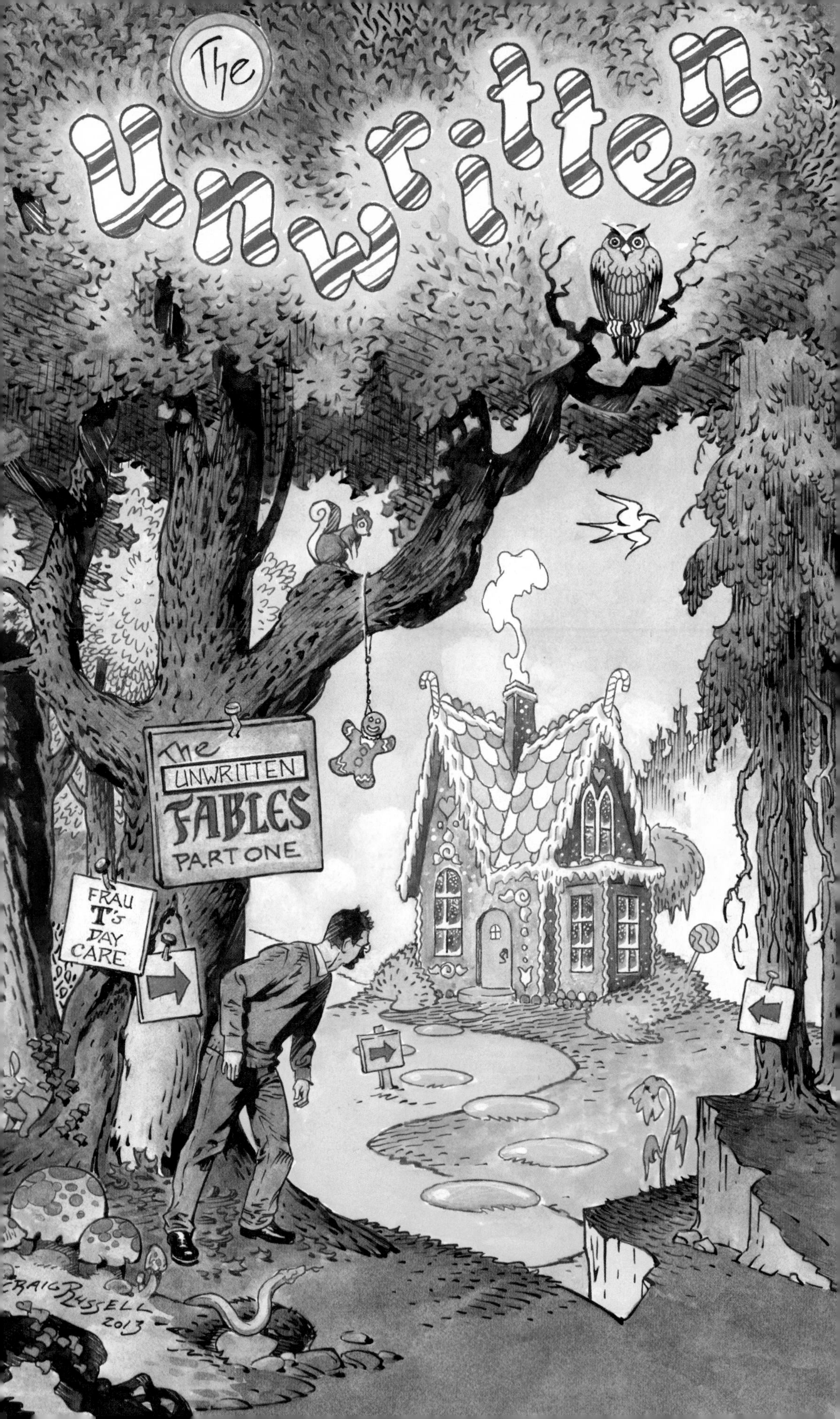
The Unwritten
The UNWRITTEN FABLES PART ONE
FRAU T's DAY CARE
CRAIG RUSSELL 2013

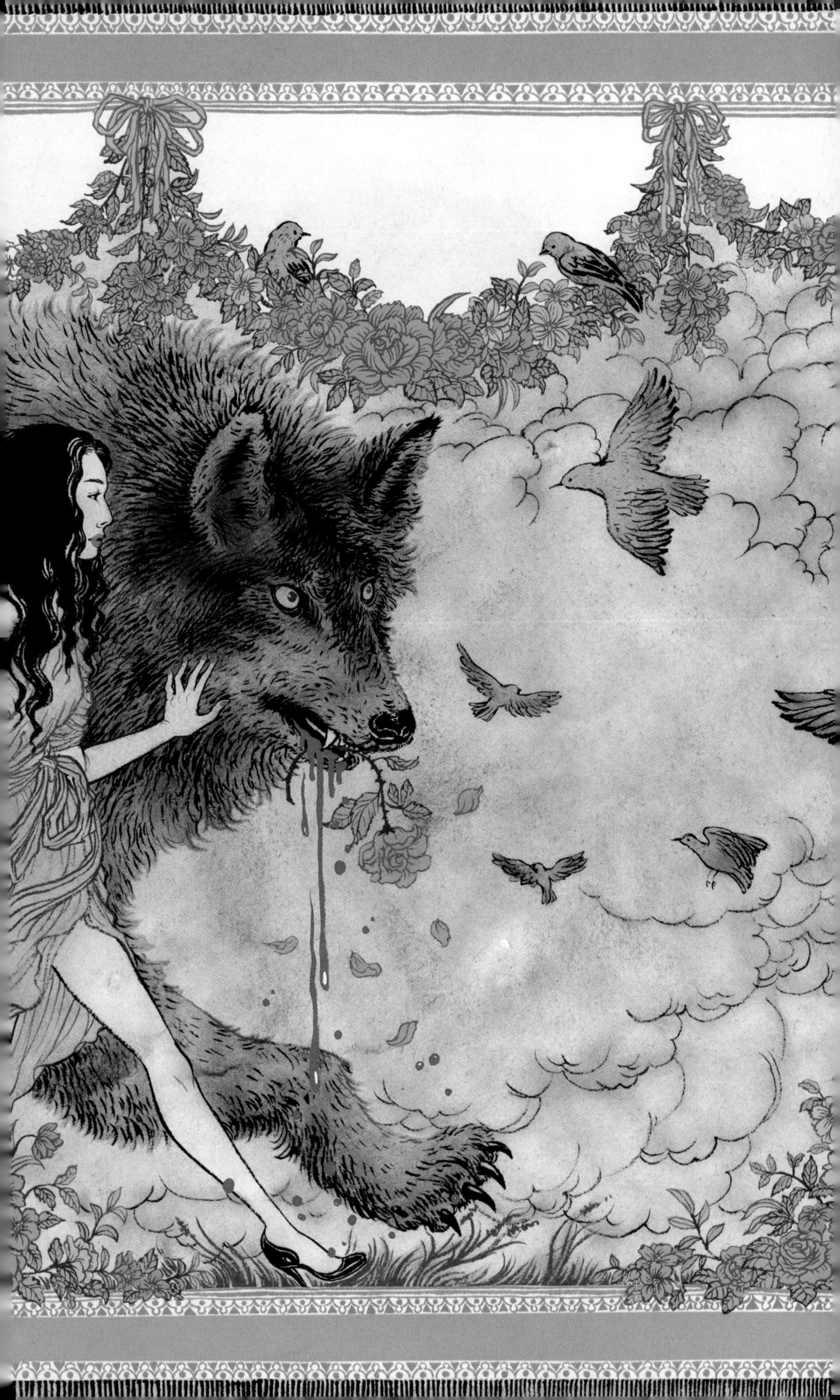

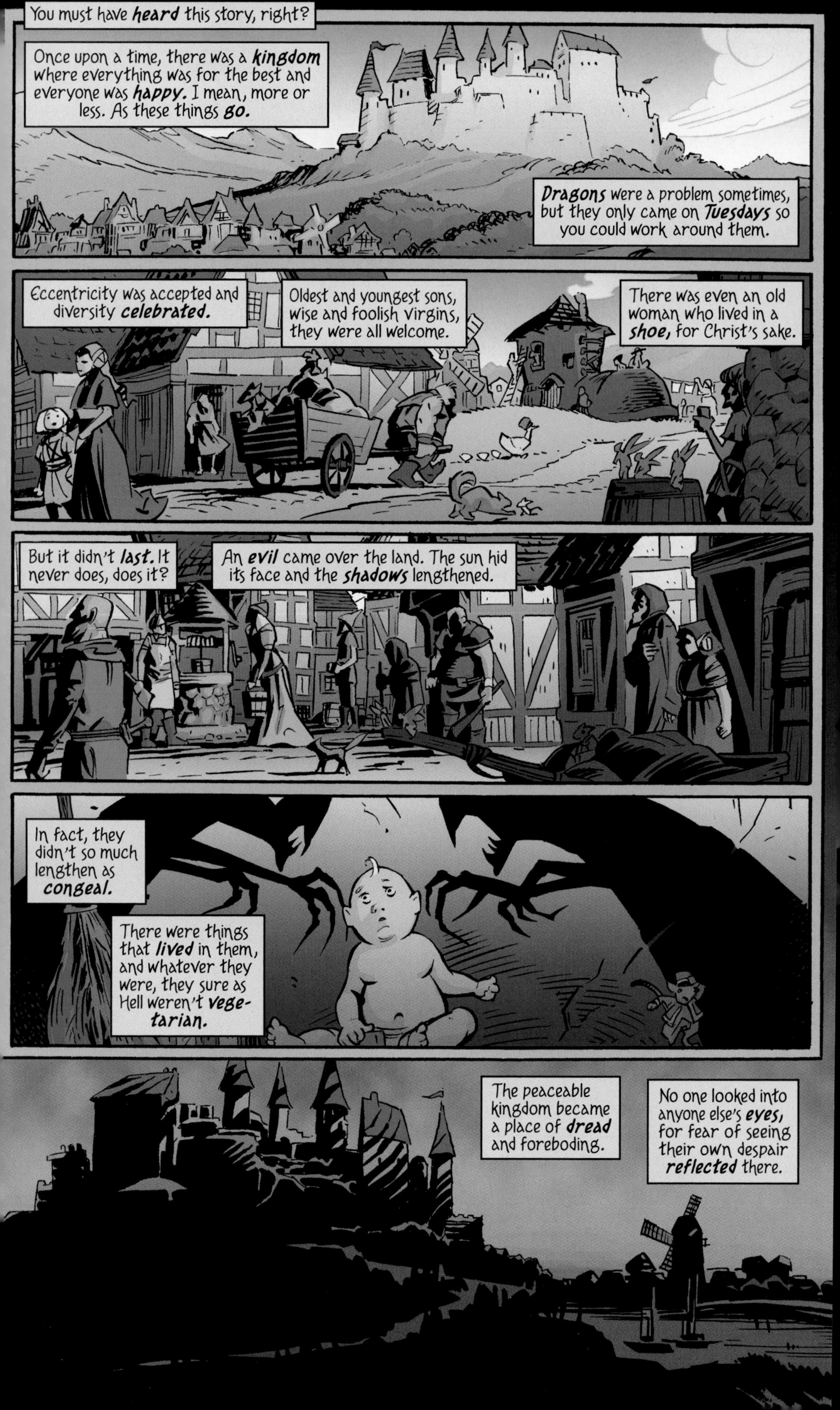
You must have heard this story, right?
Once upon a time, there was a kingdom where everything was for the best and everyone was happy. I mean, more or less. As these things go.
Dragons were a problem sometimes, but they only came on Tuesdays so you could work around them.
Eccentricity was accepted and diversity celebrated.
Oldest and youngest sons, wise and foolish virgins, they were all welcome.
There was even an old woman who lived in a shoe, for Christ's sake.
But it didn't last. It never does, does it?
An evil came over the land. The sun hid its face and the shadows lengthened.
In fact, they didn't so much lengthen as congeal.
There were things that lived in them, and whatever they were, they sure as Hell weren't vege-tarian.
The peaceable kingdom became a place of dread and foreboding.
No one looked into anyone else's eyes, for fear of seeing their own despair reflected there.

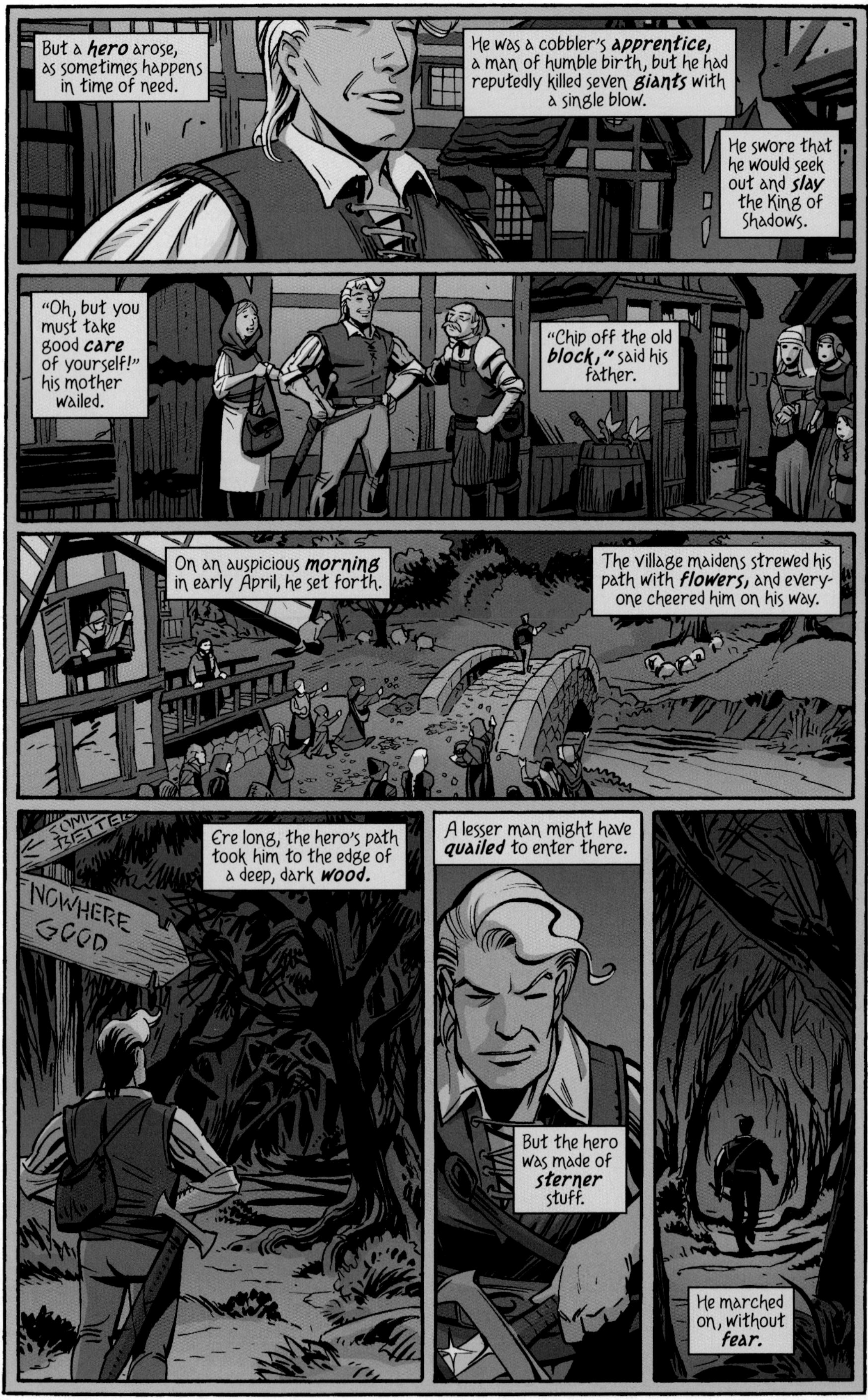

But a **hero** arose, as sometimes happens in time of need.
He was a cobbler's **apprentice,** a man of humble birth, but he had reputedly killed seven **giants** with a single blow.
He swore that he would seek out and **slay** the King of Shadows.
"Oh, but you must take good **care** of yourself!" his mother wailed.
"Chip off the old **block,"** said his father.
On an auspicious **morning** in early April, he set forth.
The village maidens strewed his path with **flowers,** and every-one cheered him on his way.
NOWHERE GOOD
Ere long, the hero's path took him to the edge of a deep, dark **wood.**
A lesser man might have **quailed** to enter there.
But the hero was made of **sterner** stuff.
He marched on, without **fear.**

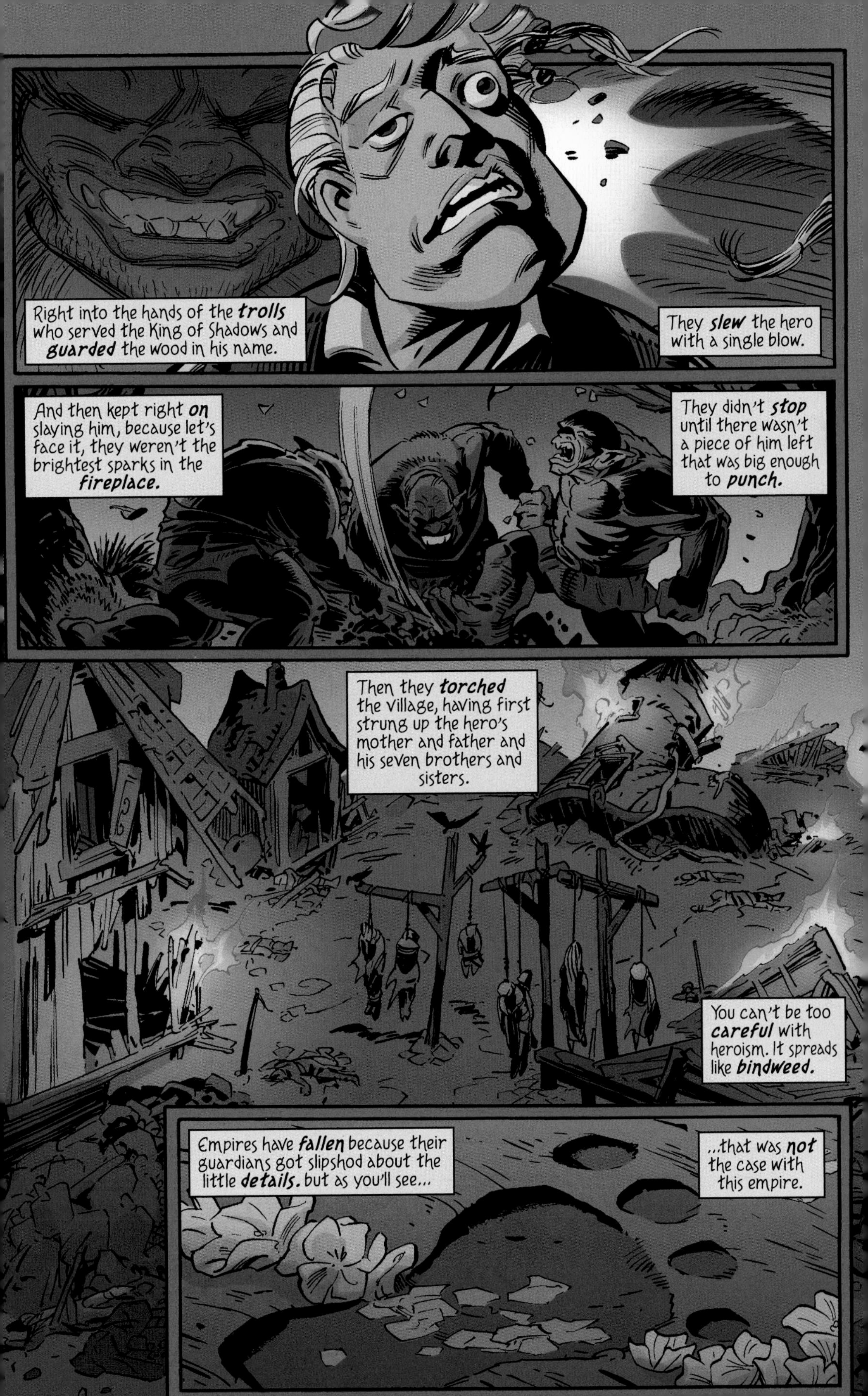
Right into the hands of the trolls who served the King of Shadows and guarded the wood in his name.
They slew the hero with a single blow.
And then kept right on slaying him, because let's face it, they weren't the brightest sparks in the fireplace.
They didn't stop until there wasn't a piece of him left that was big enough to punch.
Then they torched the village, having first strung up the hero's mother and father and his seven brothers and sisters.
You can't be too careful with heroism. It spreads like bindweed.
Empires have fallen because their guardians got slipshod about the little details. but as you'll see...
...that was not the case with this empire.

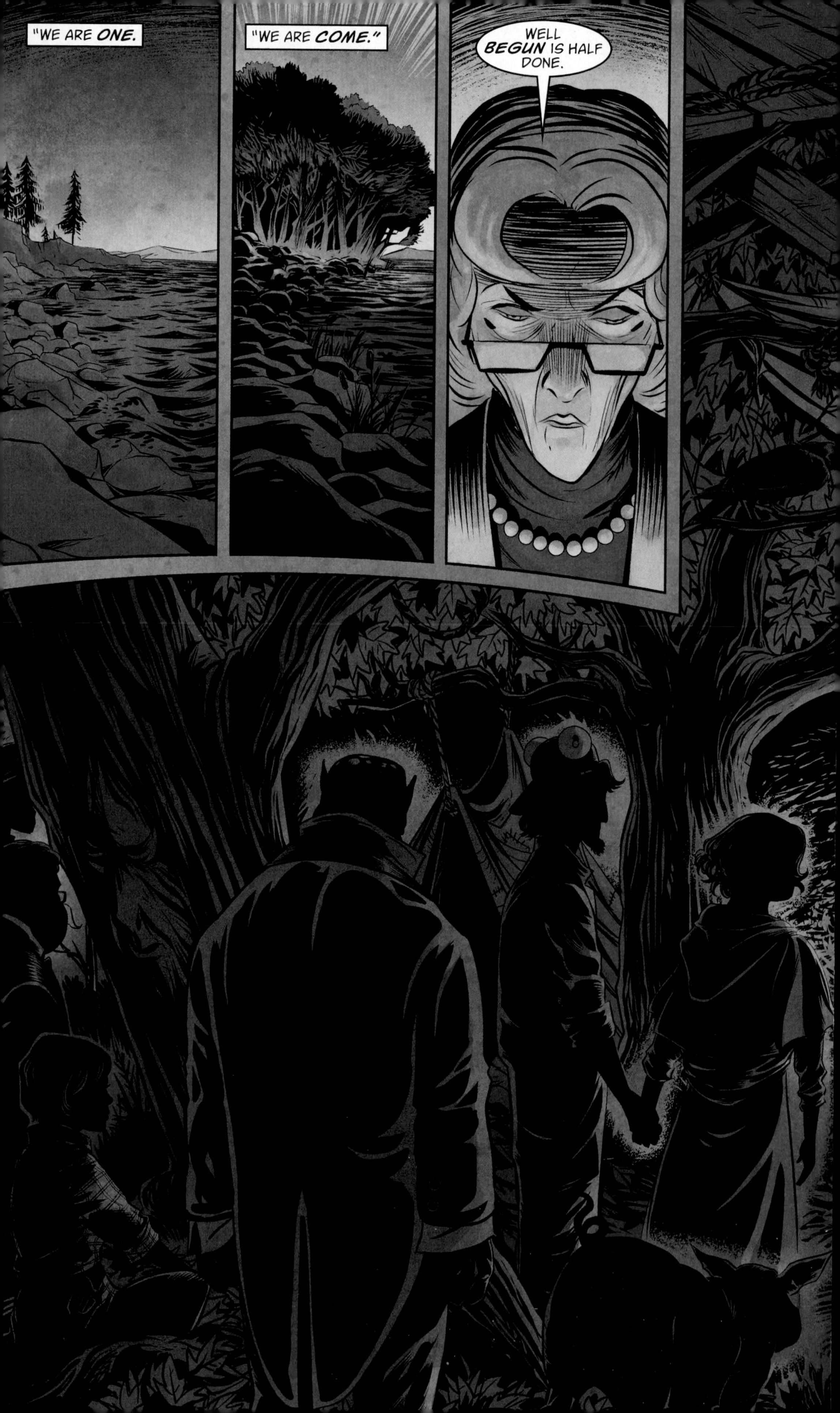
"WE ARE ONE.
"WE ARE COME."
WELL BEGUN IS HALF DONE.

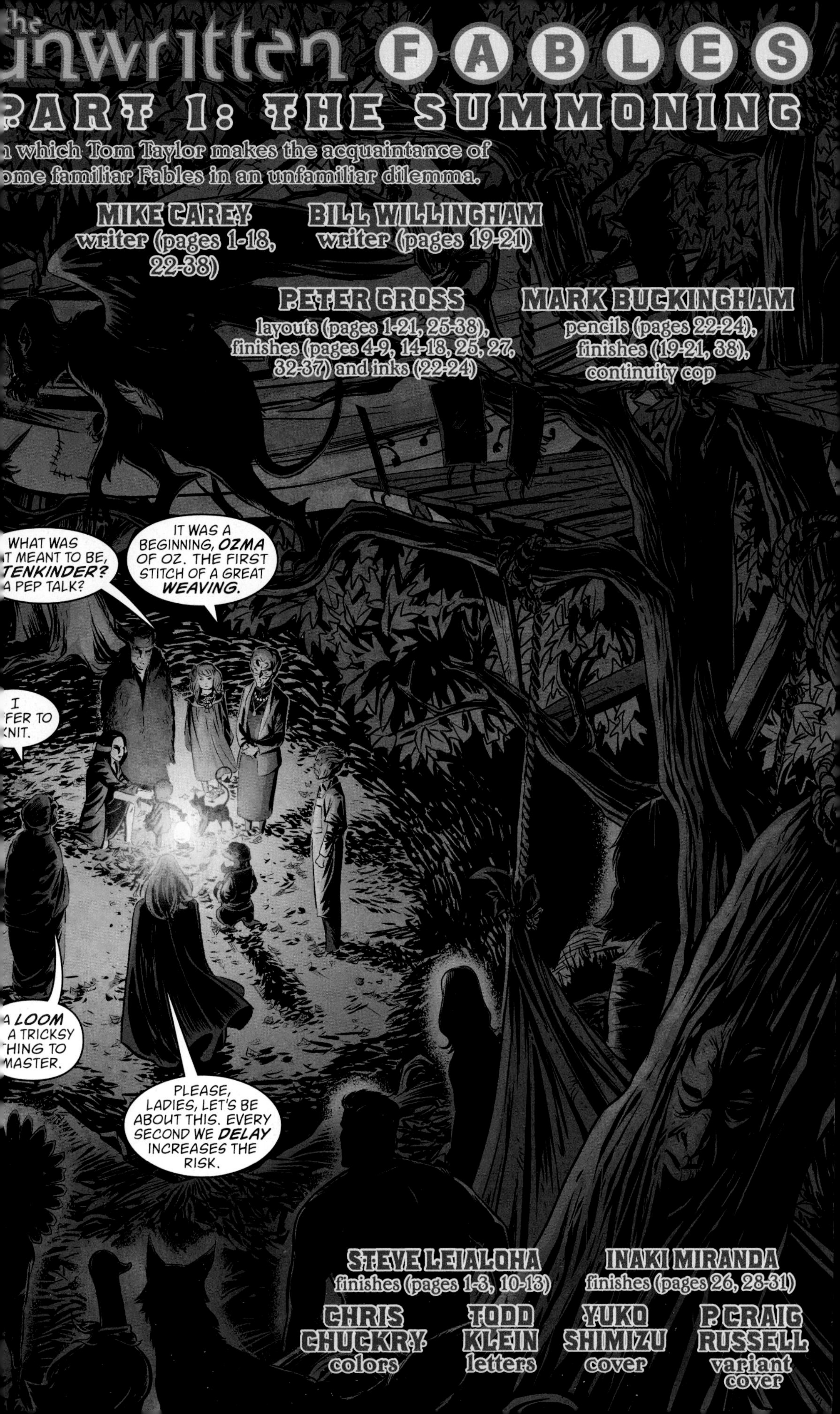
the
nwritten FABLES
PART 1: THE SUMMONING
n which Tom Taylor makes the acquaintance of
ome familiar Fables in an unfamiliar dilemma.
MIKE CAREY
writer (pages 1-18, 22-38)
BILL WILLINGHAM
writer (pages 19-21)
PETER GROSS
layouts (pages 1-21, 25-38), finishes (pages 4-9, 14-18, 25, 27, 32-37) and inks (22-24)
MARK BUCKINGHAM
pencils (pages 22-24), finishes (19-21, 38), continuity cop
WHAT WAS T MEANT TO BE, TENKINDER? A PEP TALK?
IT WAS A BEGINNING, OZMA OF OZ. THE FIRST STITCH OF A GREAT WEAVING.
I FER TO NIT.
A LOOM A TRICKSY HING TO MASTER.
PLEASE, LADIES, LET'S BE ABOUT THIS. EVERY SECOND WE DELAY INCREASES THE RISK.
STEVE LEIALOHA
finishes (pages 1-3, 10-13)
INAKI MIRANDA
finishes (pages 26, 28-31)
CHRIS CHUCKRY
colors
TODD KLEIN
letters
YUKO SHIMIZU
cover
P. CRAIG RUSSELL
variant cover

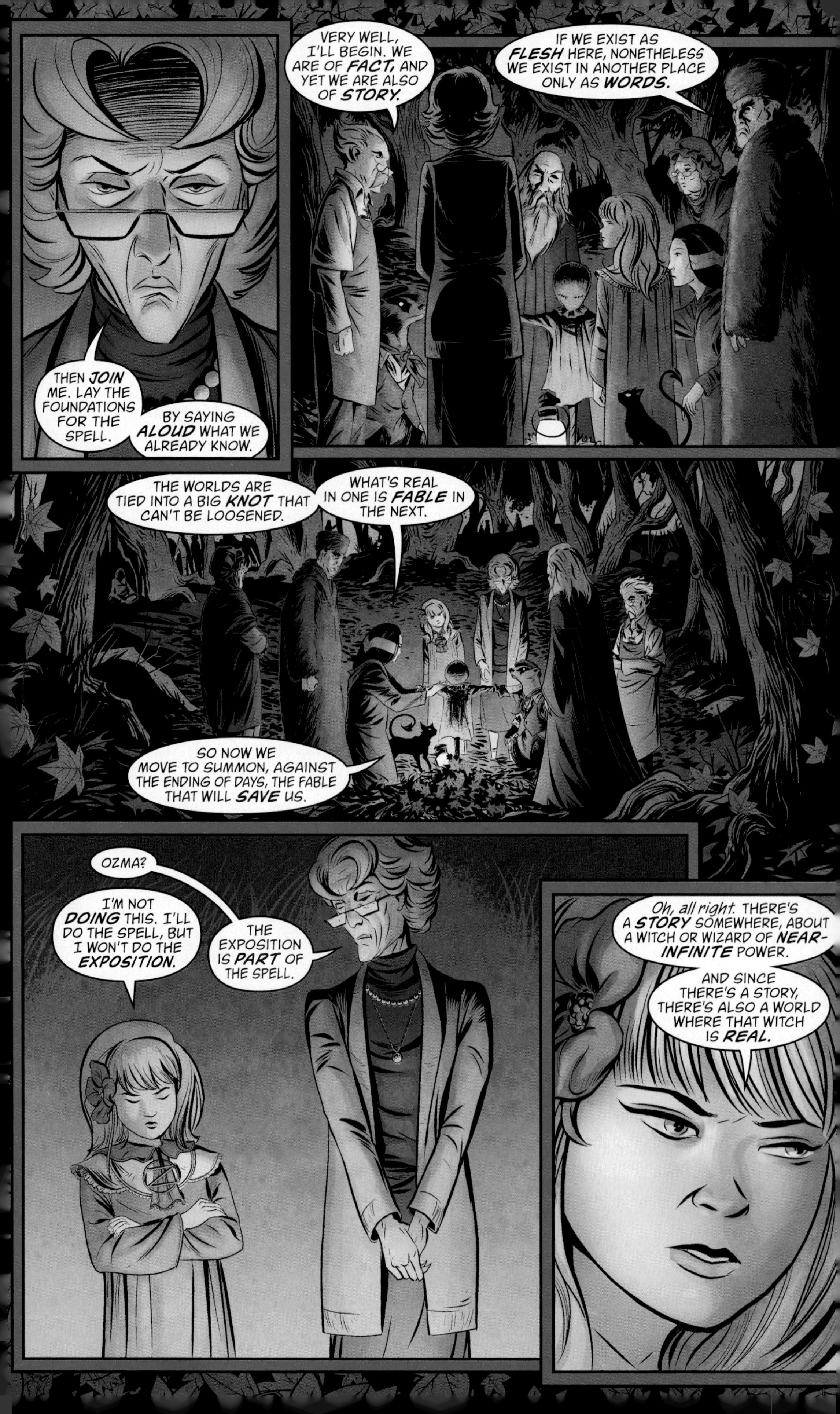

THEN JOIN ME. LAY THE FOUNDATIONS FOR THE SPELL.
BY SAYING ALOUD WHAT WE ALREADY KNOW.
VERY WELL, I'LL BEGIN. WE ARE OF FACT, AND YET WE ARE ALSO OF STORY.
IF WE EXIST AS FLESH HERE, NONETHELESS WE EXIST IN ANOTHER PLACE ONLY AS WORDS.
THE WORLDS ARE TIED INTO A BIG KNOT THAT CAN'T BE LOOSENED.
WHAT'S REAL IN ONE IS FABLE IN THE NEXT.
SO NOW WE MOVE TO SUMMON, AGAINST THE ENDING OF DAYS, THE FABLE THAT WILL SAVE US.
OZMA?
I'M NOT DOING THIS. I'LL DO THE SPELL, BUT I WON'T DO THE EXPOSITION.
THE EXPOSITION IS PART OF THE SPELL.
Oh, all right. THERE'S A STORY SOMEWHERE, ABOUT A WITCH OR WIZARD OF NEAR-INFINITE POWER.
AND SINCE THERE'S A STORY, THERE'S ALSO A WORLD WHERE THAT WITCH IS REAL.

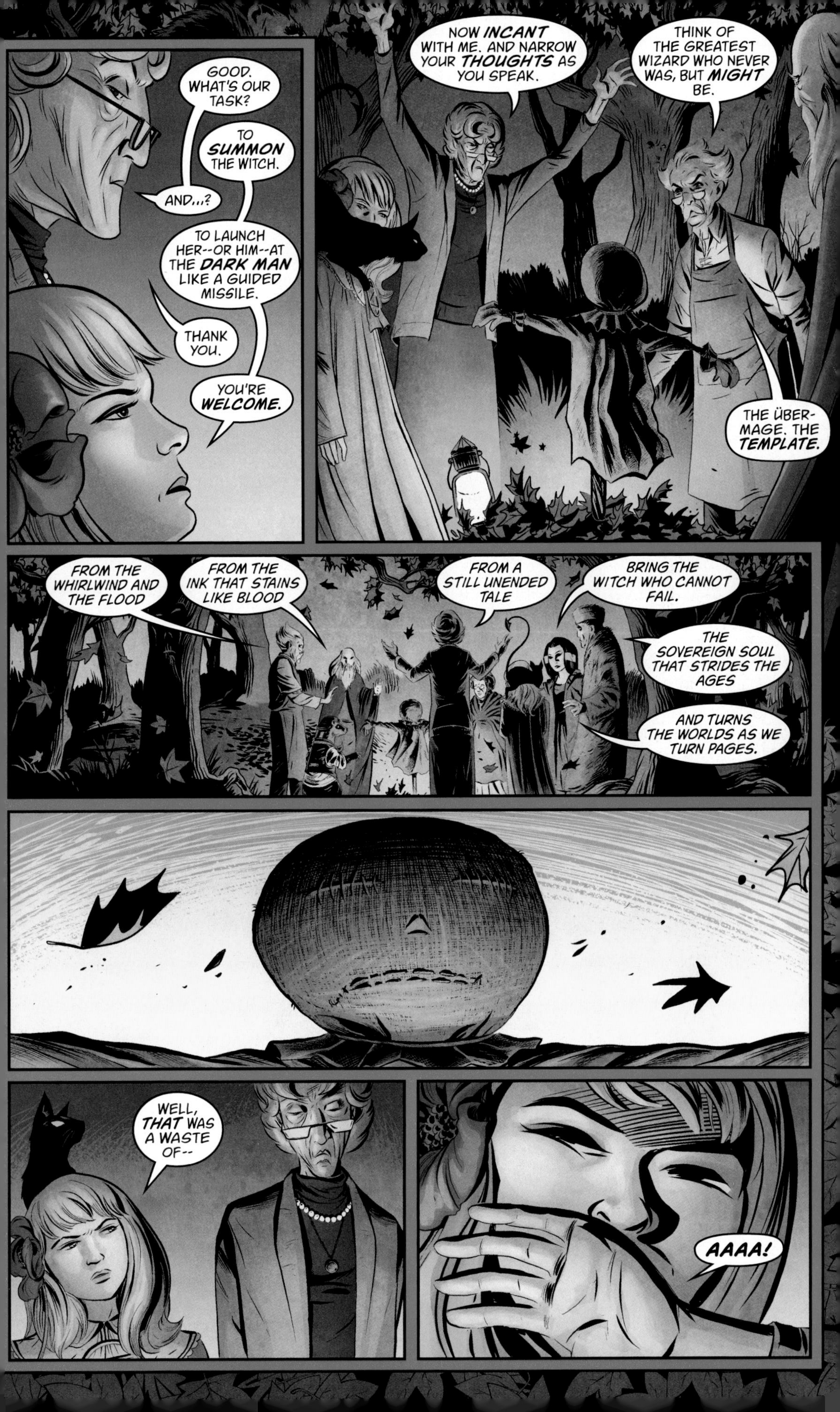

GOOD. WHAT'S OUR TASK?
TO SUMMON THE WITCH.
AND...?
TO LAUNCH HER--OR HIM--AT THE DARK MAN LIKE A GUIDED MISSILE.
THANK YOU.
YOU'RE WELCOME.
NOW INCANT WITH ME. AND NARROW YOUR THOUGHTS AS YOU SPEAK.
THINK OF THE GREATEST WIZARD WHO NEVER WAS, BUT MIGHT BE.
THE ÜBER-MAGE. THE TEMPLATE.
FROM THE WHIRLWIND AND THE FLOOD
FROM THE INK THAT STAINS LIKE BLOOD
FROM A STILL UNENDED TALE
BRING THE WITCH WHO CANNOT FAIL.
THE SOVEREIGN SOUL THAT STRIDES THE AGES
AND TURNS THE WORLDS AS WE TURN PAGES.
WELL, THAT WAS A WASTE OF--
AAAA!

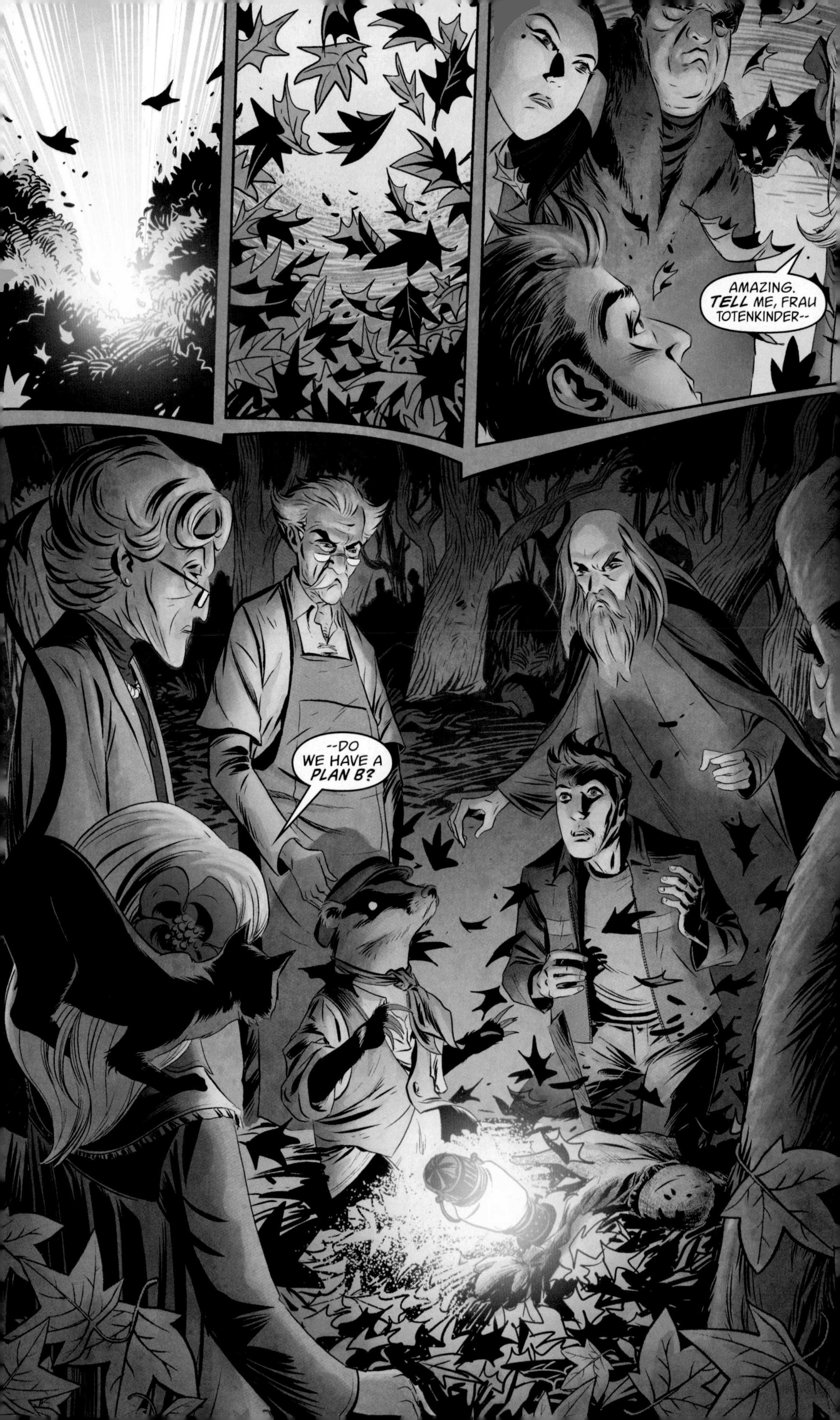
AMAZING. TELL ME, FRAU TOTENKINDER--
--DO WE HAVE A PLAN B?

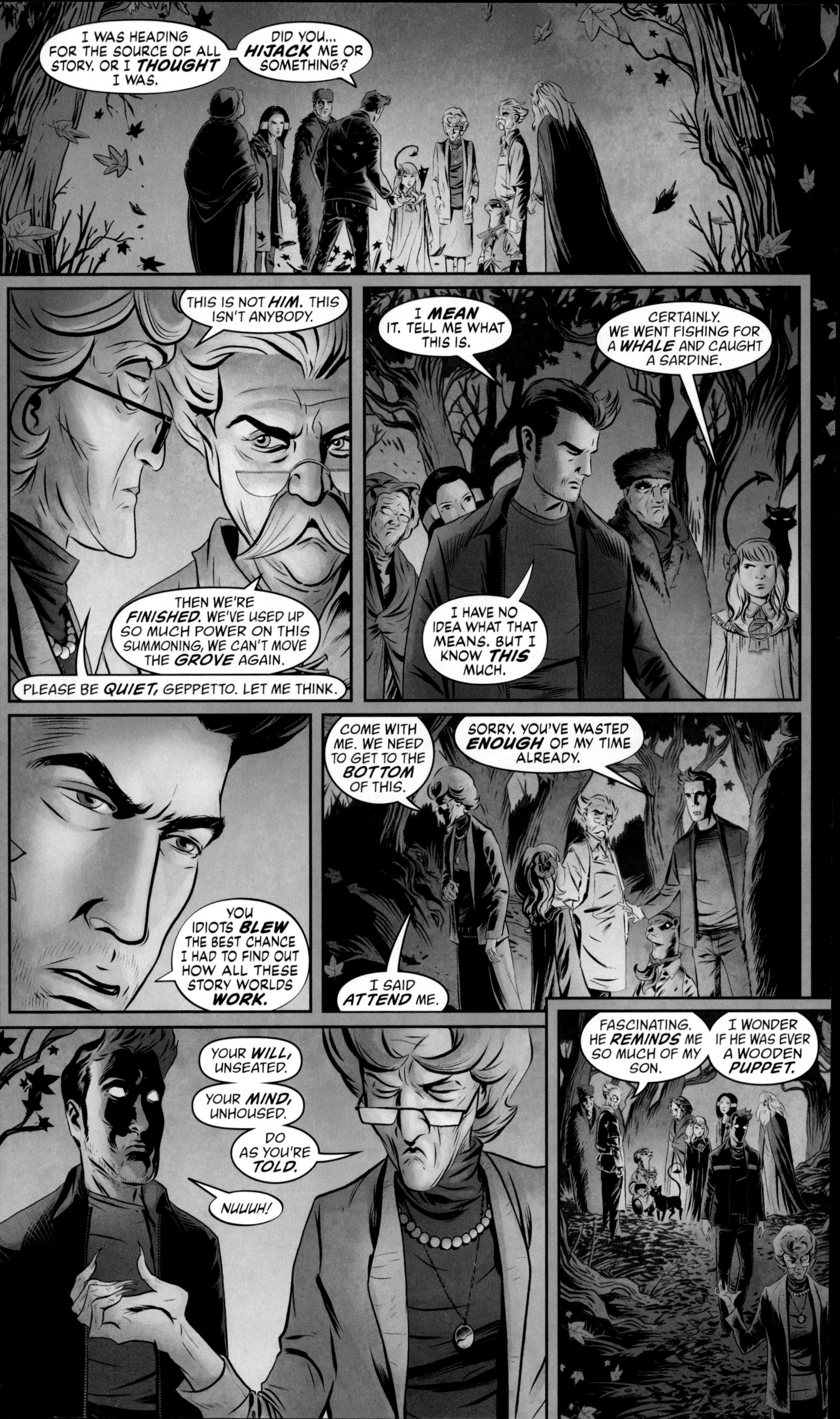
I WAS HEADING FOR THE SOURCE OF ALL STORY. OR I THOUGHT I WAS.
DID YOU... HIJACK ME OR SOMETHING?
THIS IS NOT HIM. THIS ISN'T ANYBODY.
THEN WE'RE FINISHED. WE'VE USED UP SO MUCH POWER ON THIS SUMMONING, WE CAN'T MOVE THE GROVE AGAIN.
PLEASE BE QUIET, GEPPETTO. LET ME THINK.
I MEAN IT. TELL ME WHAT THIS IS.
CERTAINLY. WE WENT FISHING FOR A WHALE AND CAUGHT A SARDINE.
I HAVE NO IDEA WHAT THAT MEANS. BUT I KNOW THIS MUCH.
YOU IDIOTS BLEW THE BEST CHANCE I HAD TO FIND OUT HOW ALL THESE STORY WORLDS WORK.
COME WITH ME. WE NEED TO GET TO THE BOTTOM OF THIS.
SORRY. YOU'VE WASTED ENOUGH OF MY TIME ALREADY.
I SAID ATTEND ME.
YOUR WILL, UNSEATED.
YOUR MIND, UNHOUSED.
DO AS YOU'RE TOLD.
NUUUH!
FASCINATING. HE REMINDS ME SO MUCH OF MY SON.
I WONDER IF HE WAS EVER A WOODEN PUPPET.

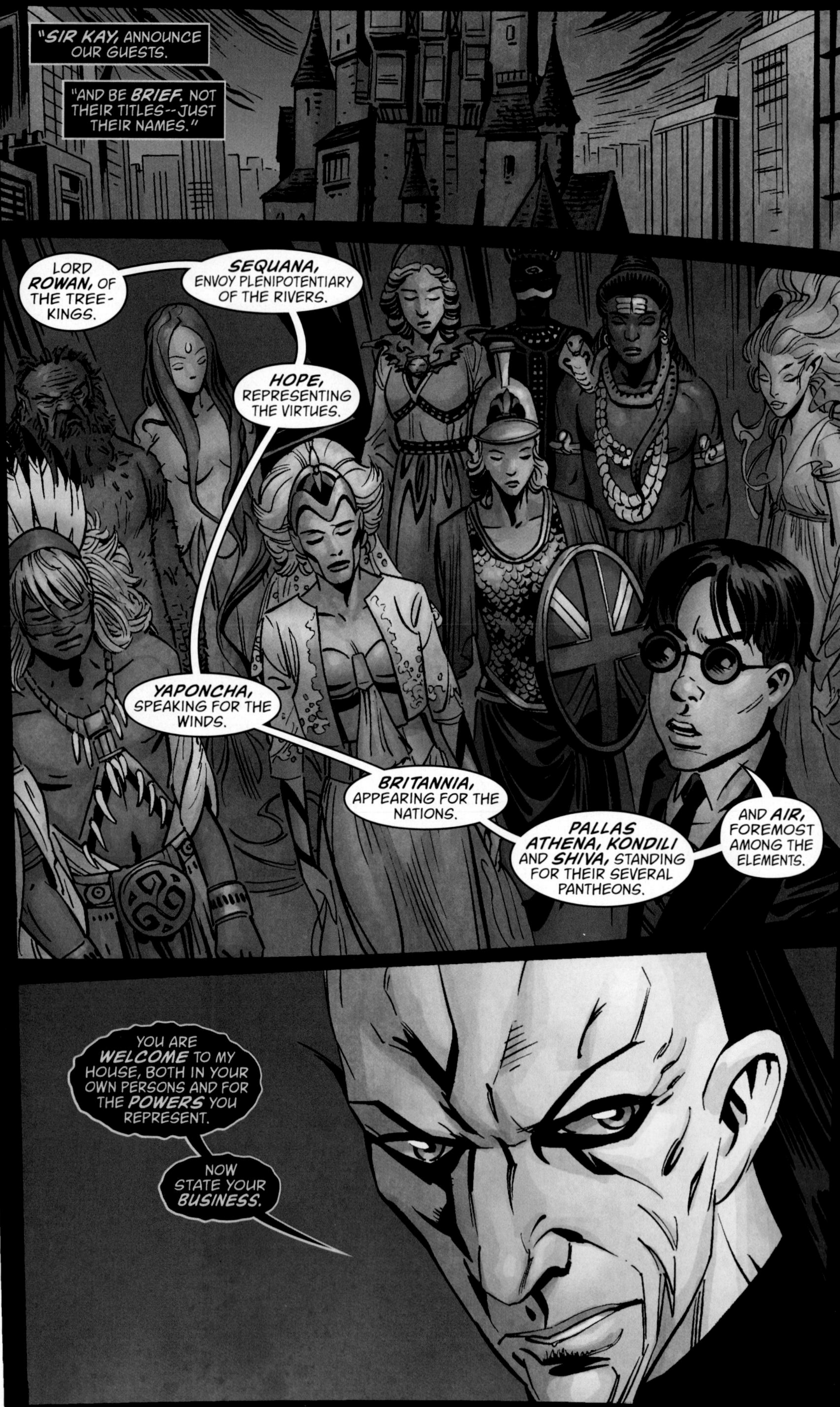
"SIR KAY, ANNOUNCE OUR GUESTS.
"AND BE BRIEF. NOT THEIR TITLES--JUST THEIR NAMES."
LORD ROWAN, OF THE TREE-KINGS.
SEQUANA, ENVOY PLENIPOTENTIARY OF THE RIVERS.
HOPE, REPRESENTING THE VIRTUES.
YAPONCHA, SPEAKING FOR THE WINDS.
BRITANNIA, APPEARING FOR THE NATIONS.
PALLAS ATHENA, KONDILI AND SHIVA, STANDING FOR THEIR SEVERAL PANTHEONS.
AND AIR, FOREMOST AMONG THE ELEMENTS.
YOU ARE WELCOME TO MY HOUSE, BOTH IN YOUR OWN PERSONS AND FOR THE POWERS YOU REPRESENT.
NOW STATE YOUR BUSINESS.

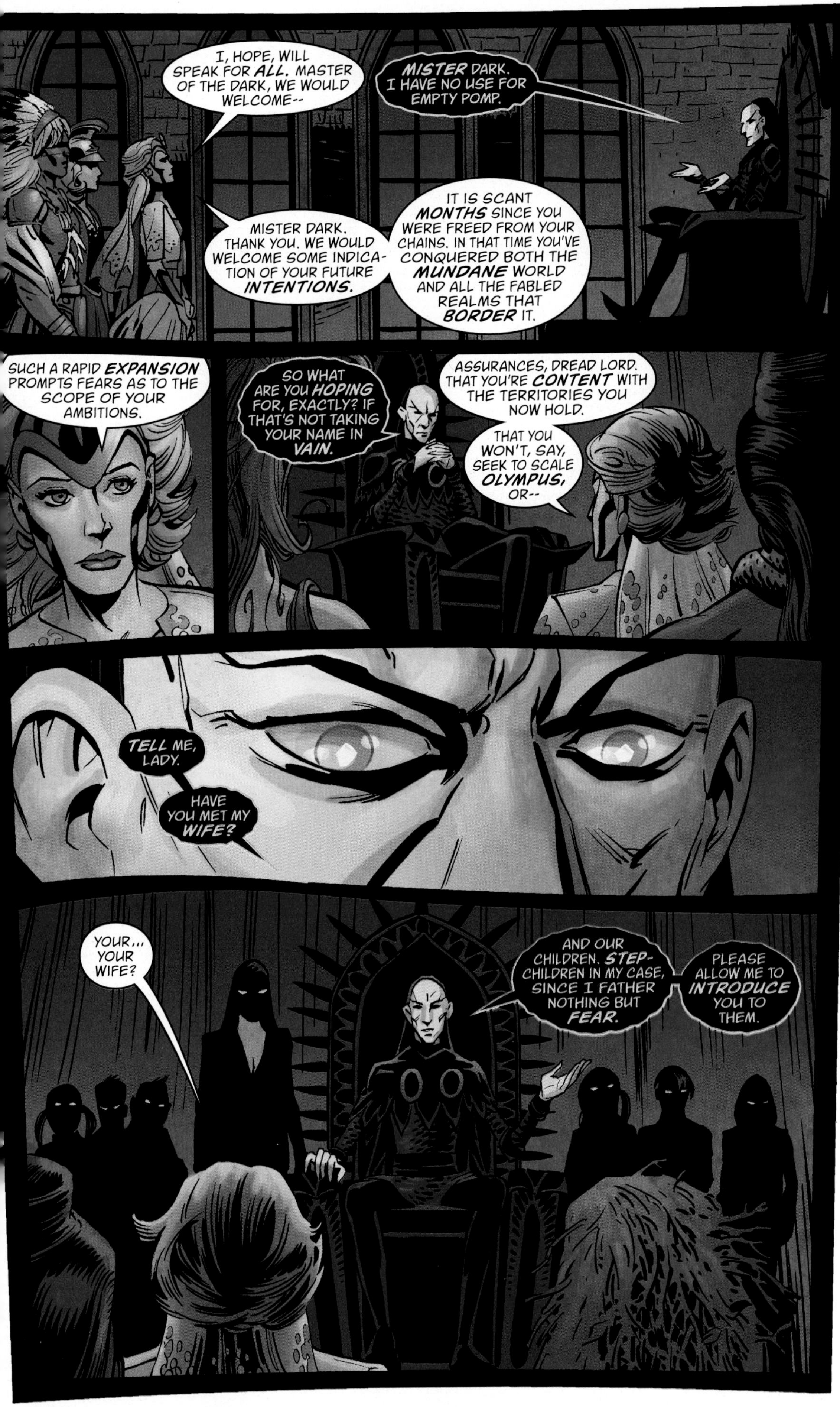
I, HOPE, WILL SPEAK FOR ALL. MASTER OF THE DARK, WE WOULD WELCOME--
MISTER DARK. I HAVE NO USE FOR EMPTY POMP.
MISTER DARK. THANK YOU. WE WOULD WELCOME SOME INDICATION OF YOUR FUTURE INTENTIONS.
IT IS SCANT MONTHS SINCE YOU WERE FREED FROM YOUR CHAINS. IN THAT TIME YOU'VE CONQUERED BOTH THE MUNDANE WORLD AND ALL THE FABLED REALMS THAT BORDER IT.
SUCH A RAPID EXPANSION PROMPTS FEARS AS TO THE SCOPE OF YOUR AMBITIONS.
SO WHAT ARE YOU HOPING FOR, EXACTLY? IF THAT'S NOT TAKING YOUR NAME IN VAIN.
ASSURANCES, DREAD LORD. THAT YOU'RE CONTENT WITH THE TERRITORIES YOU NOW HOLD.
THAT YOU WON'T, SAY, SEEK TO SCALE OLYMPUS, OR--
TELL ME, LADY.
HAVE YOU MET MY WIFE?
YOUR... YOUR WIFE?
AND OUR CHILDREN. STEP-CHILDREN IN MY CASE, SINCE I FATHER NOTHING BUT FEAR.
PLEASE ALLOW ME TO INTRODUCE YOU TO THEM.

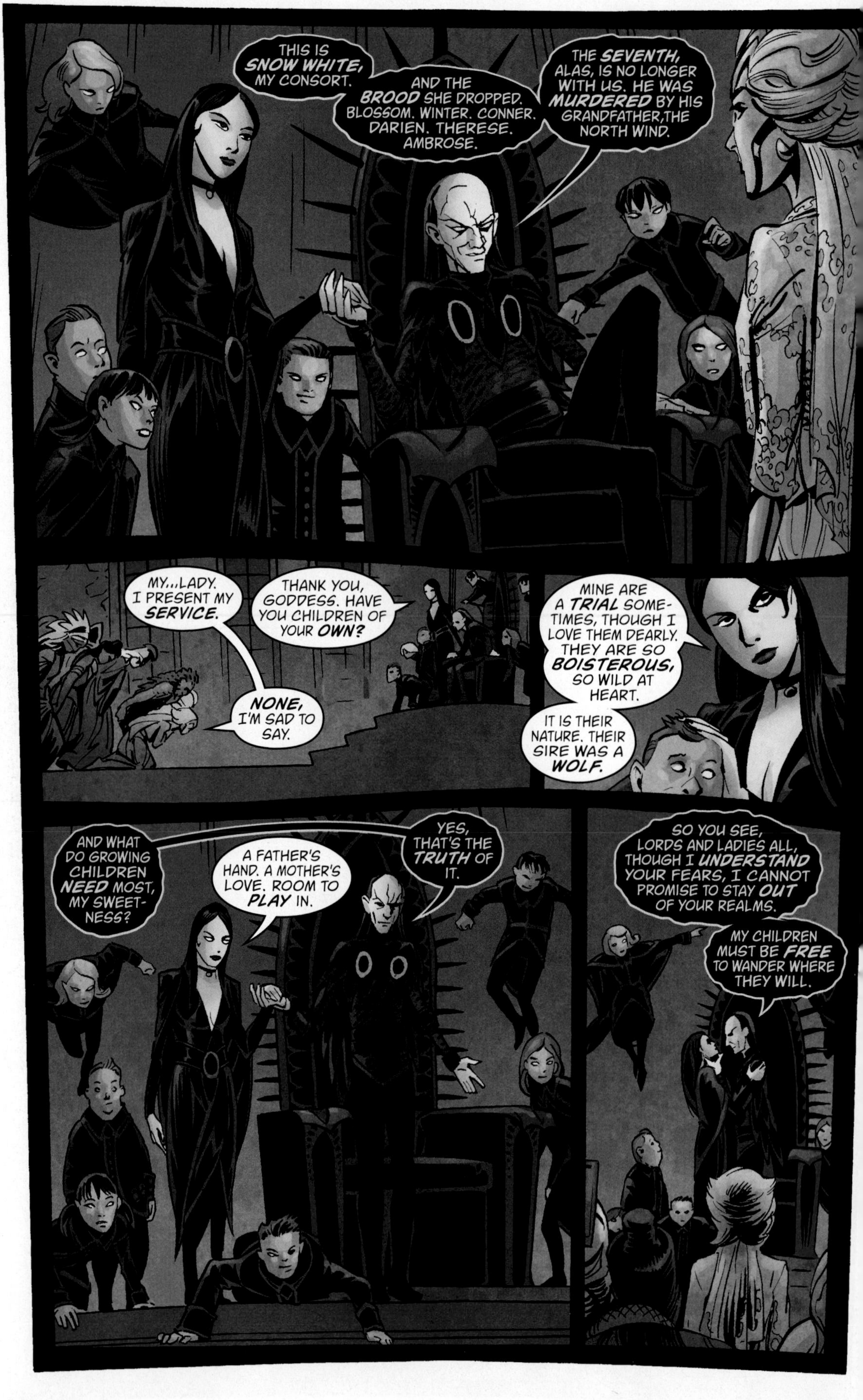

THIS IS SNOW WHITE, MY CONSORT.
AND THE BROOD SHE DROPPED. BLOSSOM. WINTER. CONNER. DARIEN. THERESE. AMBROSE.
THE SEVENTH, ALAS, IS NO LONGER WITH US. HE WAS MURDERED BY HIS GRANDFATHER, THE NORTH WIND.
MY...LADY. I PRESENT MY SERVICE.
THANK YOU, GODDESS. HAVE YOU CHILDREN OF YOUR OWN?
NONE, I'M SAD TO SAY.
MINE ARE A TRIAL SOMETIMES, THOUGH I LOVE THEM DEARLY. THEY ARE SO BOISTEROUS, SO WILD AT HEART.
IT IS THEIR NATURE. THEIR SIRE WAS A WOLF.
AND WHAT DO GROWING CHILDREN NEED MOST, MY SWEETNESS?
A FATHER'S HAND. A MOTHER'S LOVE. ROOM TO PLAY IN.
YES, THAT'S THE TRUTH OF IT.
SO YOU SEE, LORDS AND LADIES ALL, THOUGH I UNDERSTAND YOUR FEARS, I CANNOT PROMISE TO STAY OUT OF YOUR REALMS.
MY CHILDREN MUST BE FREE TO WANDER WHERE THEY WILL.

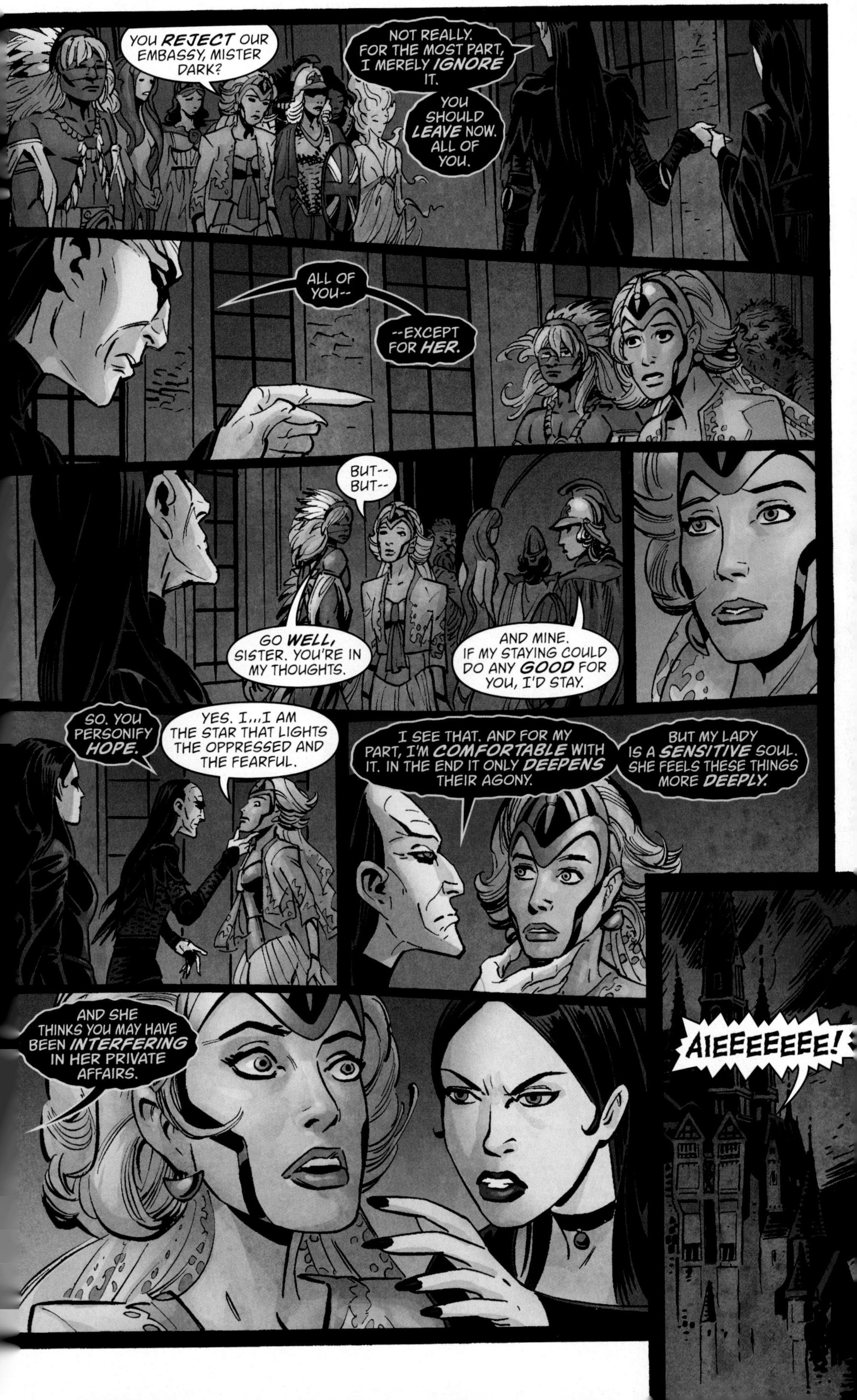

YOU REJECT OUR EMBASSY, MISTER DARK?
NOT REALLY. FOR THE MOST PART, I MERELY IGNORE IT.
YOU SHOULD LEAVE NOW. ALL OF YOU.
ALL OF YOU--
--EXCEPT FOR HER.
BUT-- BUT--
GO WELL, SISTER. YOU'RE IN MY THOUGHTS.
AND MINE. IF MY STAYING COULD DO ANY GOOD FOR YOU, I'D STAY.
SO. YOU PERSONIFY HOPE.
YES. I...I AM THE STAR THAT LIGHTS THE OPPRESSED AND THE FEARFUL.
I SEE THAT. AND FOR MY PART, I'M COMFORTABLE WITH IT. IN THE END IT ONLY DEEPENS THEIR AGONY.
BUT MY LADY IS A SENSITIVE SOUL. SHE FEELS THESE THINGS MORE DEEPLY.
AND SHE THINKS YOU MAY HAVE BEEN INTERFERING IN HER PRIVATE AFFAIRS.
AIEEEEEEE!

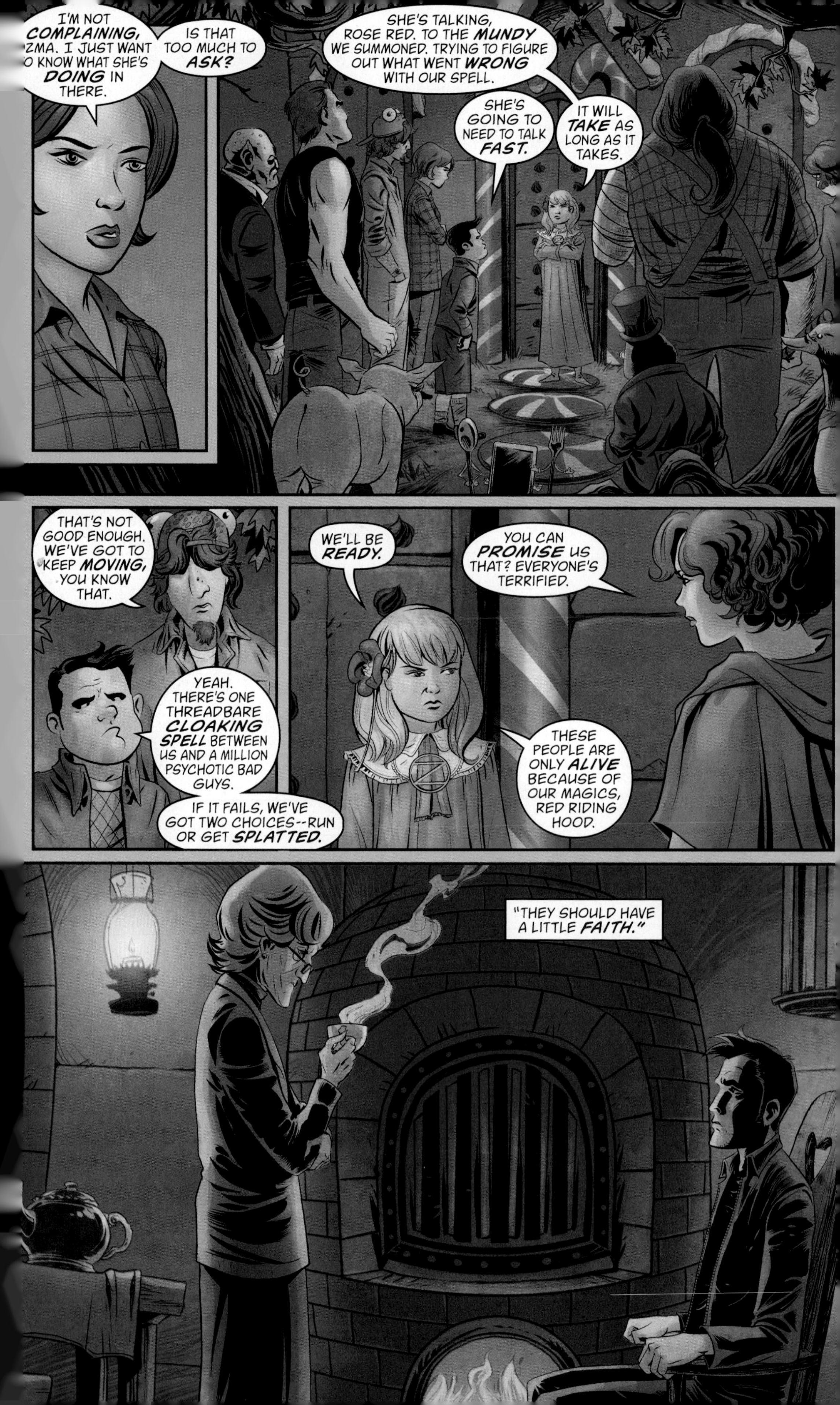
I'M NOT COMPLAINING, OZMA. I JUST WANT TO KNOW WHAT SHE'S DOING IN THERE.
IS THAT TOO MUCH TO ASK?
SHE'S TALKING, ROSE RED. TO THE MUNDY WE SUMMONED. TRYING TO FIGURE OUT WHAT WENT WRONG WITH OUR SPELL.
SHE'S GOING TO NEED TO TALK FAST.
IT WILL TAKE AS LONG AS IT TAKES.
THAT'S NOT GOOD ENOUGH. WE'VE GOT TO KEEP MOVING, YOU KNOW THAT.
YEAH. THERE'S ONE THREADBARE CLOAKING SPELL BETWEEN US AND A MILLION PSYCHOTIC BAD GUYS.
IF IT FAILS, WE'VE GOT TWO CHOICES--RUN OR GET SPLATTED.
WE'LL BE READY.
YOU CAN PROMISE US THAT? EVERYONE'S TERRIFIED.
THESE PEOPLE ARE ONLY ALIVE BECAUSE OF OUR MAGICS, RED RIDING HOOD.
"THEY SHOULD HAVE A LITTLE FAITH."

OKAY, LOOK. I'LL HELP YOU IF I CAN, IF YOU SET ME ON THE RIGHT ROAD AGAIN AFTERWARD. HOW WOULD *THAT* BE?

I'D ALSO LIKE IT IF YOU TOOK THE *SPELL* OFF ME, SO I COULD MOVE OF MY OWN FREE--

NO. THE HELP WE NEED IS VERY *SPECIFIC*. AND FAR BEYOND ANYTHING *YOU* COULD OFFER.

AS FOR FINDING THE RIGHT ROAD...WELL, YOU NEED TO KNOW WHERE YOU ARE TO *START* WITH.

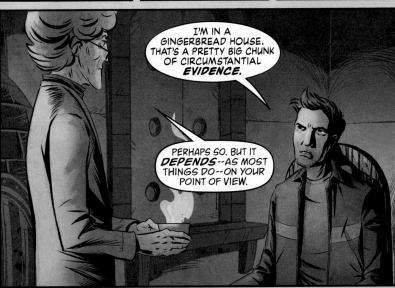

I'M IN A GINGERBREAD HOUSE. THAT'S A PRETTY BIG CHUNK OF CIRCUMSTANTIAL *EVIDENCE*.

PERHAPS SO. BUT IT *DEPENDS*--AS MOST THINGS DO--ON YOUR POINT OF VIEW.

LISTEN, I'VE DONE THIS STUFF *BEFORE*. I KNOW WHAT'S HAPPENING HERE.

THERE WAS A *STORM* THAT MIXED ALL THE STORIES TOGETHER. YOU'RE *REFUGEES*, RIGHT? YOU CAN'T FIND YOUR WAY *HOME* AGAIN.

I HAVE NO *IDEA* WHAT YOU'RE TALKING ABOUT.

THE WOUND. *LEVIATHAN'S* WOUND. IT BROKE UP ALL THE STORY WORLDS AND TURNED THEM ON THEIR HEADS.

WE FELT *NO* SUCH STORM.

AND *OUR* REALITY, ALAS, REMAINS UNCHANGED.

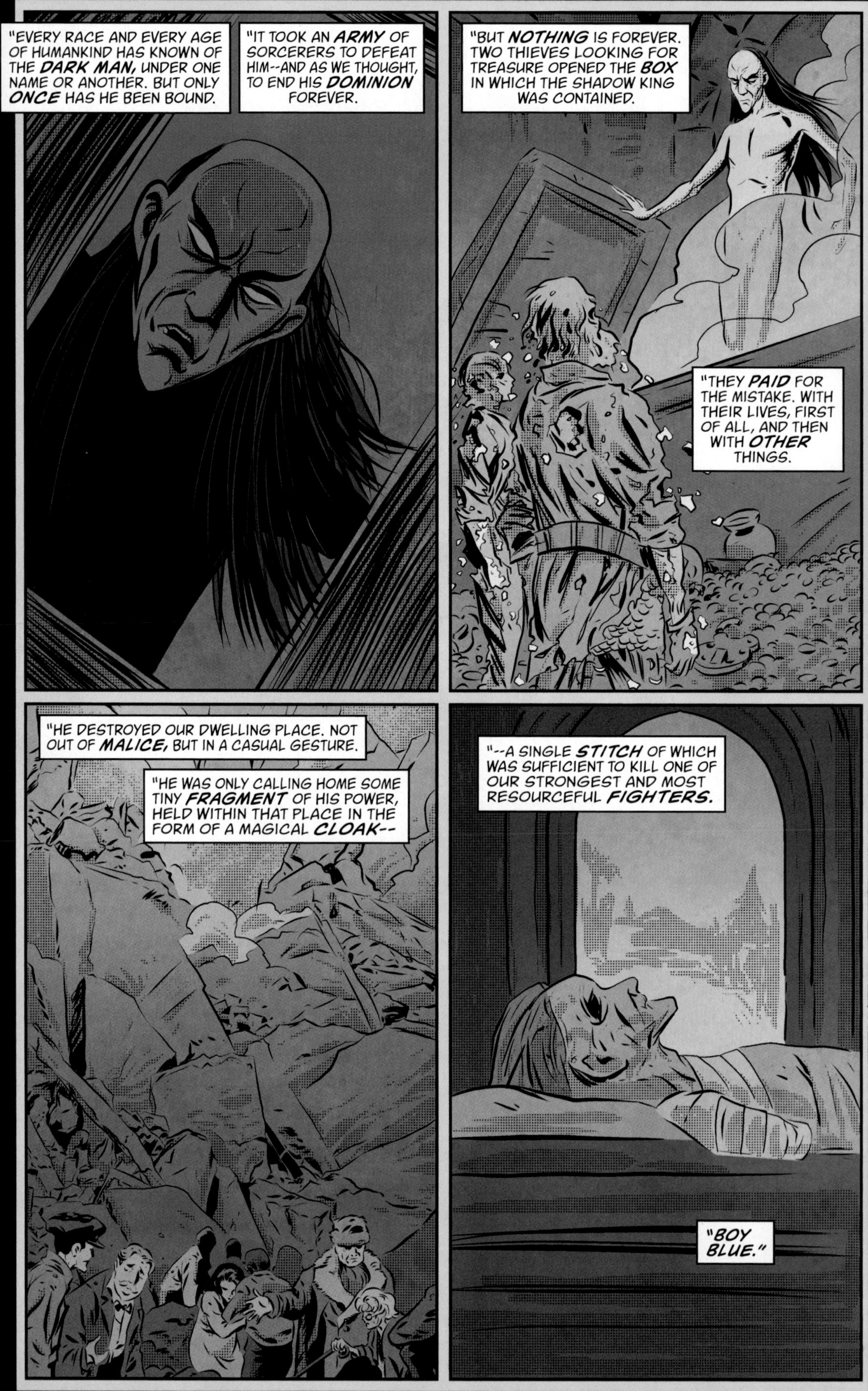
"EVERY RACE AND EVERY AGE OF HUMANKIND HAS KNOWN OF THE DARK MAN, UNDER ONE NAME OR ANOTHER. BUT ONLY ONCE HAS HE BEEN BOUND.
"IT TOOK AN ARMY OF SORCERERS TO DEFEAT HIM--AND AS WE THOUGHT, TO END HIS DOMINION FOREVER.
"BUT NOTHING IS FOREVER. TWO THIEVES LOOKING FOR TREASURE OPENED THE BOX IN WHICH THE SHADOW KING WAS CONTAINED.
"THEY PAID FOR THE MISTAKE. WITH THEIR LIVES, FIRST OF ALL, AND THEN WITH OTHER THINGS.
"HE DESTROYED OUR DWELLING PLACE. NOT OUT OF MALICE, BUT IN A CASUAL GESTURE.
"HE WAS ONLY CALLING HOME SOME TINY FRAGMENT OF HIS POWER, HELD WITHIN THAT PLACE IN THE FORM OF A MAGICAL CLOAK--
"--A SINGLE STITCH OF WHICH WAS SUFFICIENT TO KILL ONE OF OUR STRONGEST AND MOST RESOURCEFUL FIGHTERS.
"BOY BLUE."

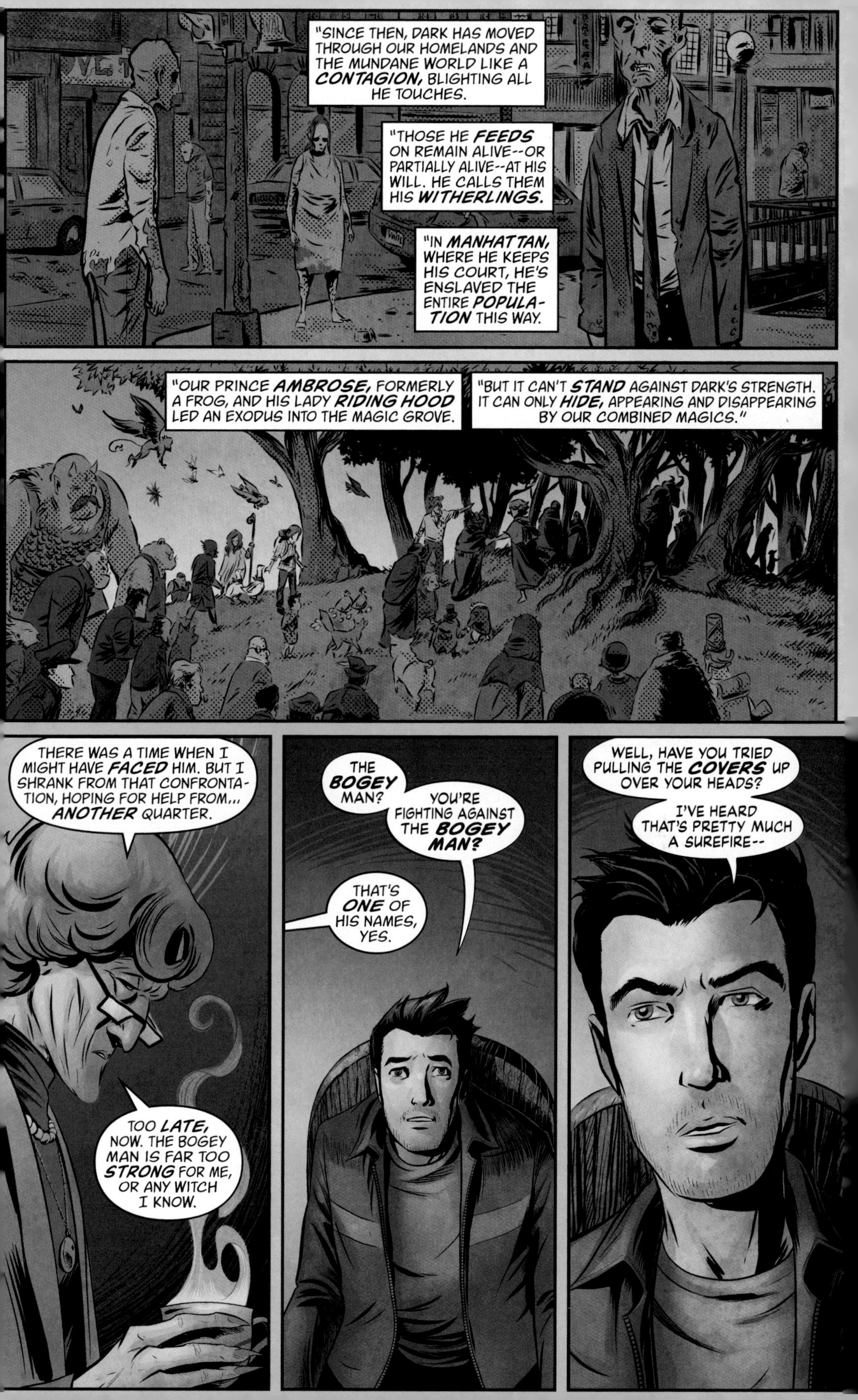
"SINCE THEN, DARK HAS MOVED THROUGH OUR HOMELANDS AND THE MUNDANE WORLD LIKE A CONTAGION, BLIGHTING ALL HE TOUCHES.
"THOSE HE FEEDS ON REMAIN ALIVE--OR PARTIALLY ALIVE--AT HIS WILL. HE CALLS THEM HIS WITHERLINGS.
"IN MANHATTAN, WHERE HE KEEPS HIS COURT, HE'S ENSLAVED THE ENTIRE POPULATION THIS WAY.
"OUR PRINCE AMBROSE, FORMERLY A FROG, AND HIS LADY RIDING HOOD LED AN EXODUS INTO THE MAGIC GROVE.
"BUT IT CAN'T STAND AGAINST DARK'S STRENGTH. IT CAN ONLY HIDE, APPEARING AND DISAPPEARING BY OUR COMBINED MAGICS."
THERE WAS A TIME WHEN I MIGHT HAVE FACED HIM. BUT I SHRANK FROM THAT CONFRONTATION, HOPING FOR HELP FROM... ANOTHER QUARTER.
TOO LATE, NOW. THE BOGEY MAN IS FAR TOO STRONG FOR ME, OR ANY WITCH I KNOW.
THE BOGEY MAN?
YOU'RE FIGHTING AGAINST THE BOGEY MAN?
THAT'S ONE OF HIS NAMES, YES.
WELL, HAVE YOU TRIED PULLING THE COVERS UP OVER YOUR HEADS?
I'VE HEARD THAT'S PRETTY MUCH A SUREFIRE--

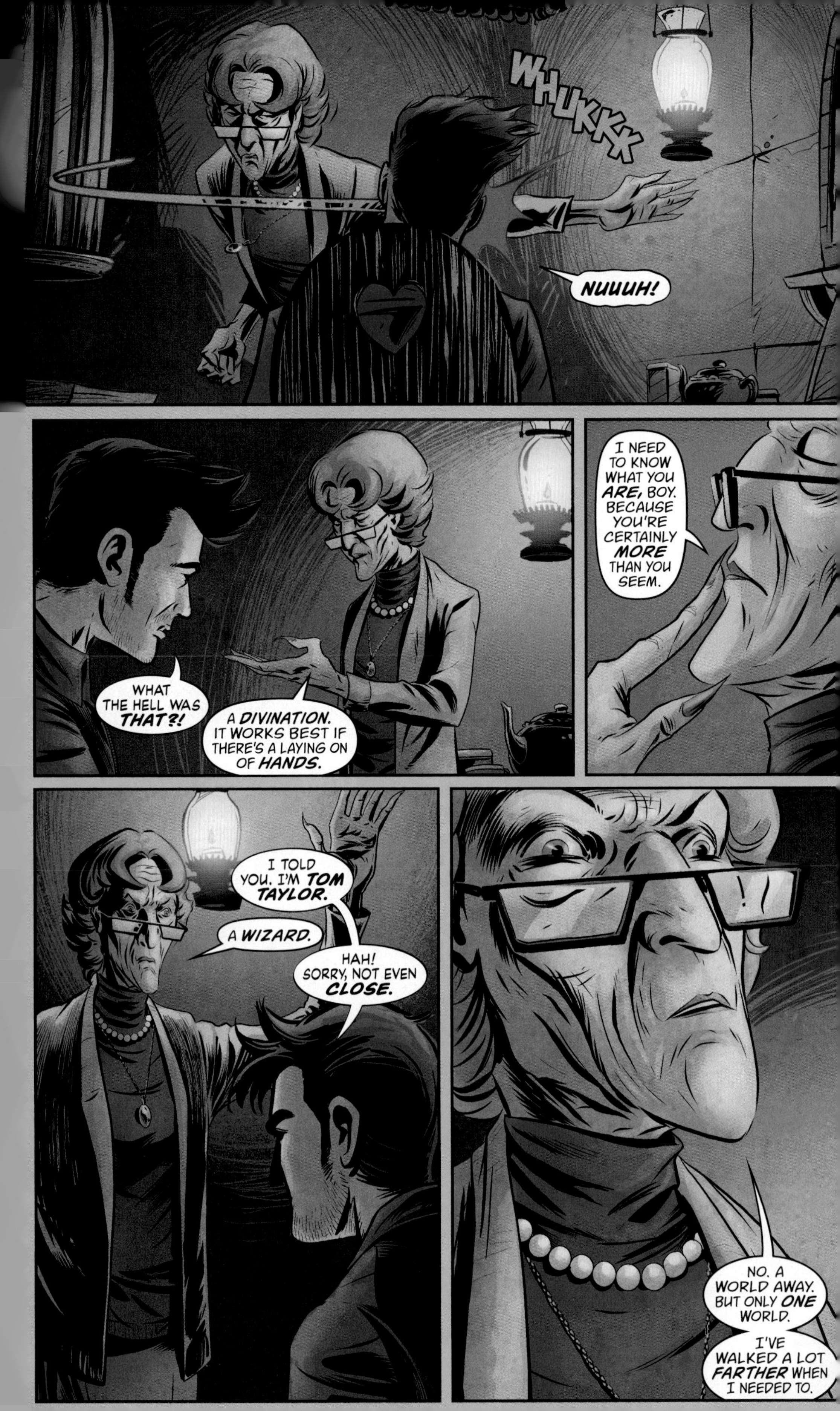
WHUKKX
NUUUH!
WHAT THE HELL WAS THAT?!
A DIVINATION. IT WORKS BEST IF THERE'S A LAYING ON OF HANDS.
I NEED TO KNOW WHAT YOU ARE, BOY. BECAUSE YOU'RE CERTAINLY MORE THAN YOU SEEM.
I TOLD YOU. I'M TOM TAYLOR.
A WIZARD.
HAH! SORRY, NOT EVEN CLOSE.
NO, A WORLD AWAY. BUT ONLY ONE WORLD.
I'VE WALKED A LOT FARTHER WHEN I NEEDED TO.

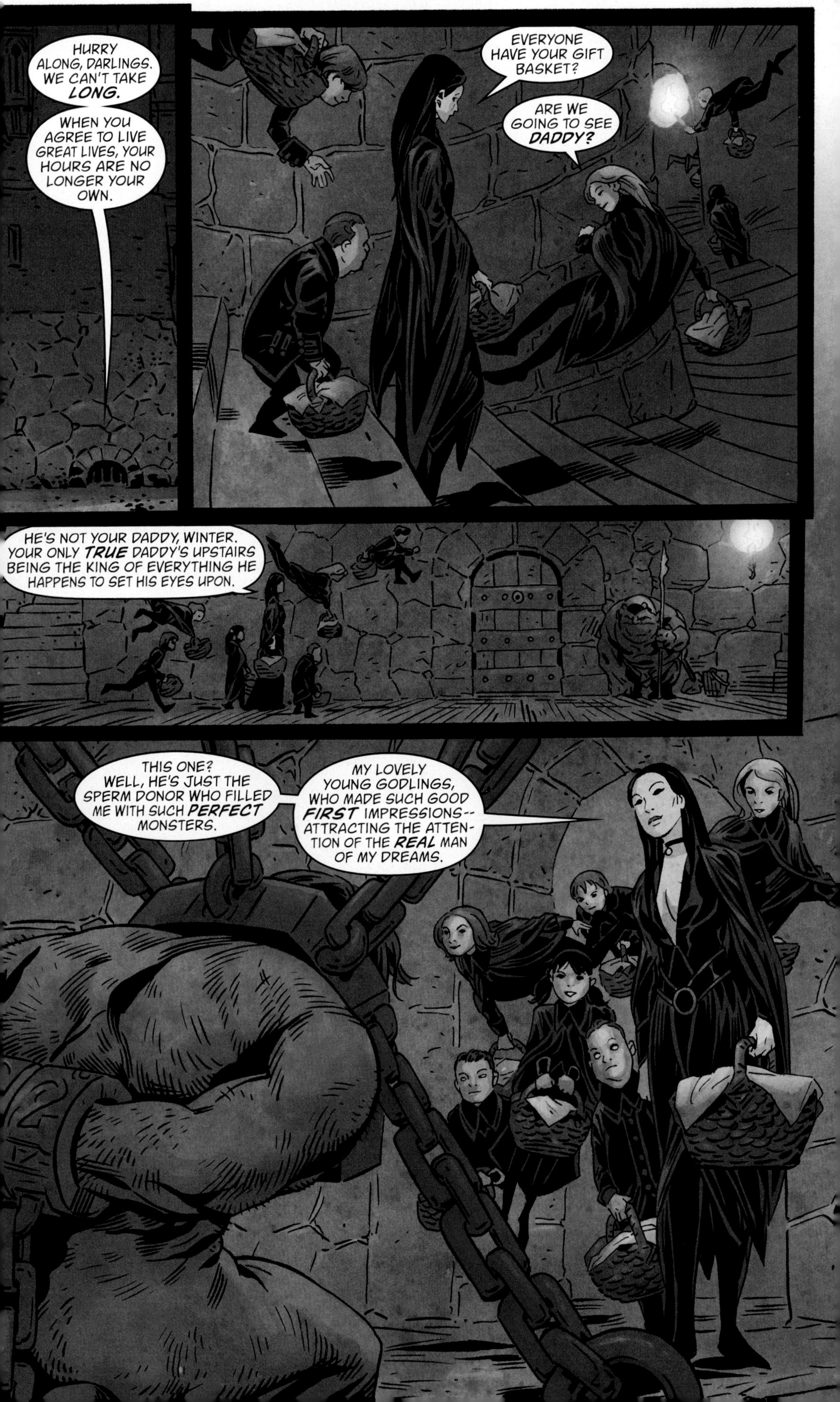
HURRY ALONG, DARLINGS. WE CAN'T TAKE LONG.
WHEN YOU AGREE TO LIVE GREAT LIVES, YOUR HOURS ARE NO LONGER YOUR OWN.
EVERYONE HAVE YOUR GIFT BASKET?
ARE WE GOING TO SEE DADDY?
HE'S NOT YOUR DADDY, WINTER. YOUR ONLY TRUE DADDY'S UPSTAIRS BEING THE KING OF EVERYTHING HE HAPPENS TO SET HIS EYES UPON.
THIS ONE? WELL, HE'S JUST THE SPERM DONOR WHO FILLED ME WITH SUCH PERFECT MONSTERS.
MY LOVELY YOUNG GODLINGS, WHO MADE SUCH GOOD FIRST IMPRESSIONS--ATTRACTING THE ATTENTION OF THE REAL MAN OF MY DREAMS.

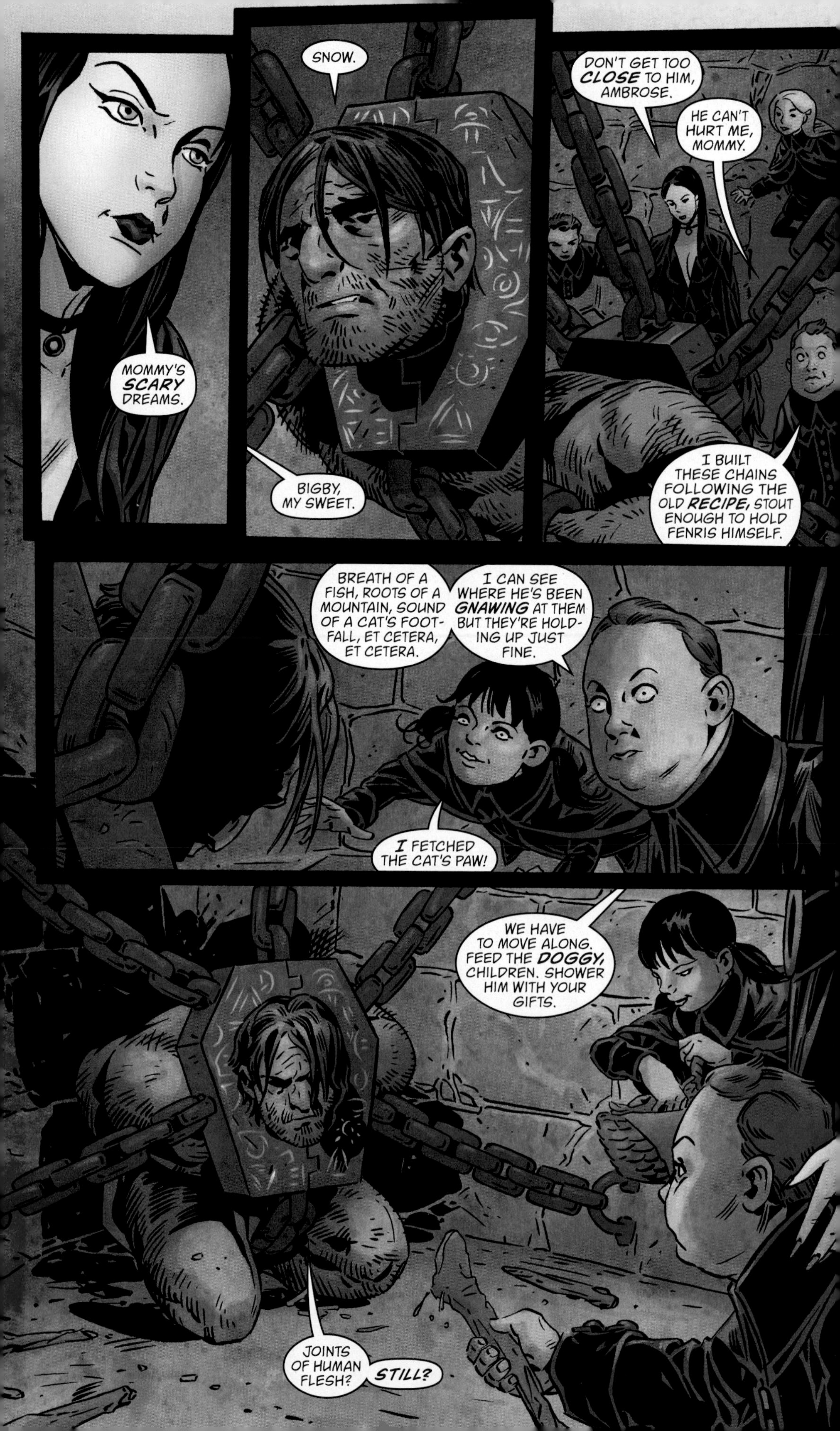
MOMMY'S SCARY DREAMS.
SNOW.
BIGBY, MY SWEET.
DON'T GET TOO CLOSE TO HIM, AMBROSE.
HE CAN'T HURT ME, MOMMY.
I BUILT THESE CHAINS FOLLOWING THE OLD RECIPE, STOUT ENOUGH TO HOLD FENRIS HIMSELF.
BREATH OF A FISH, ROOTS OF A MOUNTAIN, SOUND OF A CAT'S FOOT-FALL, ET CETERA, ET CETERA.
I CAN SEE WHERE HE'S BEEN GNAWING AT THEM BUT THEY'RE HOLD-ING UP JUST FINE.
I FETCHED THE CAT'S PAW!
WE HAVE TO MOVE ALONG. FEED THE DOGGY, CHILDREN. SHOWER HIM WITH YOUR GIFTS.
JOINTS OF HUMAN FLESH?
STILL?

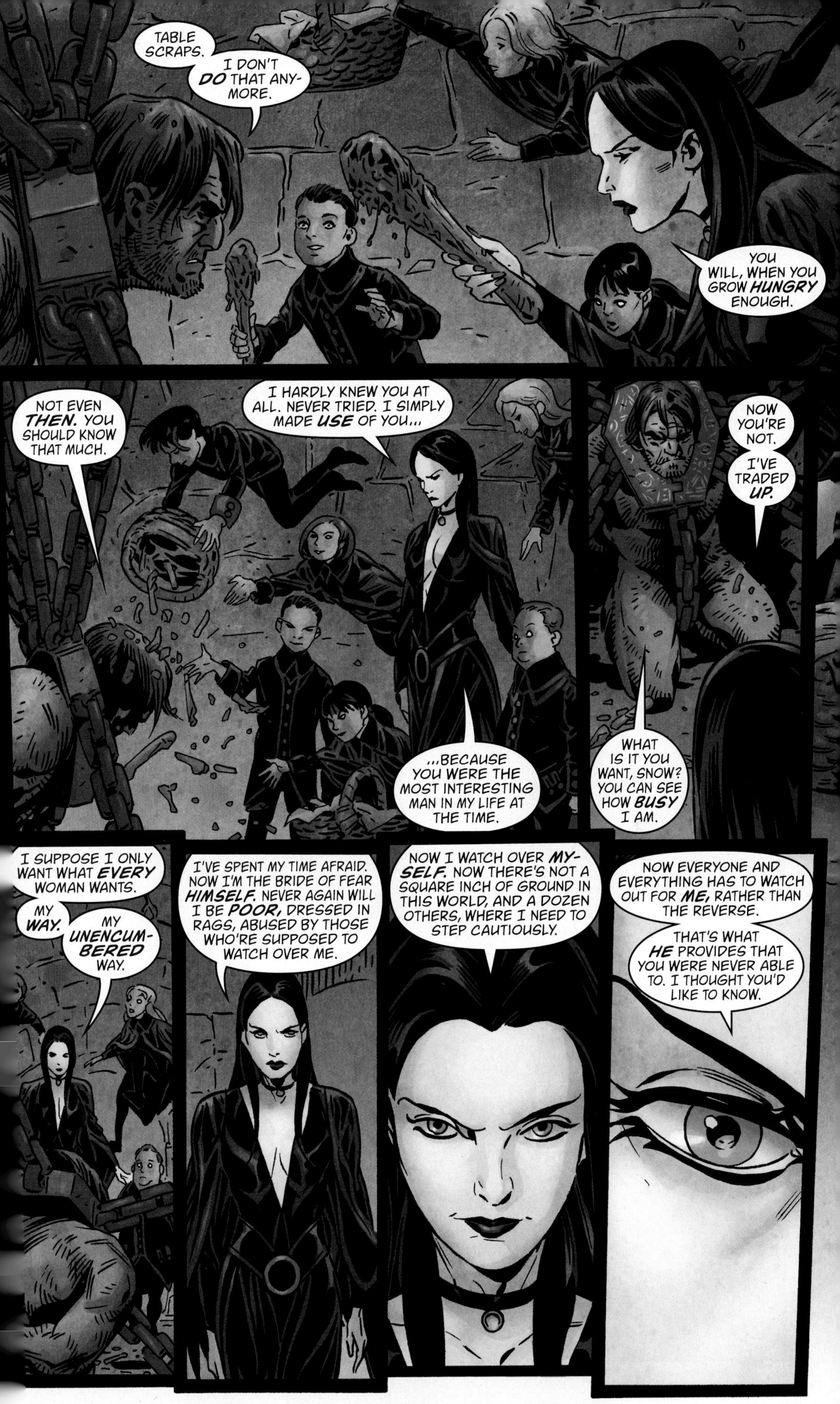
TABLE SCRAPS.
I DON'T DO THAT ANY-MORE.
YOU WILL, WHEN YOU GROW HUNGRY ENOUGH.
NOT EVEN THEN. YOU SHOULD KNOW THAT MUCH.
I HARDLY KNEW YOU AT ALL. NEVER TRIED. I SIMPLY MADE USE OF YOU...
...BECAUSE YOU WERE THE MOST INTERESTING MAN IN MY LIFE AT THE TIME.
NOW YOU'RE NOT.
I'VE TRADED UP.
WHAT IS IT YOU WANT, SNOW? YOU CAN SEE HOW BUSY I AM.
I SUPPOSE I ONLY WANT WHAT EVERY WOMAN WANTS.
MY WAY.
MY UNENCUMBERED WAY.
I'VE SPENT MY TIME AFRAID. NOW I'M THE BRIDE OF FEAR HIMSELF. NEVER AGAIN WILL I BE POOR, DRESSED IN RAGS, ABUSED BY THOSE WHO'RE SUPPOSED TO WATCH OVER ME.
NOW I WATCH OVER MY-SELF. NOW THERE'S NOT A SQUARE INCH OF GROUND IN THIS WORLD, AND A DOZEN OTHERS, WHERE I NEED TO STEP CAUTIOUSLY.
NOW EVERYONE AND EVERYTHING HAS TO WATCH OUT FOR ME, RATHER THAN THE REVERSE.
THAT'S WHAT HE PROVIDES THAT YOU WERE NEVER ABLE TO. I THOUGHT YOU'D LIKE TO KNOW.

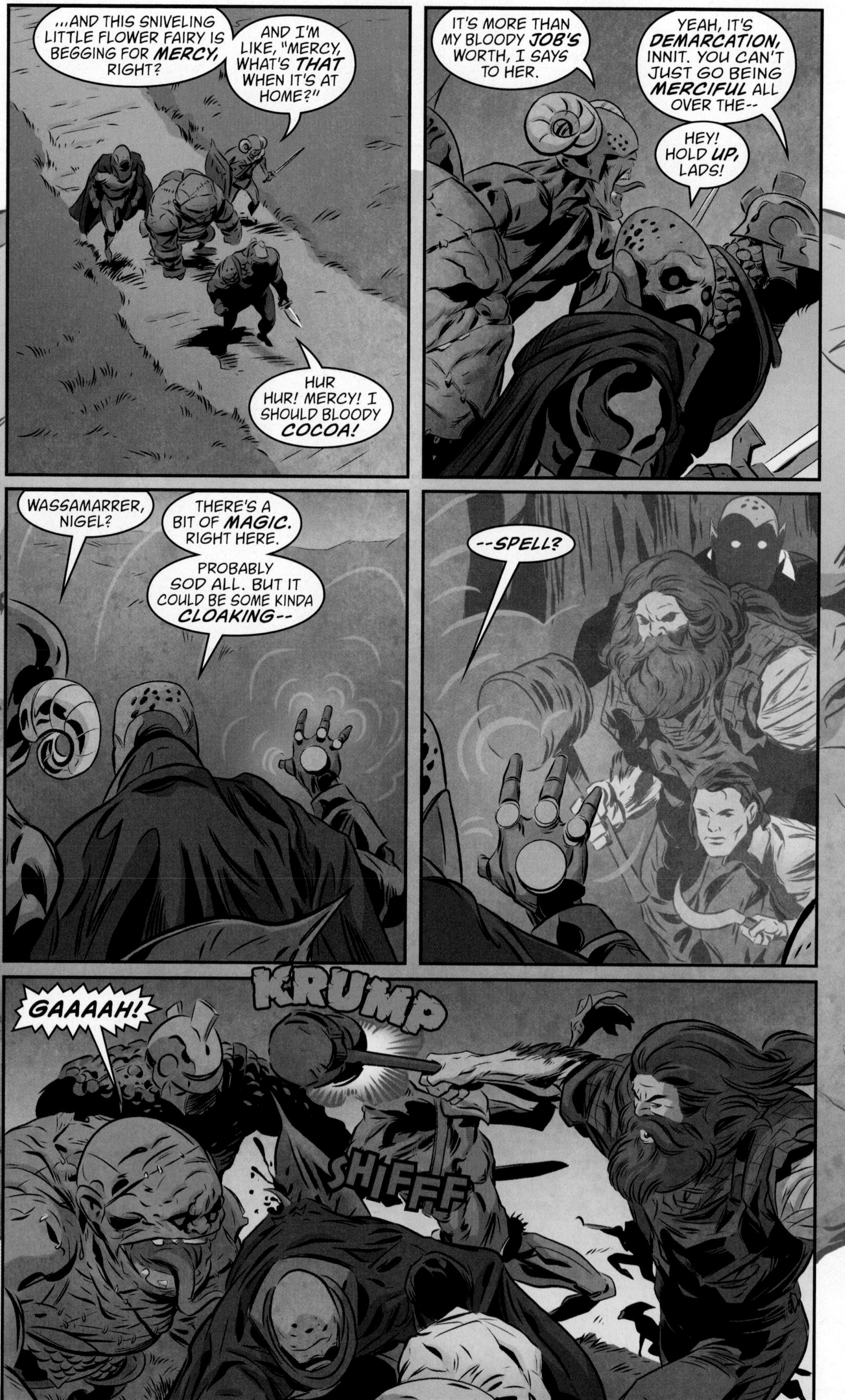
...AND THIS SNIVELING LITTLE FLOWER FAIRY IS BEGGING FOR MERCY, RIGHT?
AND I'M LIKE, "MERCY, WHAT'S THAT WHEN IT'S AT HOME?"
HUR HUR! MERCY! I SHOULD BLOODY COCOA!
IT'S MORE THAN MY BLOODY JOB'S WORTH, I SAYS TO HER.
YEAH, IT'S DEMARCATION, INNIT. YOU CAN'T JUST GO BEING MERCIFUL ALL OVER THE--
HEY! HOLD UP, LADS!
WASSAMARRER, NIGEL?
THERE'S A BIT OF MAGIC. RIGHT HERE.
PROBABLY SOD ALL. BUT IT COULD BE SOME KINDA CLOAKING--
--SPELL?
GAAAAH!
KRUMP
SHIFFF

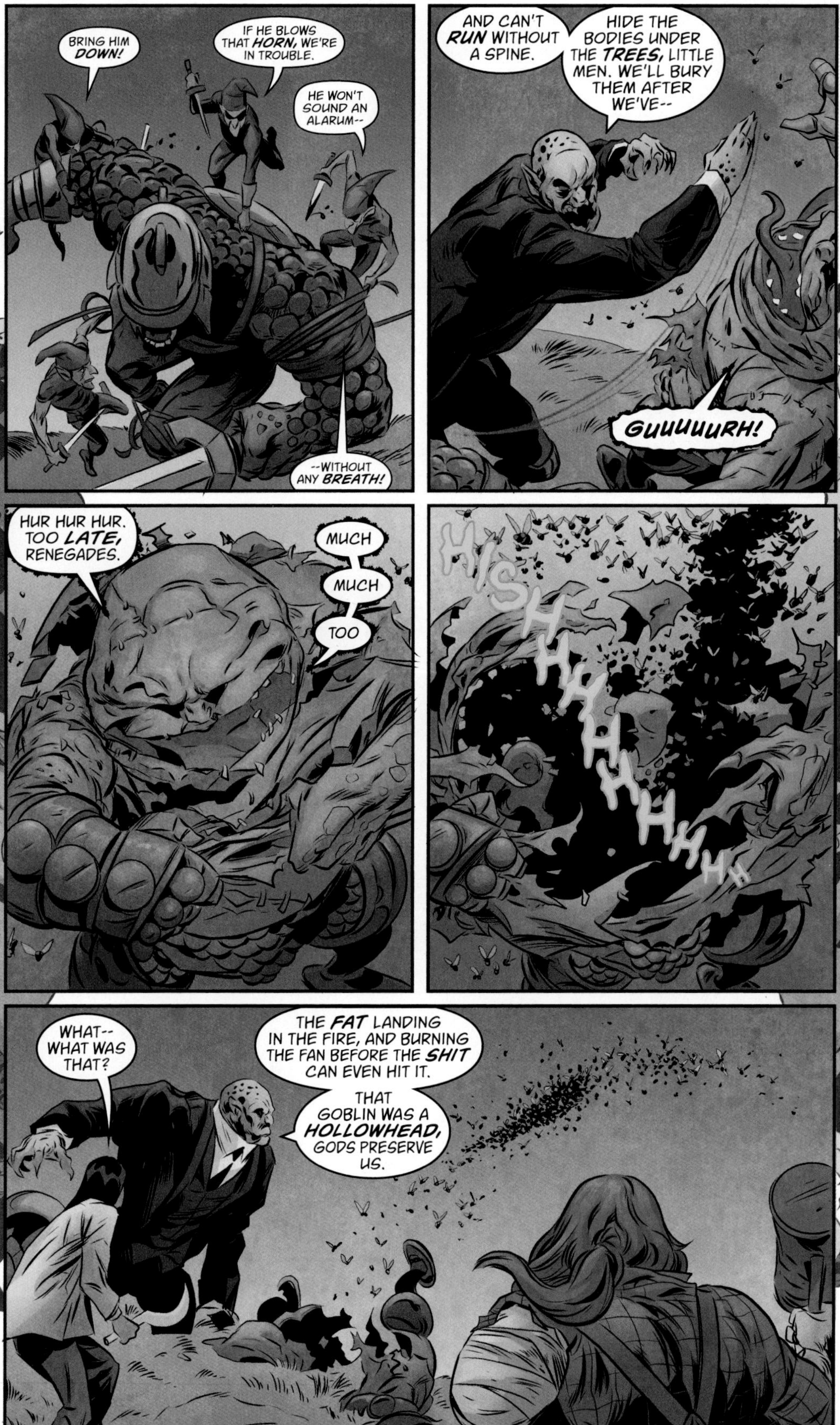
BRING HIM DOWN!
IF HE BLOWS THAT HORN, WE'RE IN TROUBLE.
HE WON'T SOUND AN ALARUM--
--WITHOUT ANY BREATH!
AND CAN'T RUN WITHOUT A SPINE.
HIDE THE BODIES UNDER THE TREES, LITTLE MEN. WE'LL BURY THEM AFTER WE'VE--
GUUUUURH!
HUR HUR HUR. TOO LATE, RENEGADES.
MUCH
MUCH
TOO
HISHHHHHHHHHHH
WHAT-- WHAT WAS THAT?
THE FAT LANDING IN THE FIRE, AND BURNING THE FAN BEFORE THE SHIT CAN EVEN HIT IT.
THAT GOBLIN WAS A HOLLOWHEAD, GODS PRESERVE US.

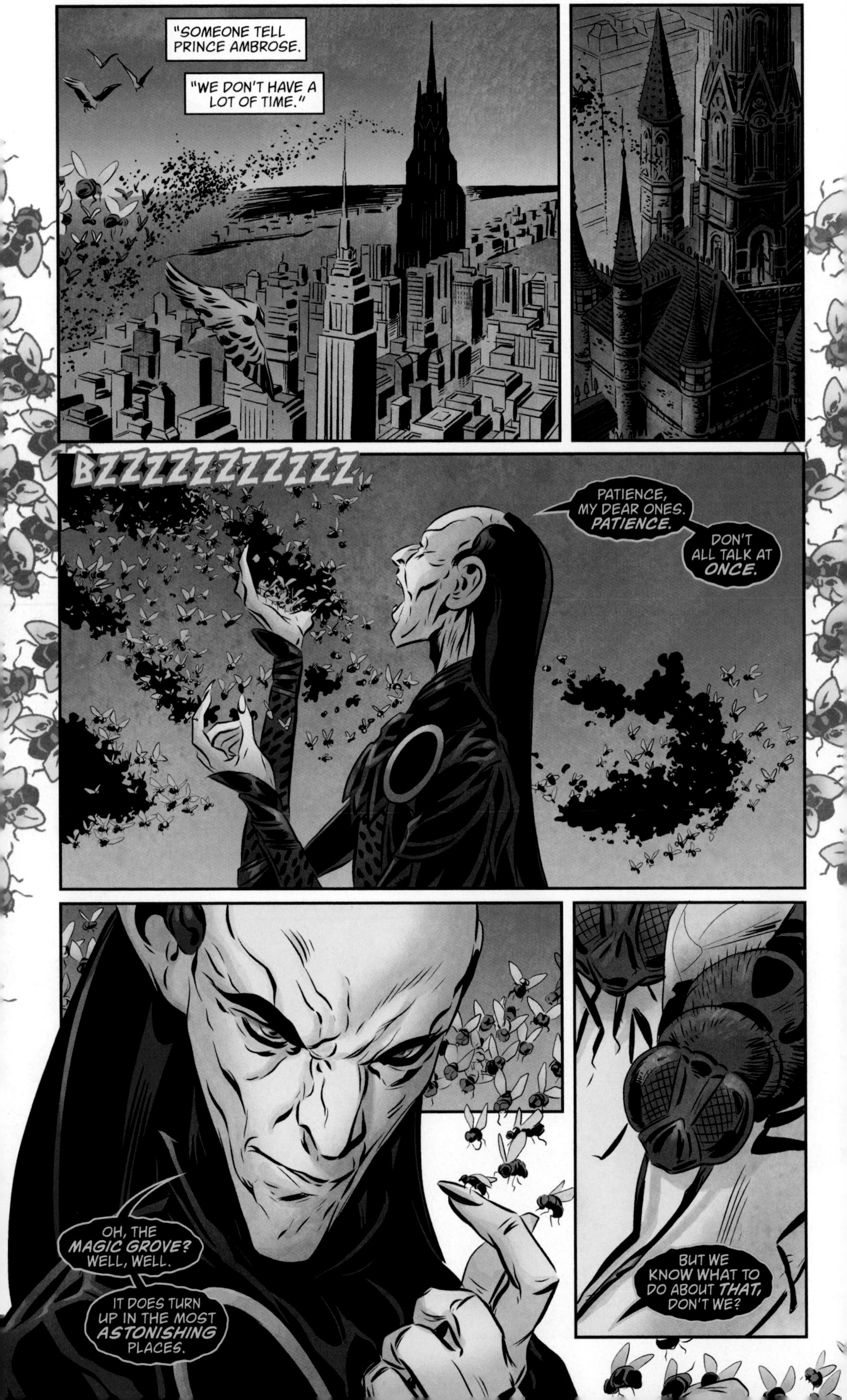

"SOMEONE TELL PRINCE AMBROSE.
"WE DON'T HAVE A LOT OF TIME."
BZZZZZZZZZZZZ
PATIENCE, MY DEAR ONES. PATIENCE.
DON'T ALL TALK AT ONCE.
OH, THE MAGIC GROVE? WELL, WELL.
IT DOES TURN UP IN THE MOST ASTONISHING PLACES.
BUT WE KNOW WHAT TO DO ABOUT THAT, DON'T WE?

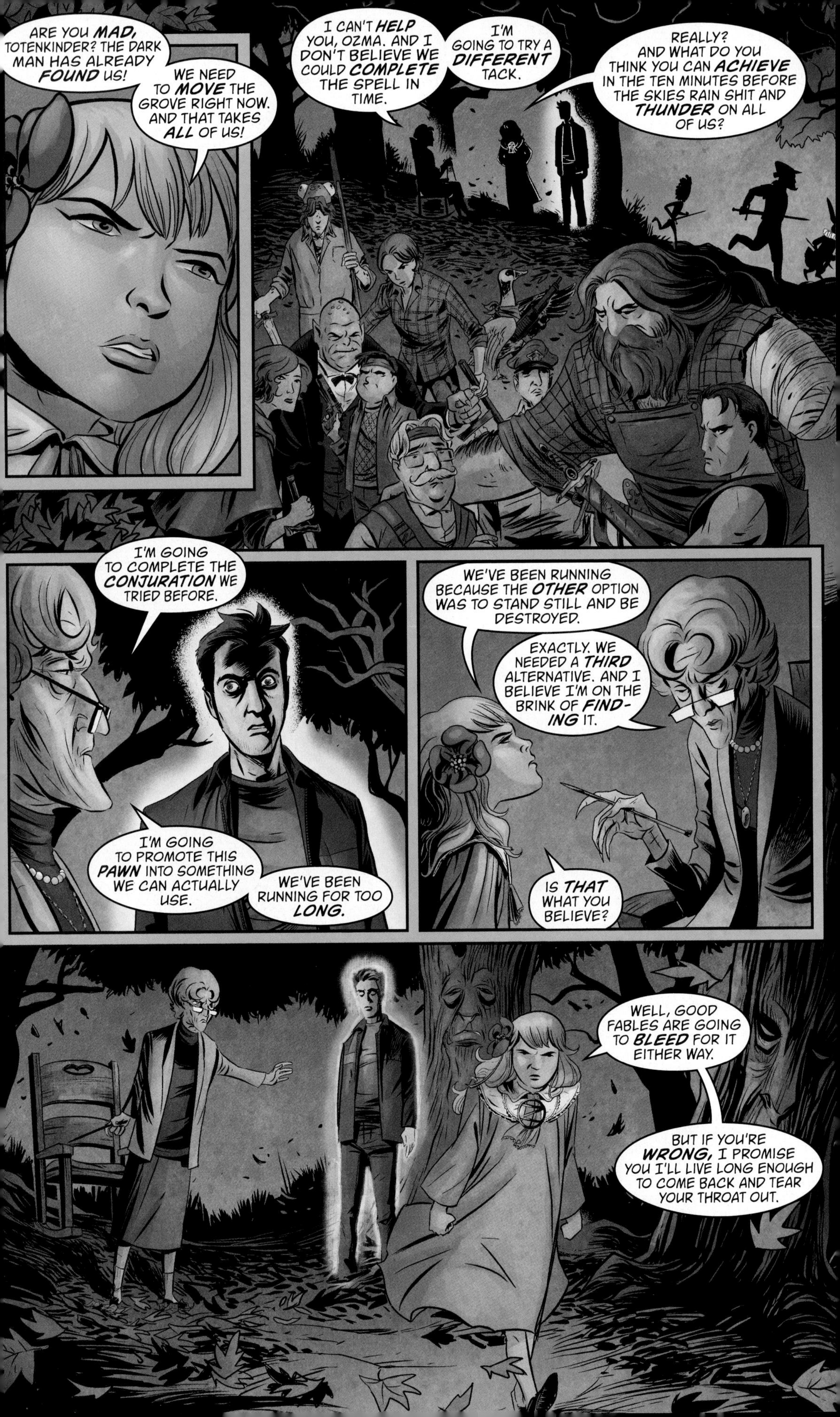

ARE YOU MAD, TOTENKINDER? THE DARK MAN HAS ALREADY FOUND US!
WE NEED TO MOVE THE GROVE RIGHT NOW. AND THAT TAKES ALL OF US!
I CAN'T HELP YOU, OZMA. AND I DON'T BELIEVE WE COULD COMPLETE THE SPELL IN TIME.
I'M GOING TO TRY A DIFFERENT TACK.
REALLY? AND WHAT DO YOU THINK YOU CAN ACHIEVE IN THE TEN MINUTES BEFORE THE SKIES RAIN SHIT AND THUNDER ON ALL OF US?
I'M GOING TO COMPLETE THE CONJURATION WE TRIED BEFORE.
I'M GOING TO PROMOTE THIS PAWN INTO SOMETHING WE CAN ACTUALLY USE.
WE'VE BEEN RUNNING FOR TOO LONG.
WE'VE BEEN RUNNING BECAUSE THE OTHER OPTION WAS TO STAND STILL AND BE DESTROYED.
EXACTLY. WE NEEDED A THIRD ALTERNATIVE. AND I BELIEVE I'M ON THE BRINK OF FINDING IT.
IS THAT WHAT YOU BELIEVE?
WELL, GOOD FABLES ARE GOING TO BLEED FOR IT EITHER WAY.
BUT IF YOU'RE WRONG, I PROMISE YOU I'LL LIVE LONG ENOUGH TO COME BACK AND TEAR YOUR THROAT OUT.

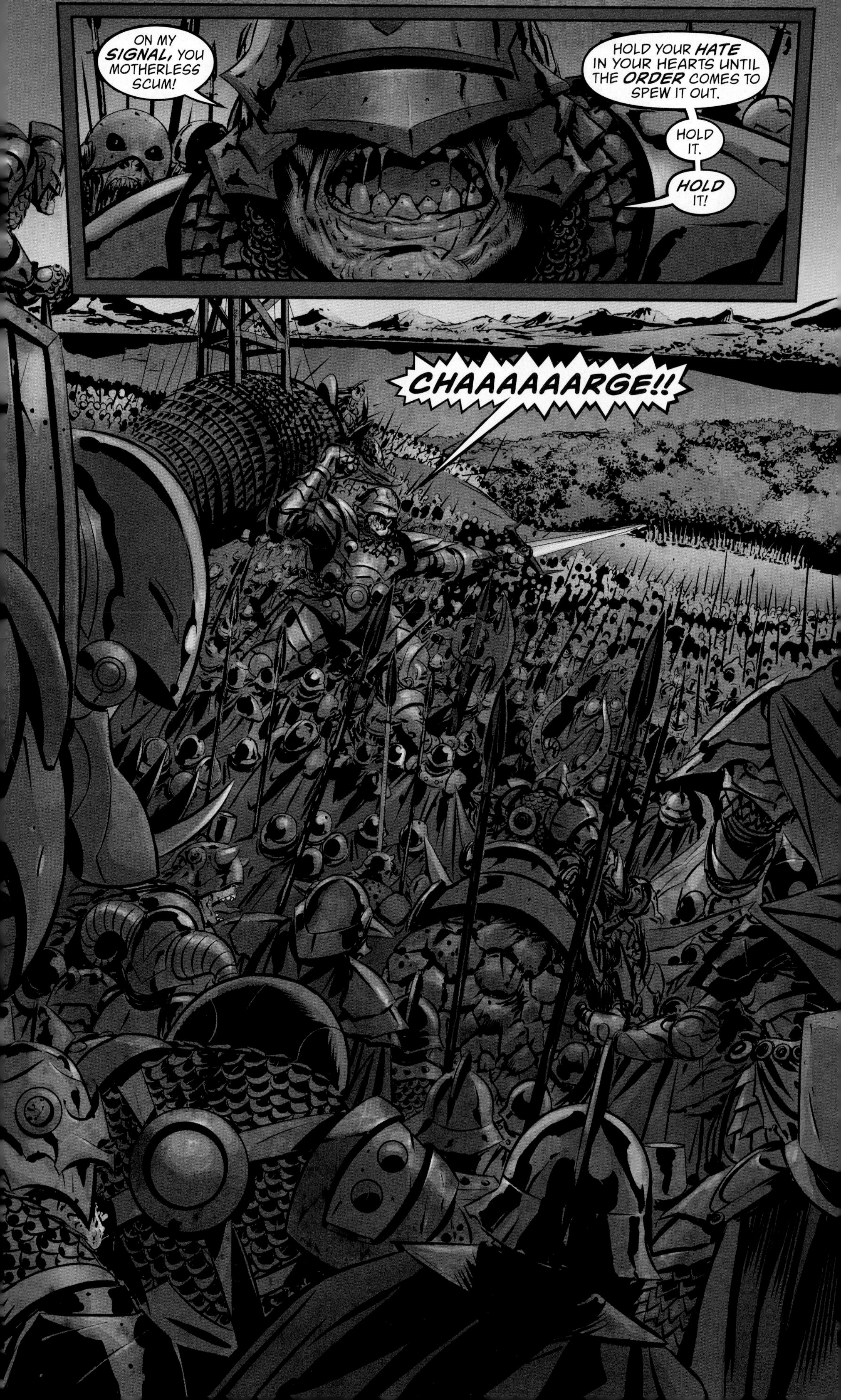
ON MY SIGNAL, YOU MOTHERLESS SCUM!
HOLD YOUR HATE IN YOUR HEARTS UNTIL THE ORDER COMES TO SPEW IT OUT.
HOLD IT.
HOLD IT!
CHAAAAAAARGE!!

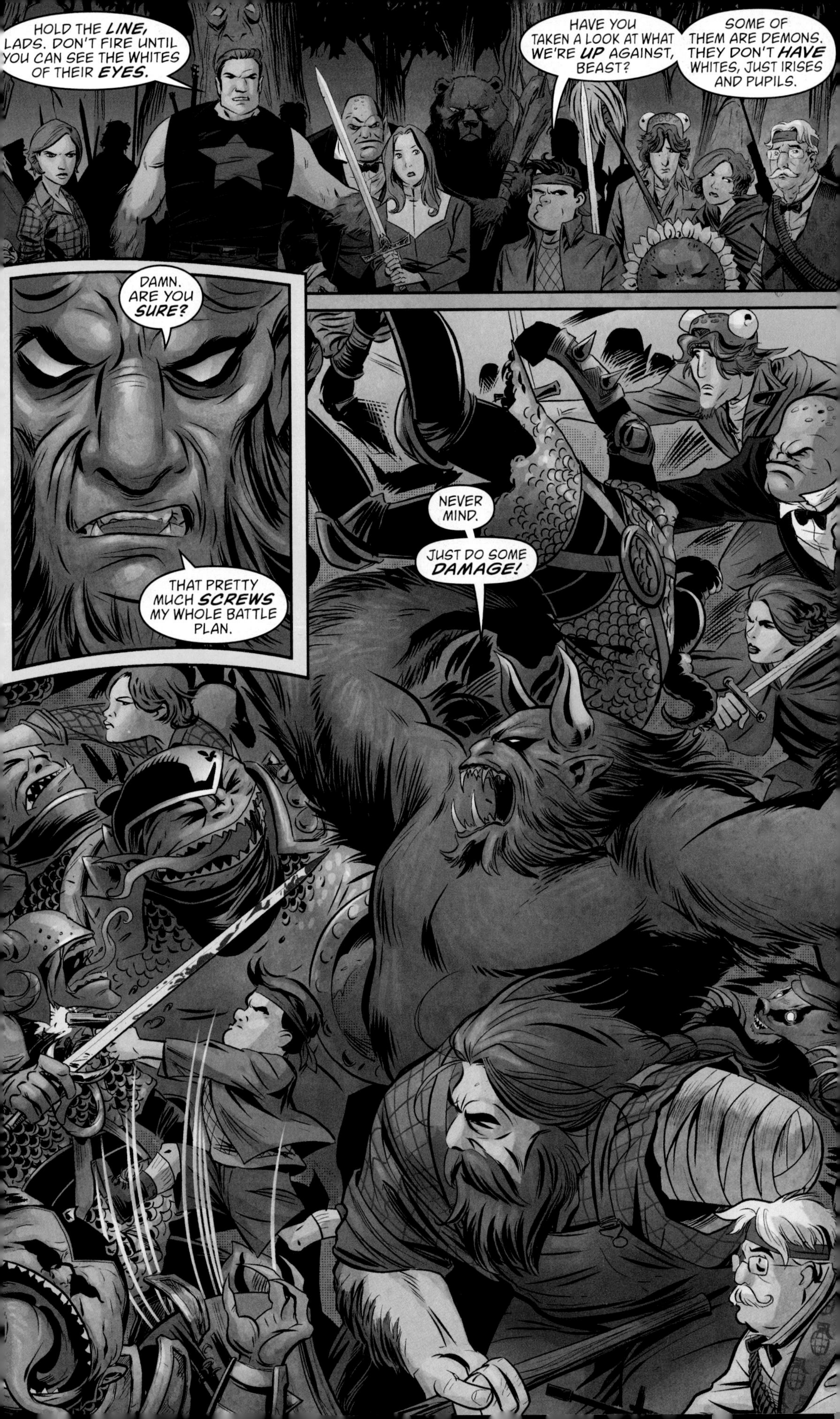
HOLD THE LINE, LADS. DON'T FIRE UNTIL YOU CAN SEE THE WHITES OF THEIR EYES.
HAVE YOU TAKEN A LOOK AT WHAT WE'RE UP AGAINST, BEAST?
SOME OF THEM ARE DEMONS. THEY DON'T HAVE WHITES, JUST IRISES AND PUPILS.
DAMN. ARE YOU SURE?
THAT PRETTY MUCH SCREWS MY WHOLE BATTLE PLAN.
NEVER MIND.
JUST DO SOME DAMAGE!

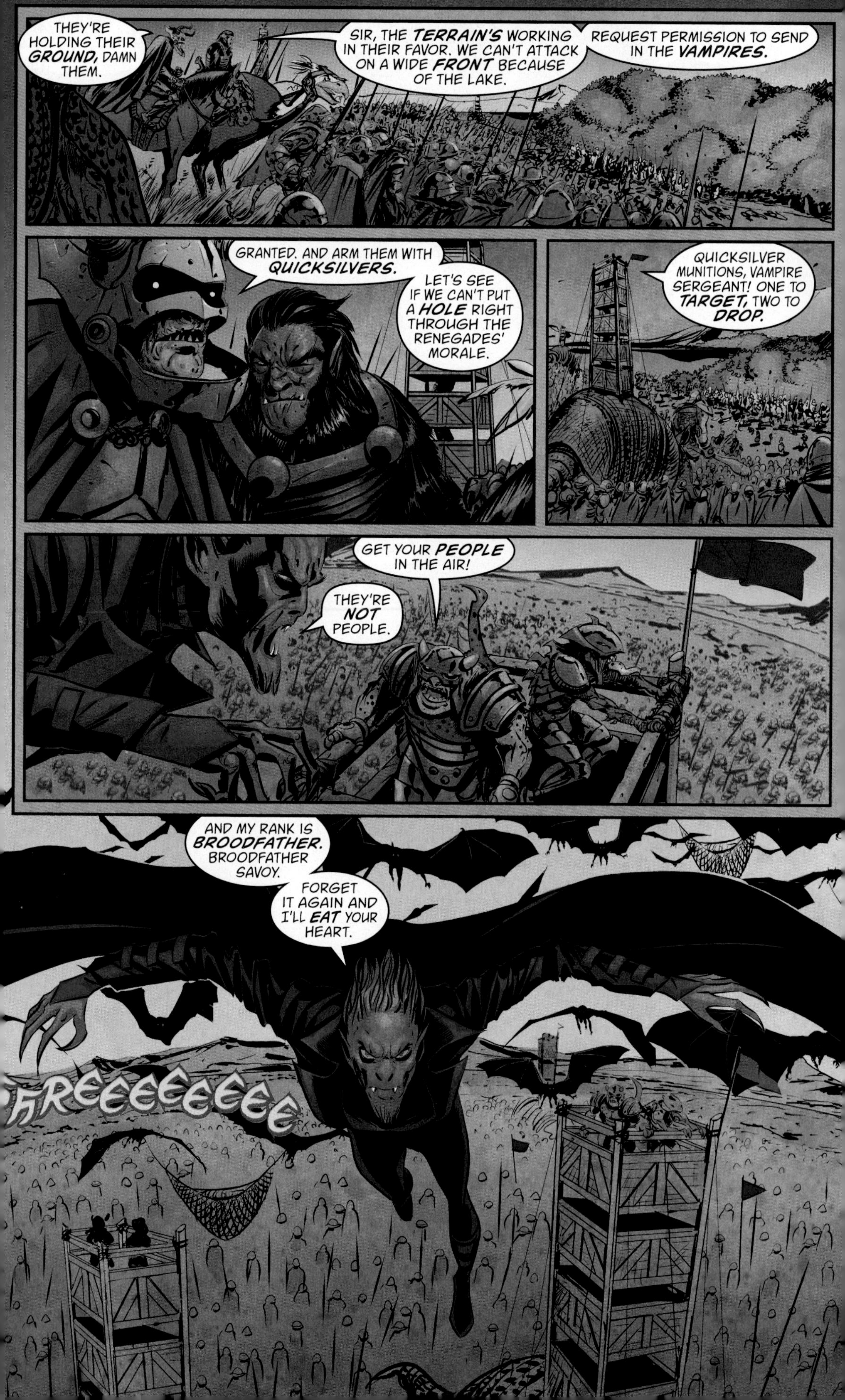
THEY'RE HOLDING THEIR GROUND, DAMN THEM.
SIR, THE TERRAIN'S WORKING IN THEIR FAVOR. WE CAN'T ATTACK ON A WIDE FRONT BECAUSE OF THE LAKE.
REQUEST PERMISSION TO SEND IN THE VAMPIRES.
GRANTED. AND ARM THEM WITH QUICKSILVERS.
LET'S SEE IF WE CAN'T PUT A HOLE RIGHT THROUGH THE RENEGADES' MORALE.
QUICKSILVER MUNITIONS, VAMPIRE SERGEANT! ONE TO TARGET, TWO TO DROP.
GET YOUR PEOPLE IN THE AIR!
THEY'RE NOT PEOPLE.
AND MY RANK IS BROODFATHER. BROODFATHER SAVOY.
FORGET IT AGAIN AND I'LL EAT YOUR HEART.
FREEEEEEEEE

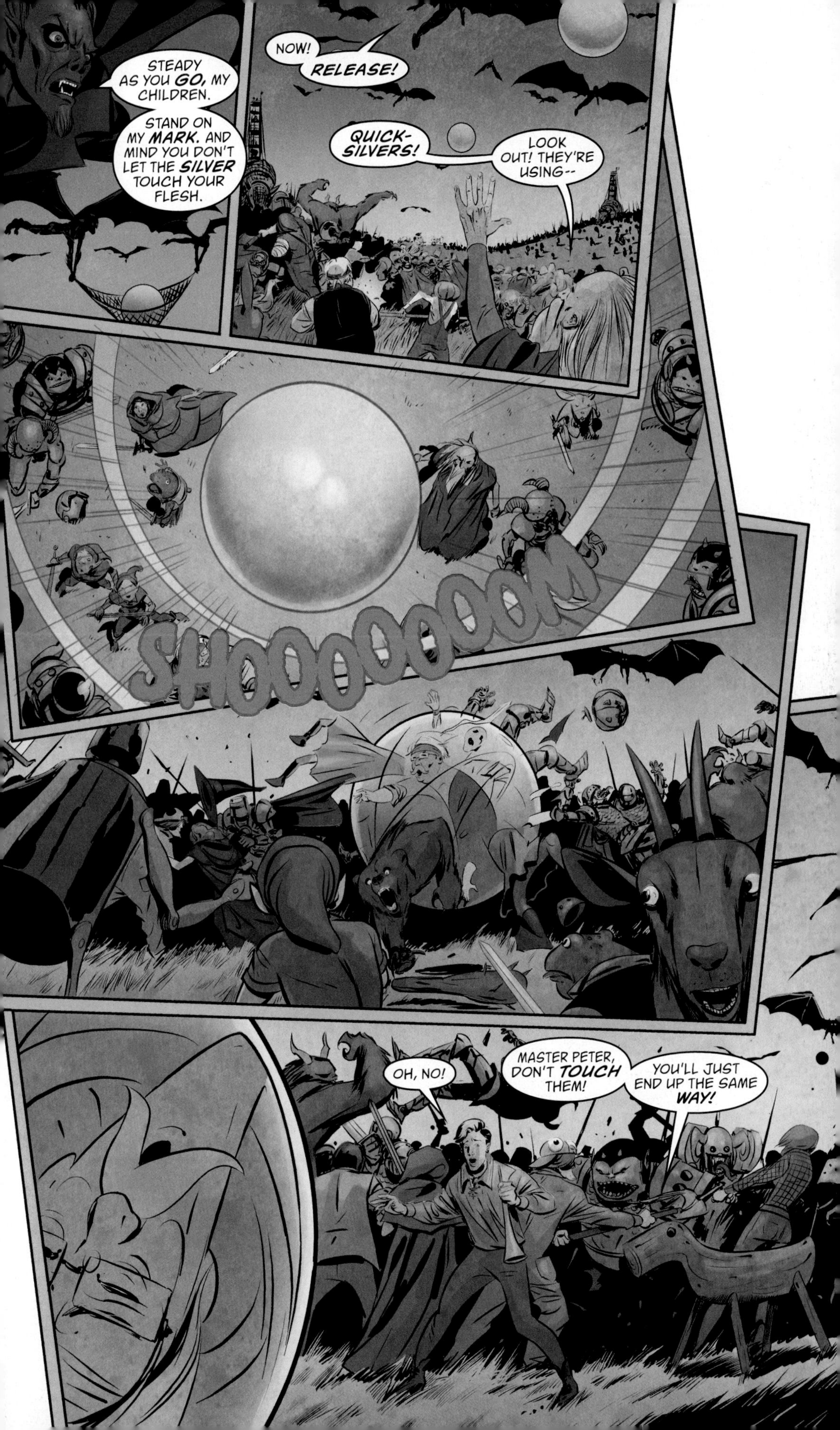
STEADY AS YOU GO, MY CHILDREN.
STAND ON MY MARK. AND MIND YOU DON'T LET THE SILVER TOUCH YOUR FLESH.
NOW! RELEASE!
QUICK-SILVERS!
LOOK OUT! THEY'RE USING--
SHOOOOOOOM
OH, NO!
MASTER PETER, DON'T TOUCH THEM!
YOU'LL JUST END UP THE SAME WAY!

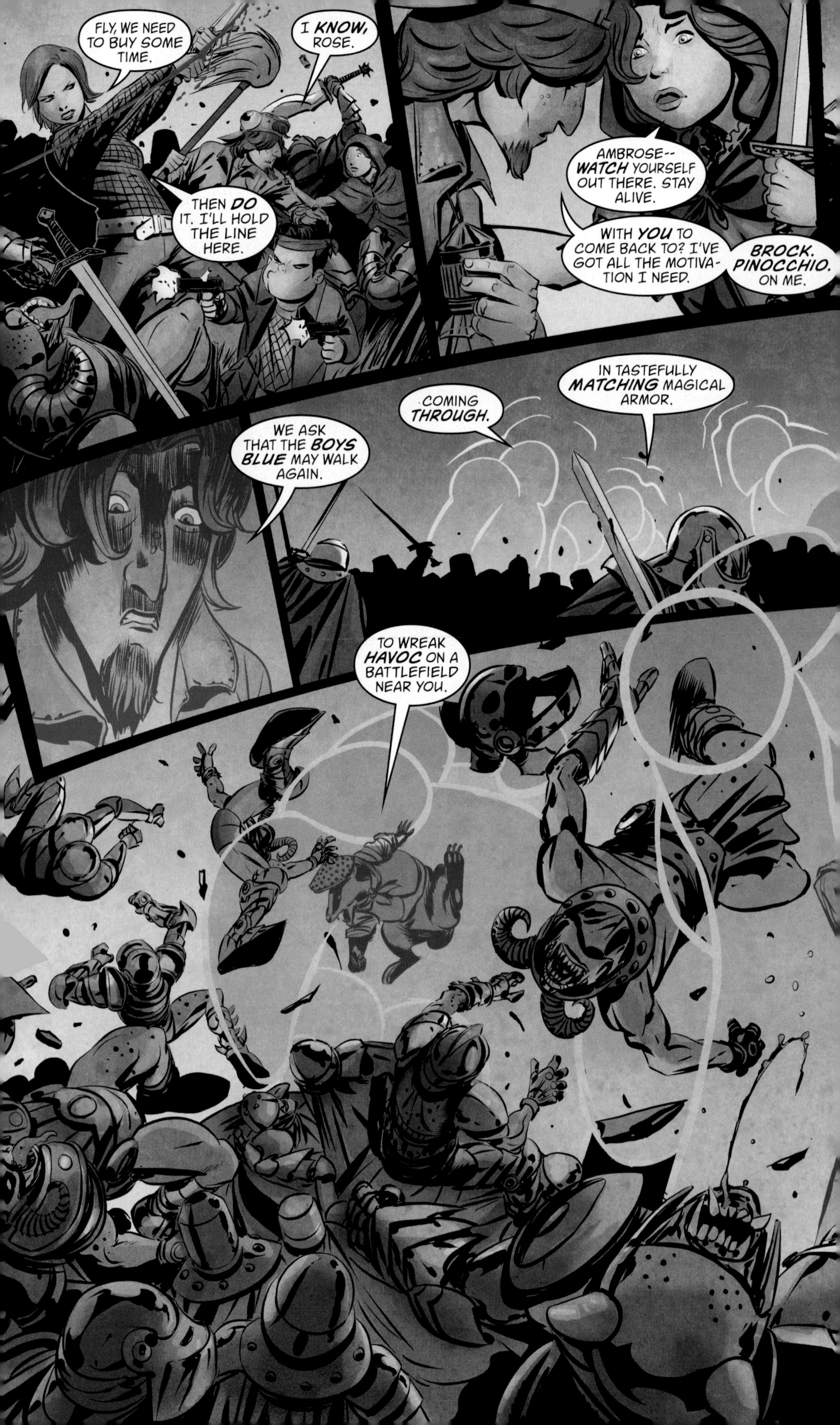
FLY, WE NEED TO BUY SOME TIME.
I KNOW, ROSE.
THEN DO IT. I'LL HOLD THE LINE HERE.
AMBROSE-- WATCH YOURSELF OUT THERE. STAY ALIVE.
WITH YOU TO COME BACK TO? I'VE GOT ALL THE MOTIVATION I NEED.
BROCK. PINOCCHIO. ON ME.
WE ASK THAT THE BOYS BLUE MAY WALK AGAIN.
COMING THROUGH.
IN TASTEFULLY MATCHING MAGICAL ARMOR.
TO WREAK HAVOC ON A BATTLEFIELD NEAR YOU.

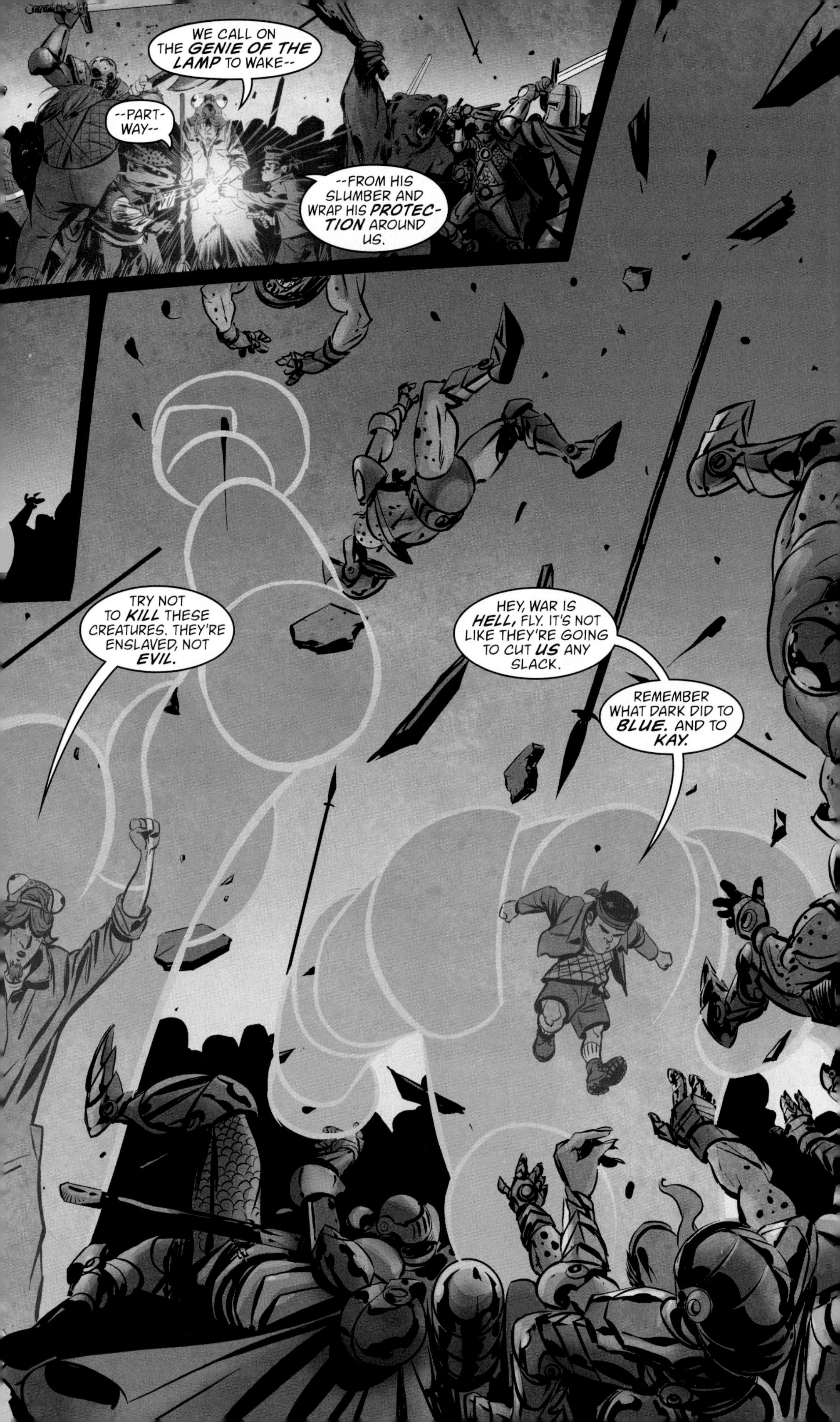
WE CALL ON THE GENIE OF THE LAMP TO WAKE--
--PART-WAY--
--FROM HIS SLUMBER AND WRAP HIS PROTEC-TION AROUND US.
TRY NOT TO KILL THESE CREATURES. THEY'RE ENSLAVED, NOT EVIL.
HEY, WAR IS HELL, FLY. IT'S NOT LIKE THEY'RE GOING TO CUT US ANY SLACK.
REMEMBER WHAT DARK DID TO BLUE. AND TO KAY.

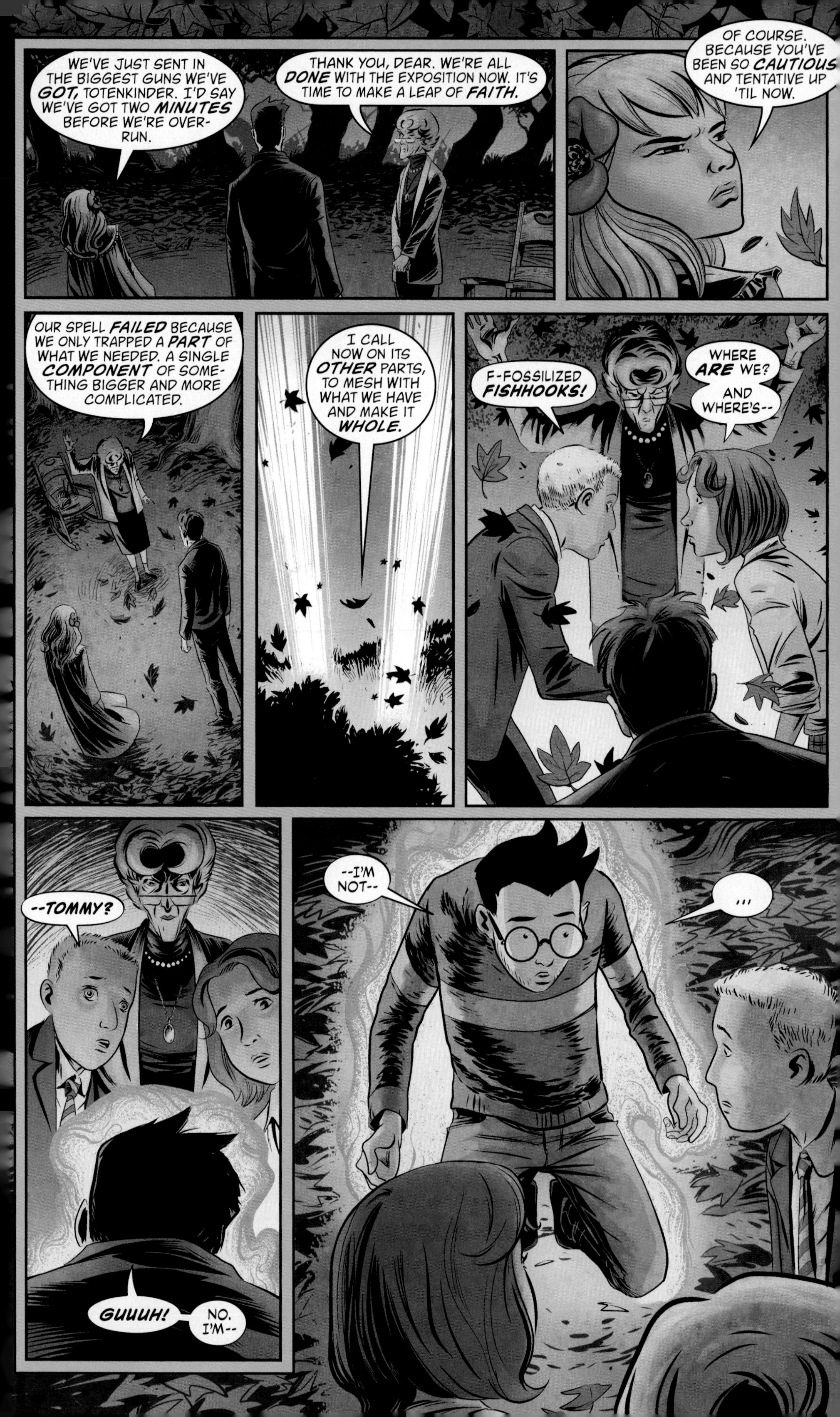

WE'VE JUST SENT IN THE BIGGEST GUNS WE'VE GOT, TOTENKINDER. I'D SAY WE'VE GOT TWO MINUTES BEFORE WE'RE OVER-RUN.
THANK YOU, DEAR. WE'RE ALL DONE WITH THE EXPOSITION NOW. IT'S TIME TO MAKE A LEAP OF FAITH.
OF COURSE. BECAUSE YOU'VE BEEN SO CAUTIOUS AND TENTATIVE UP 'TIL NOW.
OUR SPELL FAILED BECAUSE WE ONLY TRAPPED A PART OF WHAT WE NEEDED. A SINGLE COMPONENT OF SOME-THING BIGGER AND MORE COMPLICATED.
I CALL NOW ON ITS OTHER PARTS, TO MESH WITH WHAT WE HAVE AND MAKE IT WHOLE.
F-FOSSILIZED FISHHOOKS!
WHERE ARE WE?
AND WHERE'S--
--TOMMY?
GUUUH!
NO. I'M--
--I'M NOT--
...

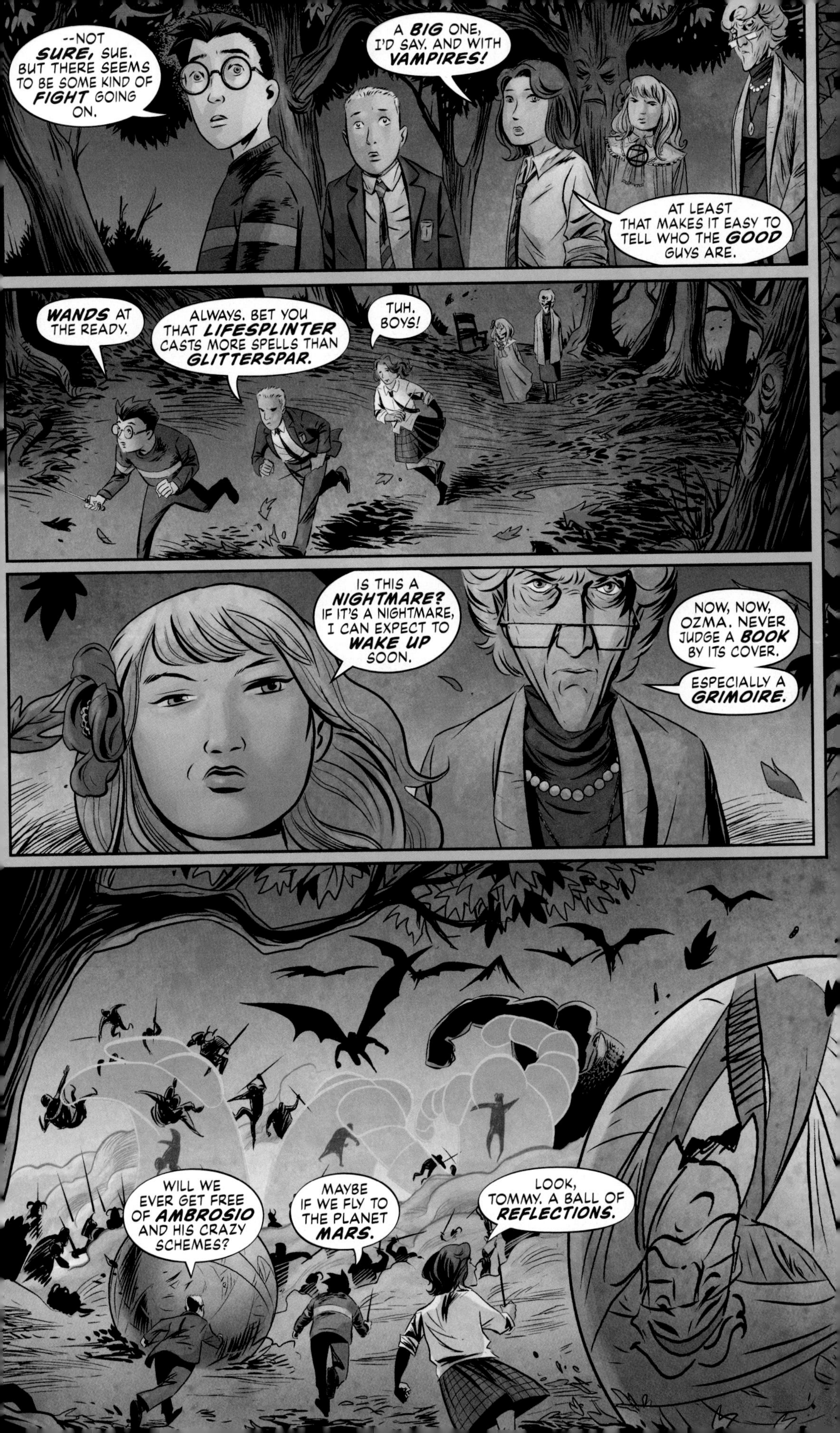
--NOT SURE, SUE. BUT THERE SEEMS TO BE SOME KIND OF FIGHT GOING ON.
A BIG ONE, I'D SAY. AND WITH VAMPIRES!
AT LEAST THAT MAKES IT EASY TO TELL WHO THE GOOD GUYS ARE.
WANDS AT THE READY.
ALWAYS. BET YOU THAT LIFESPLINTER CASTS MORE SPELLS THAN GLITTERSPAR.
TUH. BOYS!
IS THIS A NIGHTMARE? IF IT'S A NIGHTMARE, I CAN EXPECT TO WAKE UP SOON.
NOW, NOW, OZMA. NEVER JUDGE A BOOK BY ITS COVER.
ESPECIALLY A GRIMOIRE.
WILL WE EVER GET FREE OF AMBROSIO AND HIS CRAZY SCHEMES?
MAYBE IF WE FLY TO THE PLANET MARS.
LOOK, TOMMY. A BALL OF REFLECTIONS.

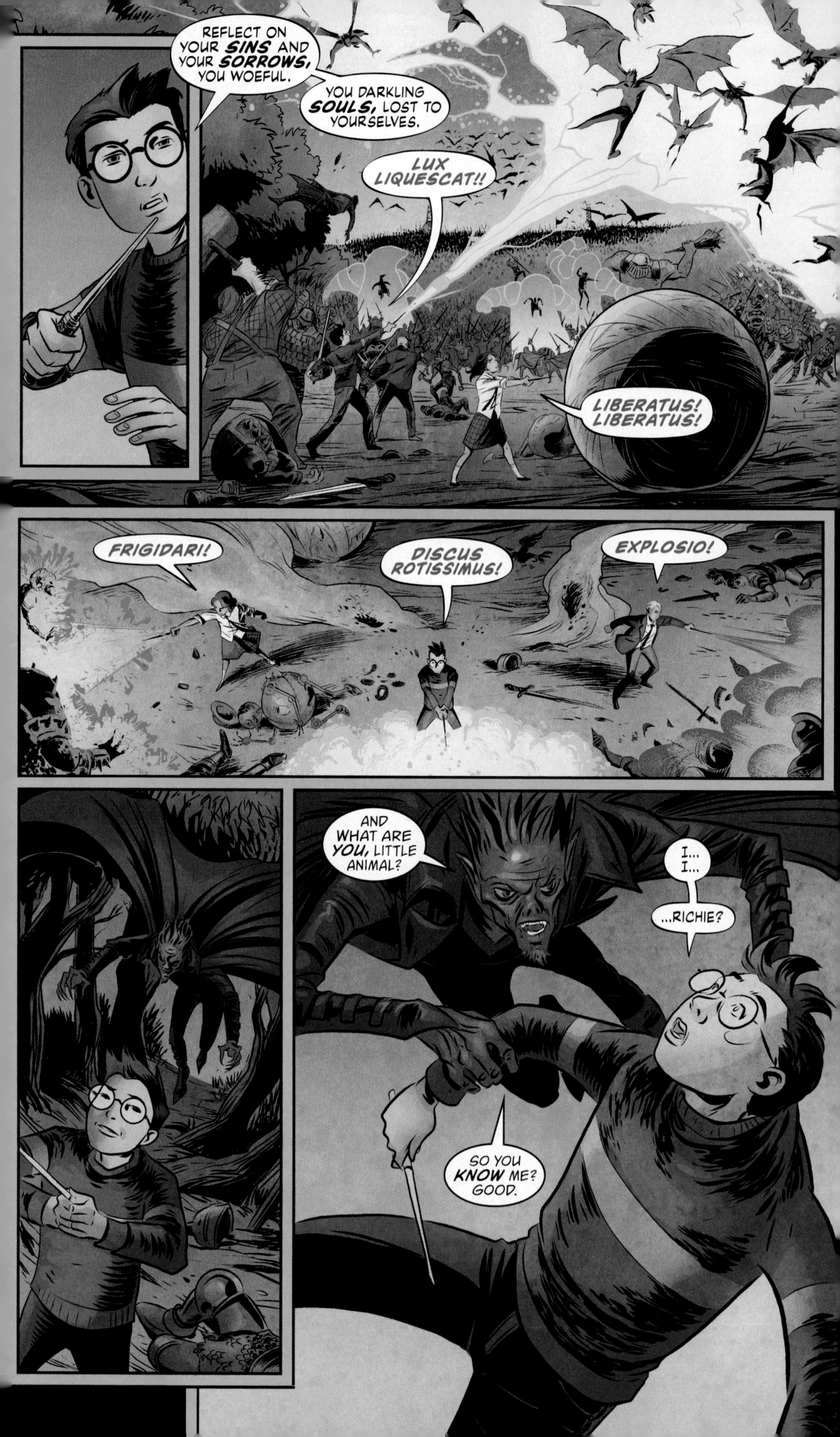

REFLECT ON YOUR SINS AND YOUR SORROWS, YOU WOEFUL.
YOU DARKLING SOULS, LOST TO YOURSELVES.
LUX LIQUESCAT!!
LIBERATUS! LIBERATUS!
FRIGIDARI!
DISCUS ROTISSIMUS!
EXPLOSIO!
AND WHAT ARE YOU, LITTLE ANIMAL?
I... I...
...RICHIE?
SO YOU KNOW ME? GOOD.

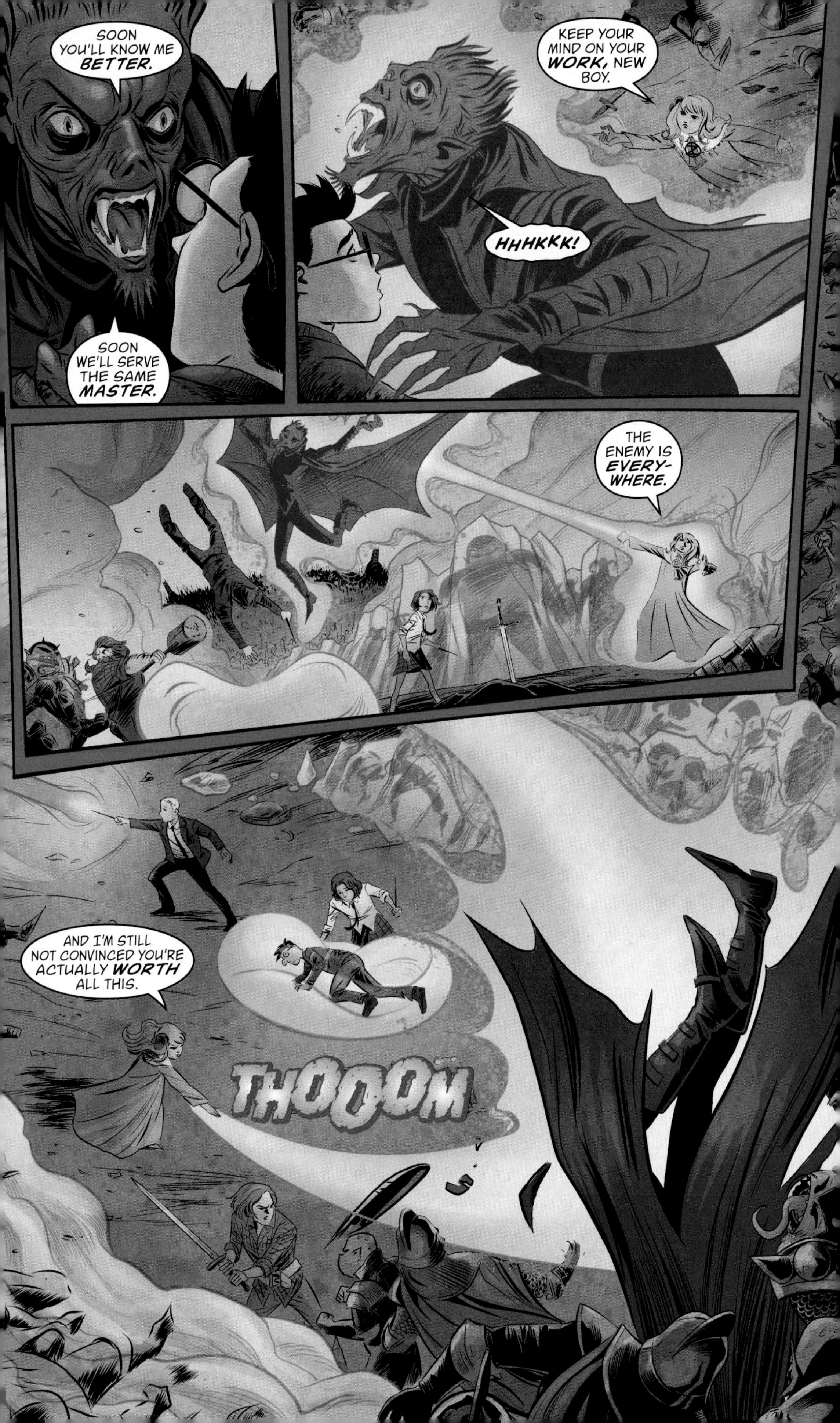
SOON YOU'LL KNOW ME BETTER.
SOON WE'LL SERVE THE SAME MASTER.
KEEP YOUR MIND ON YOUR WORK, NEW BOY.
HHHKKK!
THE ENEMY IS EVERY-WHERE.
AND I'M STILL NOT CONVINCED YOU'RE ACTUALLY WORTH ALL THIS.
THOOOM

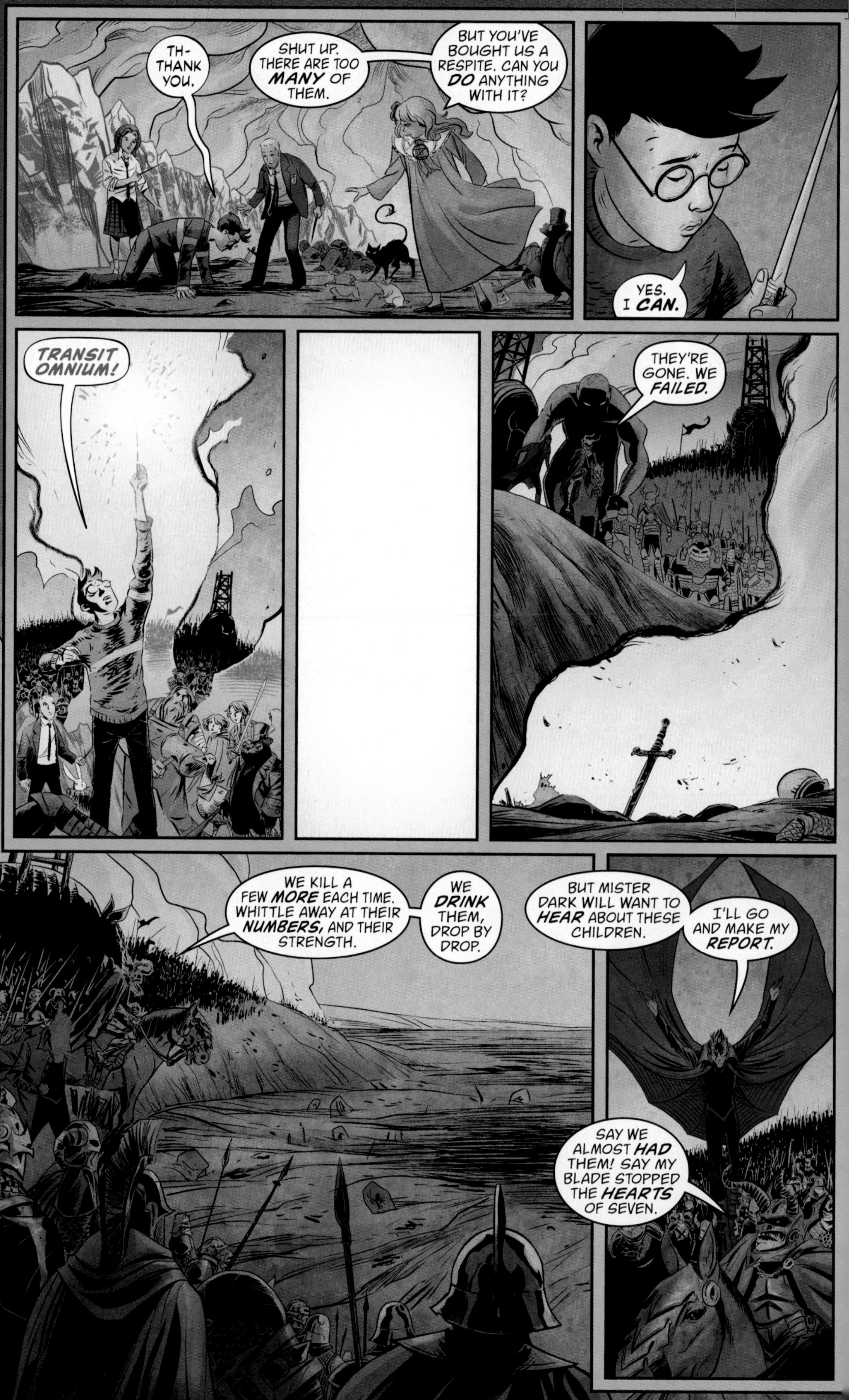

TH-THANK YOU.
SHUT UP. THERE ARE TOO MANY OF THEM.
BUT YOU'VE BOUGHT US A RESPITE. CAN YOU DO ANYTHING WITH IT?
YES. I CAN.
TRANSIT OMNIUM!
THEY'RE GONE. WE FAILED.
WE KILL A FEW MORE EACH TIME. WHITTLE AWAY AT THEIR NUMBERS, AND THEIR STRENGTH.
WE DRINK THEM, DROP BY DROP.
BUT MISTER DARK WILL WANT TO HEAR ABOUT THESE CHILDREN.
I'LL GO AND MAKE MY REPORT.
SAY WE ALMOST HAD THEM! SAY MY BLADE STOPPED THE HEARTS OF SEVEN.

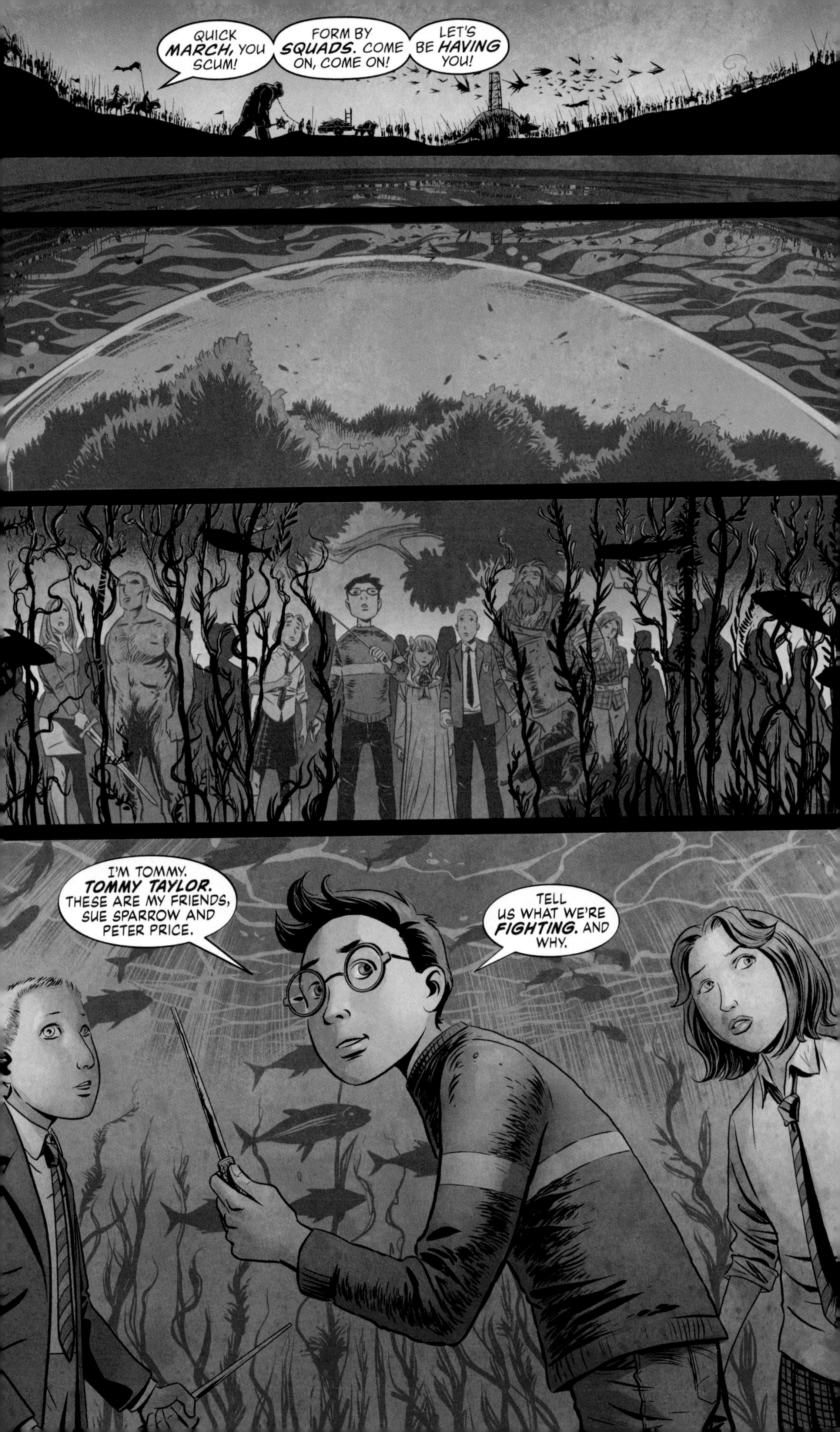
QUICK MARCH, YOU SCUM!
FORM BY SQUADS. COME ON, COME ON!
LET'S BE HAVING YOU!
I'M TOMMY. TOMMY TAYLOR. THESE ARE MY FRIENDS, SUE SPARROW AND PETER PRICE.
TELL US WHAT WE'RE FIGHTING. AND WHY.

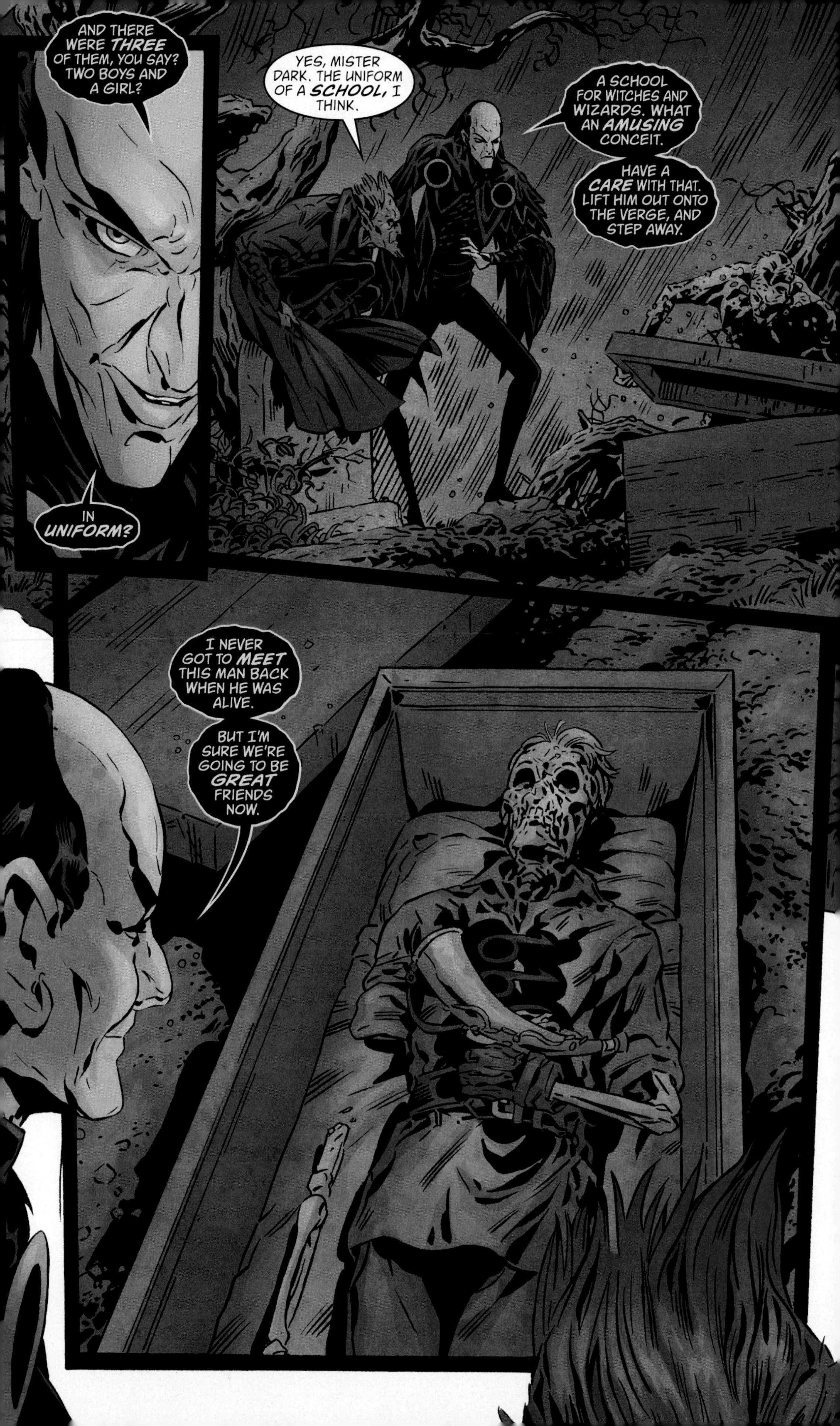
AND THERE WERE THREE OF THEM, YOU SAY? TWO BOYS AND A GIRL?
YES, MISTER DARK. THE UNIFORM OF A SCHOOL, I THINK.
IN UNIFORM?
A SCHOOL FOR WITCHES AND WIZARDS. WHAT AN AMUSING CONCEIT.
HAVE A CARE WITH THAT. LIFT HIM OUT ONTO THE VERGE, AND STEP AWAY.
I NEVER GOT TO MEET THIS MAN BACK WHEN HE WAS ALIVE.
BUT I'M SURE WE'RE GOING TO BE GREAT FRIENDS NOW.

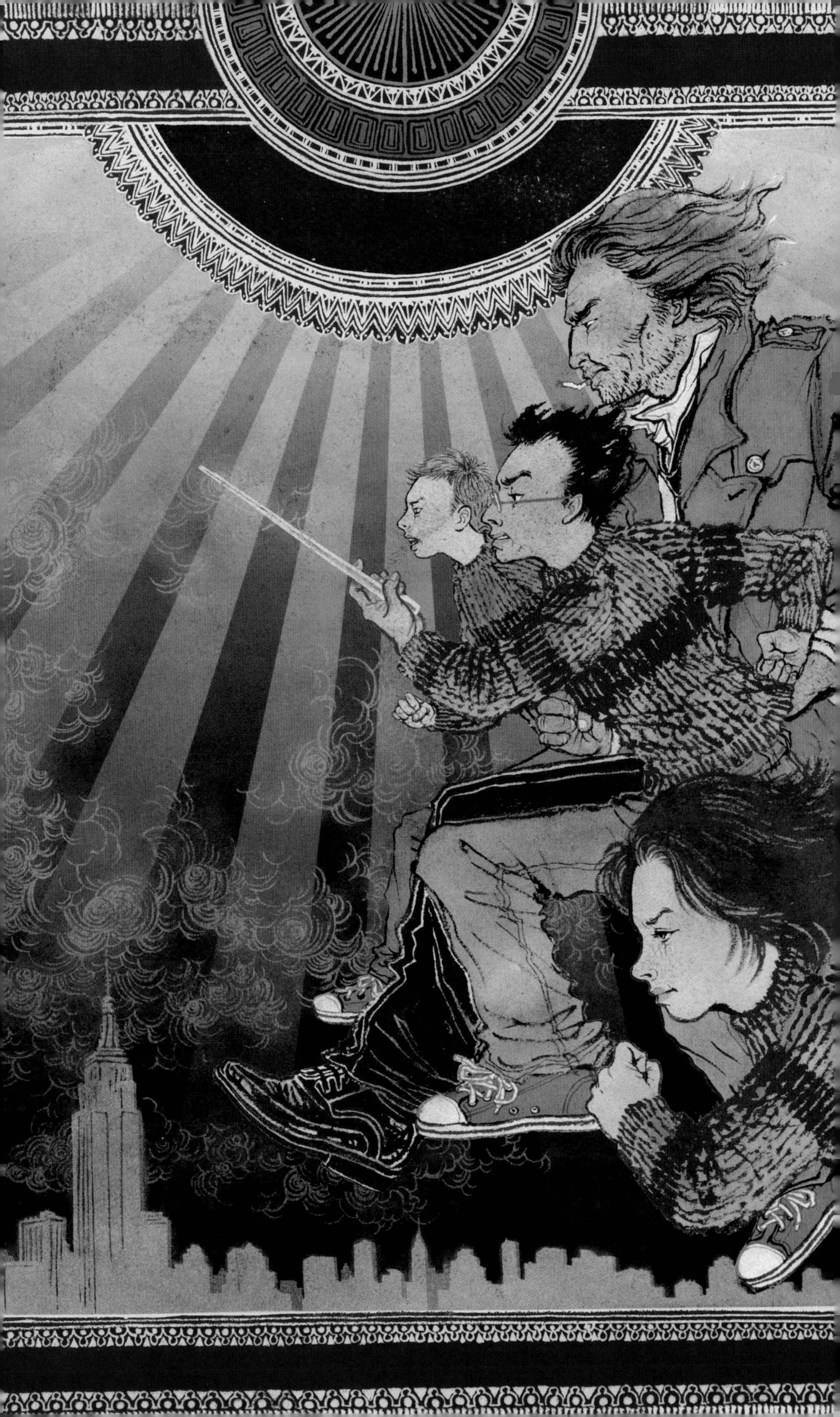

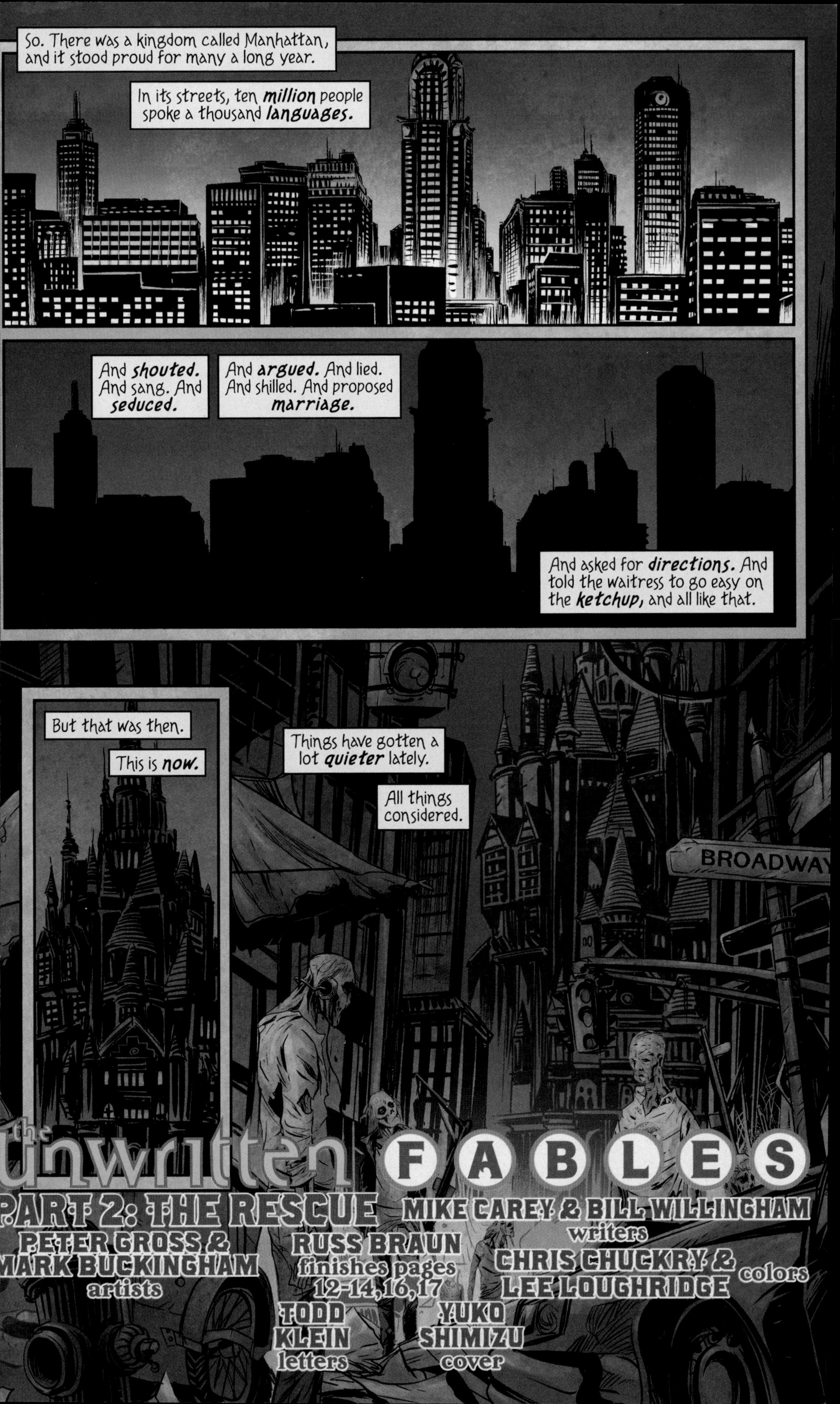

So. There was a kingdom called Manhattan, and it stood proud for many a long year.
In its streets, ten **million** people spoke a thousand **languages.**
And **shouted.** And sang. And **seduced.**
And **argued.** And lied. And shilled. And proposed **marriage.**
And asked for **directions.** And told the waitress to go easy on the **ketchup,** and all like that.
But that was then.
This is **now.**
Things have gotten a lot **quieter** lately.
All things considered.
BROADWAY
the Unwritten FABLES
PART 2: THE RESCUE
MIKE CAREY & BILL WILLINGHAM writers
PETER GROSS & MARK BUCKINGHAM artists
RUSS BRAUN finishes pages 12-14, 16, 17
CHRIS CHUCKRY & LEE LOUGHRIDGE colors
TODD KLEIN letters
YUKO SHIMIZU cover

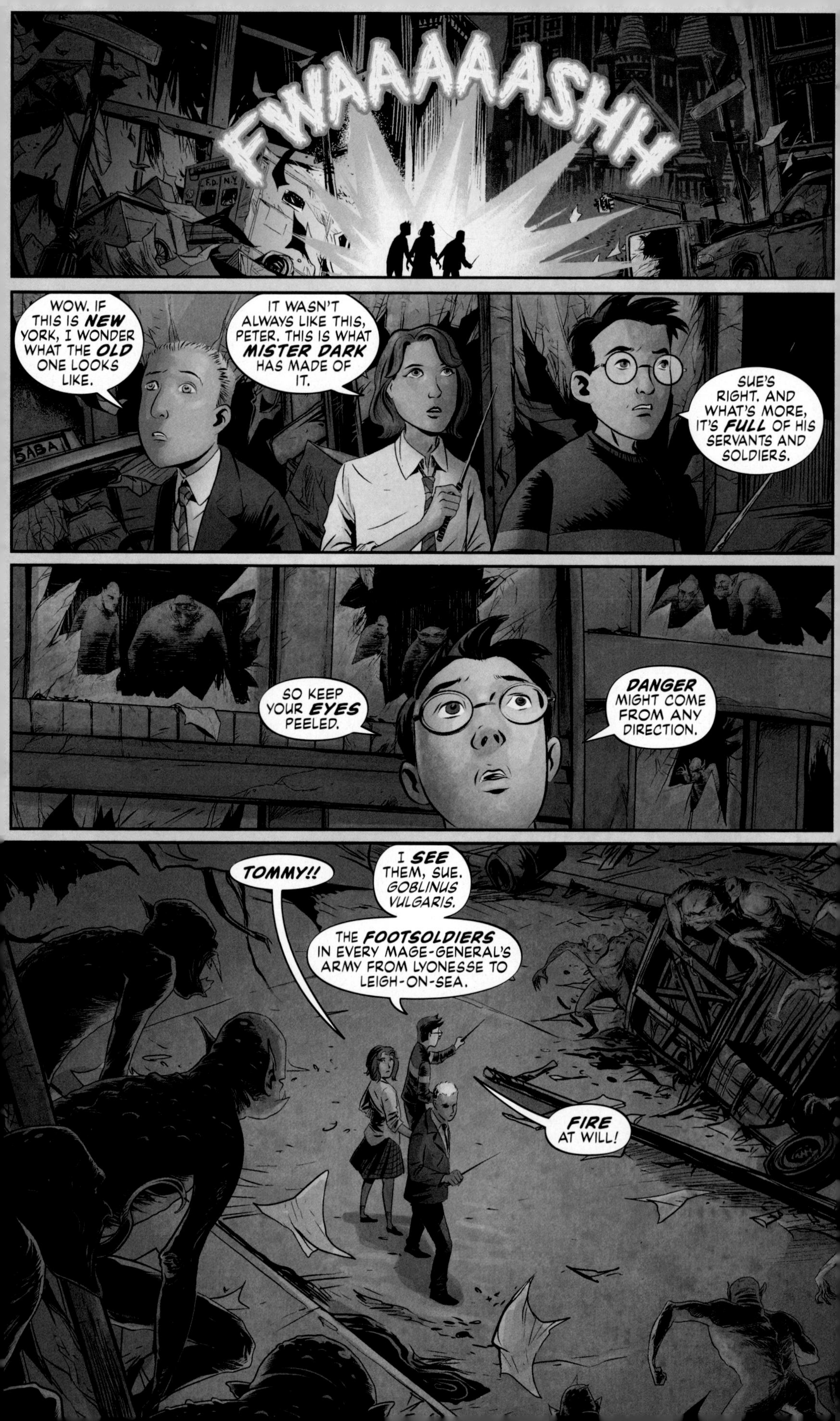
FWAAAAASHH
WOW. IF THIS IS NEW YORK, I WONDER WHAT THE OLD ONE LOOKS LIKE.
IT WASN'T ALWAYS LIKE THIS, PETER. THIS IS WHAT MISTER DARK HAS MADE OF IT.
SUE'S RIGHT. AND WHAT'S MORE, IT'S FULL OF HIS SERVANTS AND SOLDIERS.
SO KEEP YOUR EYES PEELED.
DANGER MIGHT COME FROM ANY DIRECTION.
TOMMY!!
I SEE THEM, SUE. GOBLINUS VULGARIS.
THE FOOTSOLDIERS IN EVERY MAGE-GENERAL'S ARMY FROM LYONESSE TO LEIGH-ON-SEA.
FIRE AT WILL!

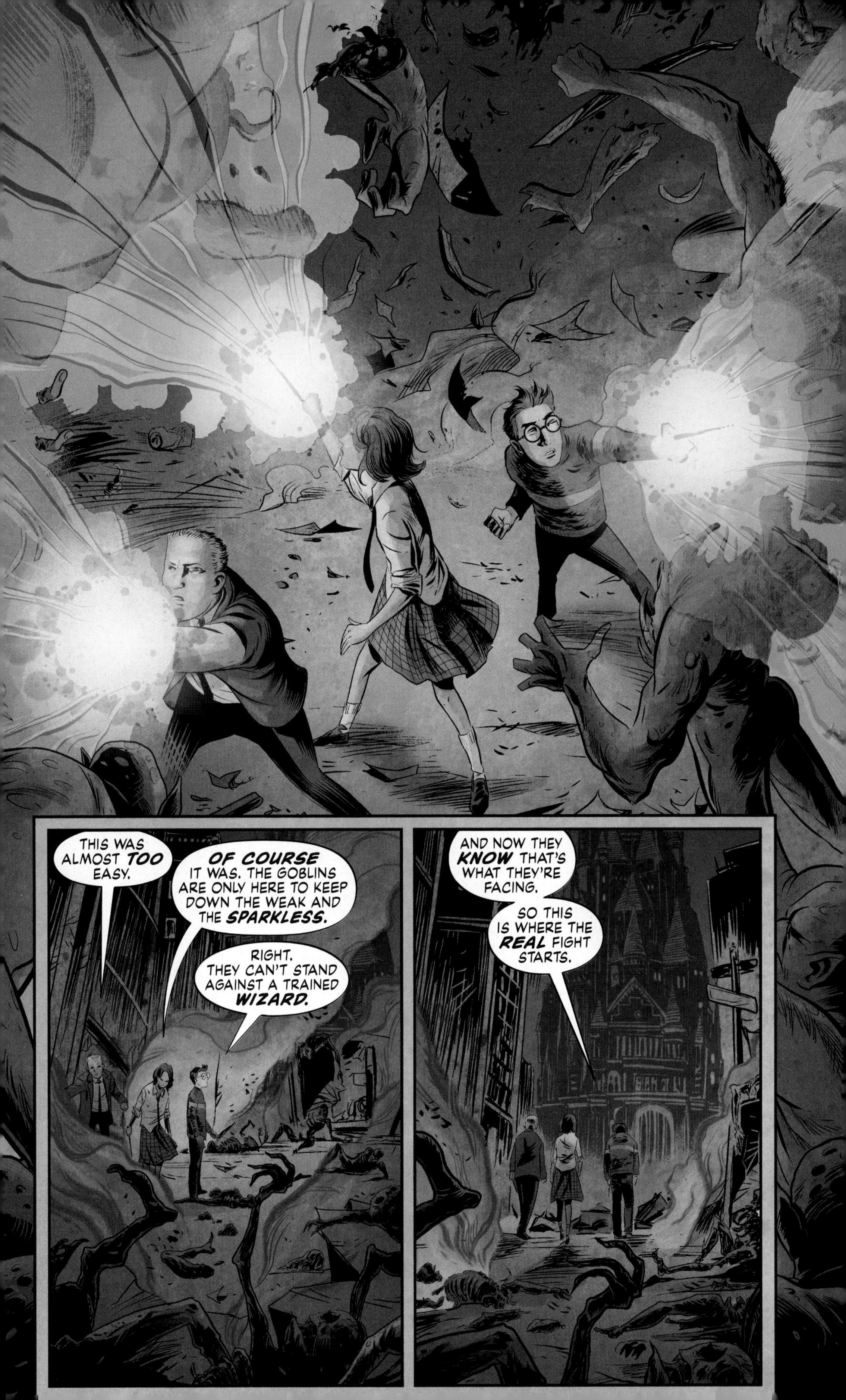
THIS WAS ALMOST TOO EASY.
OF COURSE IT WAS. THE GOBLINS ARE ONLY HERE TO KEEP DOWN THE WEAK AND THE SPARKLESS.
RIGHT. THEY CAN'T STAND AGAINST A TRAINED WIZARD.
AND NOW THEY KNOW THAT'S WHAT THEY'RE FACING.
SO THIS IS WHERE THE REAL FIGHT STARTS.

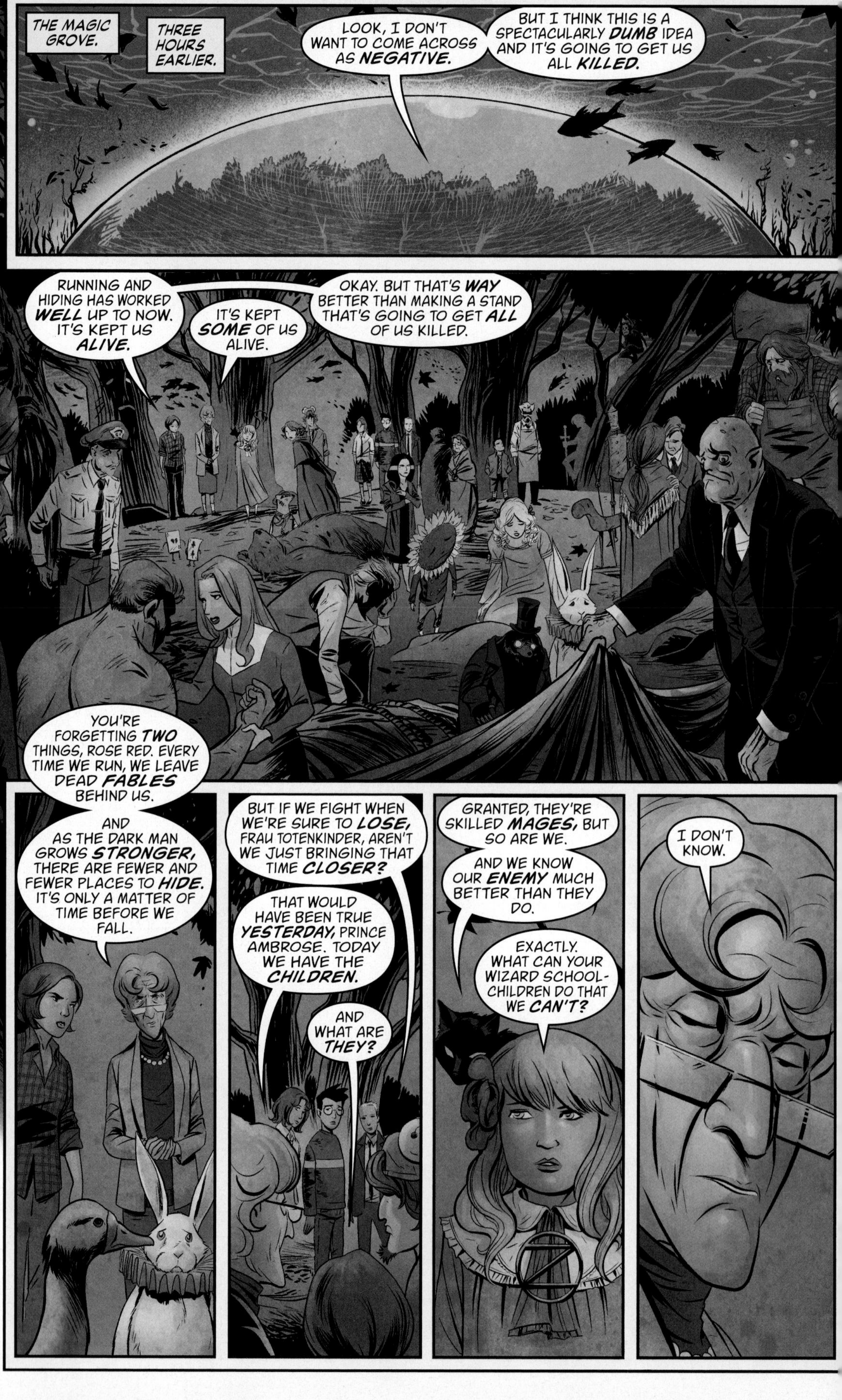
THE MAGIC GROVE.
THREE HOURS EARLIER.
LOOK, I DON'T WANT TO COME ACROSS AS NEGATIVE.
BUT I THINK THIS IS A SPECTACULARLY DUMB IDEA AND IT'S GOING TO GET US ALL KILLED.
RUNNING AND HIDING HAS WORKED WELL UP TO NOW. IT'S KEPT US ALIVE.
IT'S KEPT SOME OF US ALIVE.
OKAY. BUT THAT'S WAY BETTER THAN MAKING A STAND THAT'S GOING TO GET ALL OF US KILLED.
YOU'RE FORGETTING TWO THINGS, ROSE RED. EVERY TIME WE RUN, WE LEAVE DEAD FABLES BEHIND US.
AND AS THE DARK MAN GROWS STRONGER, THERE ARE FEWER AND FEWER PLACES TO HIDE. IT'S ONLY A MATTER OF TIME BEFORE WE FALL.
BUT IF WE FIGHT WHEN WE'RE SURE TO LOSE, FRAU TOTENKINDER, AREN'T WE JUST BRINGING THAT TIME CLOSER?
THAT WOULD HAVE BEEN TRUE YESTERDAY, PRINCE AMBROSE. TODAY WE HAVE THE CHILDREN.
AND WHAT ARE THEY?
GRANTED, THEY'RE SKILLED MAGES, BUT SO ARE WE.
AND WE KNOW OUR ENEMY MUCH BETTER THAN THEY DO.
EXACTLY. WHAT CAN YOUR WIZARD SCHOOL-CHILDREN DO THAT WE CAN'T?
I DON'T KNOW.

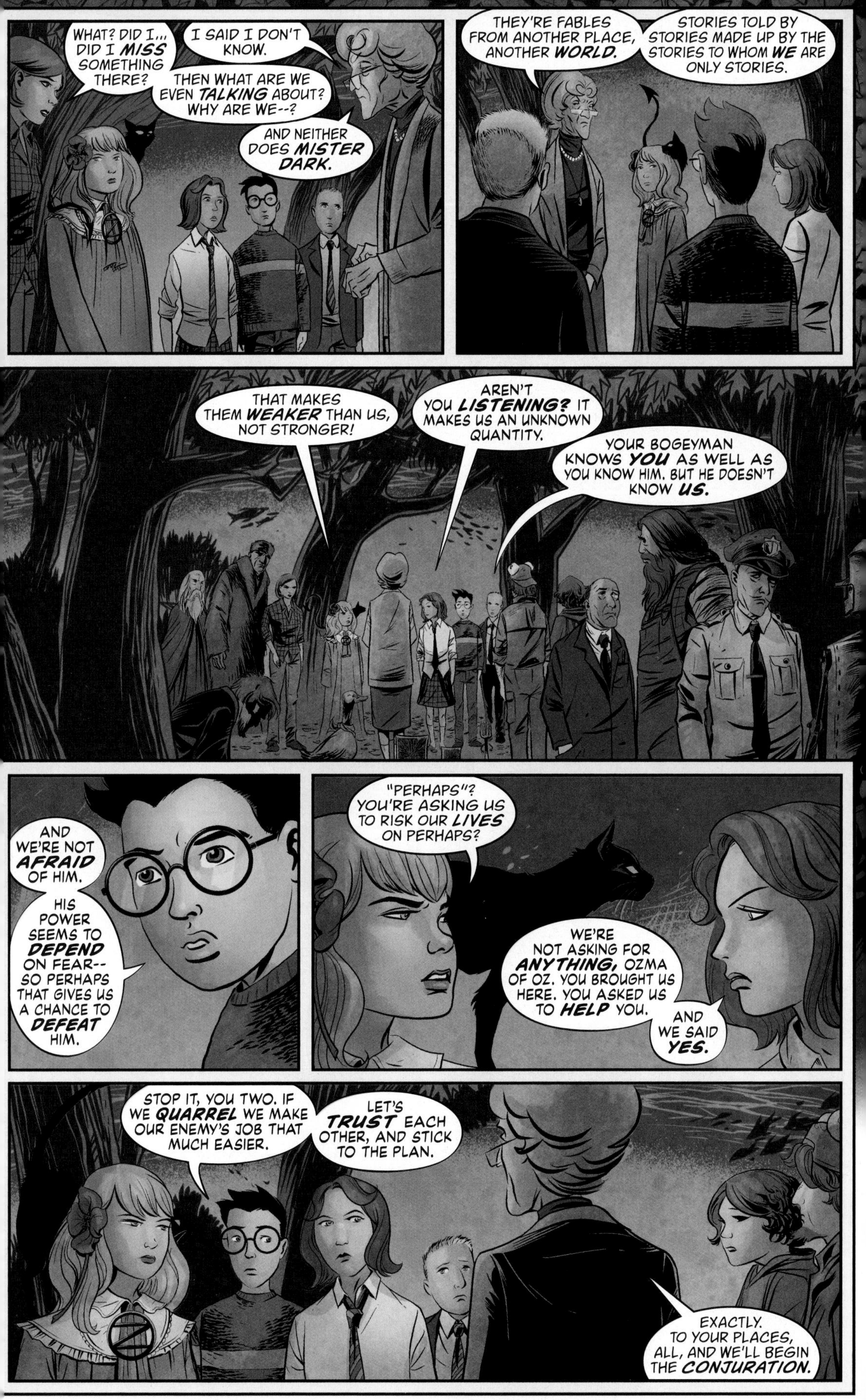
WHAT? DID I... DID I MISS SOMETHING THERE?
I SAID I DON'T KNOW.
THEN WHAT ARE WE EVEN TALKING ABOUT? WHY ARE WE--?
AND NEITHER DOES MISTER DARK.
THEY'RE FABLES FROM ANOTHER PLACE, ANOTHER WORLD.
STORIES TOLD BY STORIES MADE UP BY THE STORIES TO WHOM WE ARE ONLY STORIES.
THAT MAKES THEM WEAKER THAN US, NOT STRONGER!
AREN'T YOU LISTENING? IT MAKES US AN UNKNOWN QUANTITY.
YOUR BOGEYMAN KNOWS YOU AS WELL AS YOU KNOW HIM. BUT HE DOESN'T KNOW US.
AND WE'RE NOT AFRAID OF HIM.
HIS POWER SEEMS TO DEPEND ON FEAR-- SO PERHAPS THAT GIVES US A CHANCE TO DEFEAT HIM.
"PERHAPS"? YOU'RE ASKING US TO RISK OUR LIVES ON PERHAPS?
WE'RE NOT ASKING FOR ANYTHING, OZMA OF OZ. YOU BROUGHT US HERE. YOU ASKED US TO HELP YOU.
AND WE SAID YES.
STOP IT, YOU TWO. IF WE QUARREL WE MAKE OUR ENEMY'S JOB THAT MUCH EASIER.
LET'S TRUST EACH OTHER, AND STICK TO THE PLAN.
EXACTLY. TO YOUR PLACES, ALL, AND WE'LL BEGIN THE CONJURATION.

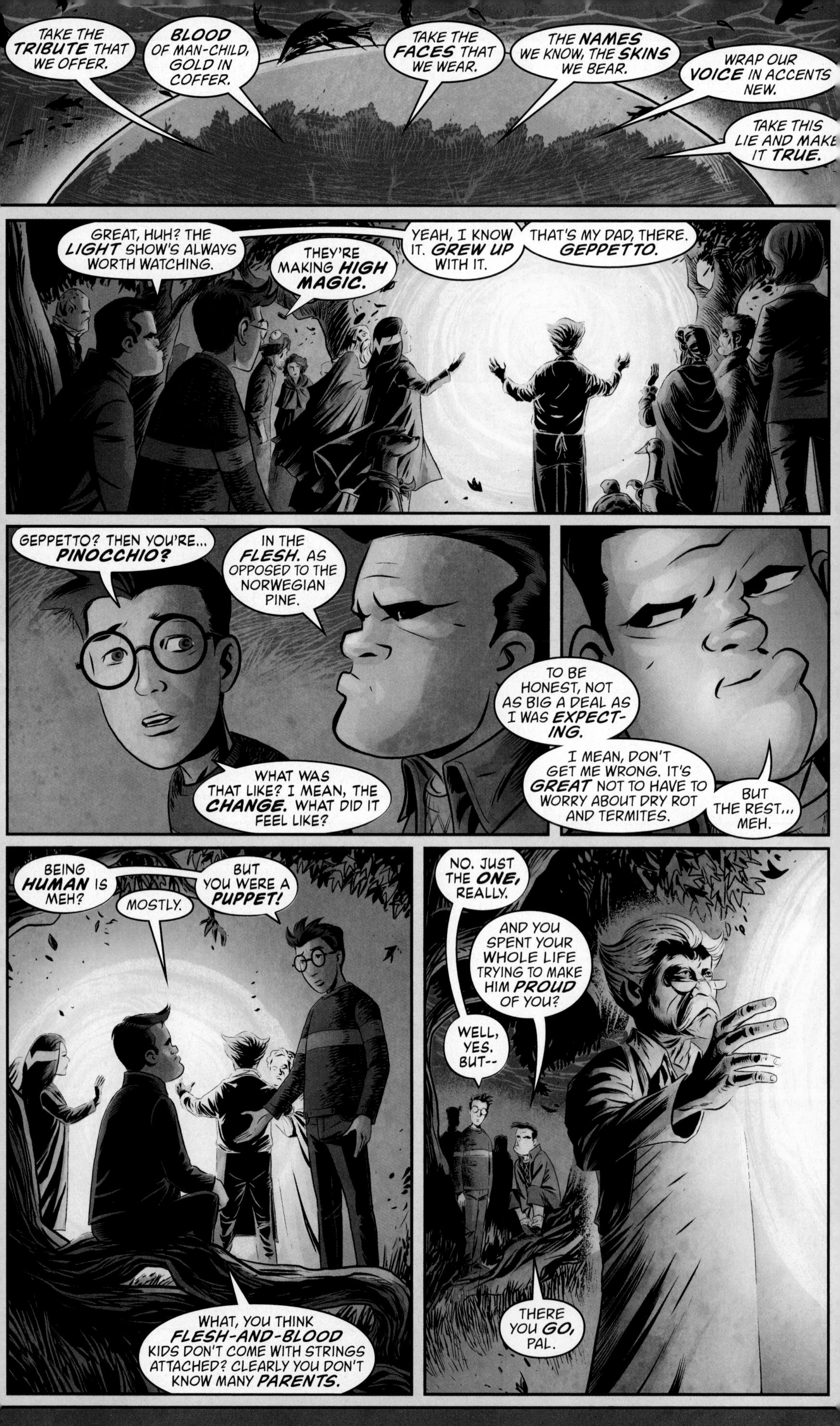

TAKE THE TRIBUTE THAT WE OFFER.
BLOOD OF MAN-CHILD, GOLD IN COFFER.
TAKE THE FACES THAT WE WEAR.
THE NAMES WE KNOW, THE SKINS WE BEAR.
WRAP OUR VOICE IN ACCENTS NEW.
TAKE THIS LIE AND MAKE IT TRUE.
GREAT, HUH? THE LIGHT SHOW'S ALWAYS WORTH WATCHING.
THEY'RE MAKING HIGH MAGIC.
YEAH, I KNOW IT. GREW UP WITH IT.
THAT'S MY DAD, THERE. GEPPETTO.
GEPPETTO? THEN YOU'RE... PINOCCHIO?
IN THE FLESH. AS OPPOSED TO THE NORWEGIAN PINE.
WHAT WAS THAT LIKE? I MEAN, THE CHANGE. WHAT DID IT FEEL LIKE?
TO BE HONEST, NOT AS BIG A DEAL AS I WAS EXPECT-ING.
I MEAN, DON'T GET ME WRONG. IT'S GREAT NOT TO HAVE TO WORRY ABOUT DRY ROT AND TERMITES.
BUT THE REST... MEH.
BEING HUMAN IS MEH?
MOSTLY.
BUT YOU WERE A PUPPET!
WHAT, YOU THINK FLESH-AND-BLOOD KIDS DON'T COME WITH STRINGS ATTACHED? CLEARLY YOU DON'T KNOW MANY PARENTS.
NO. JUST THE ONE, REALLY.
AND YOU SPENT YOUR WHOLE LIFE TRYING TO MAKE HIM PROUD OF YOU?
WELL, YES. BUT--
THERE YOU GO, PAL.

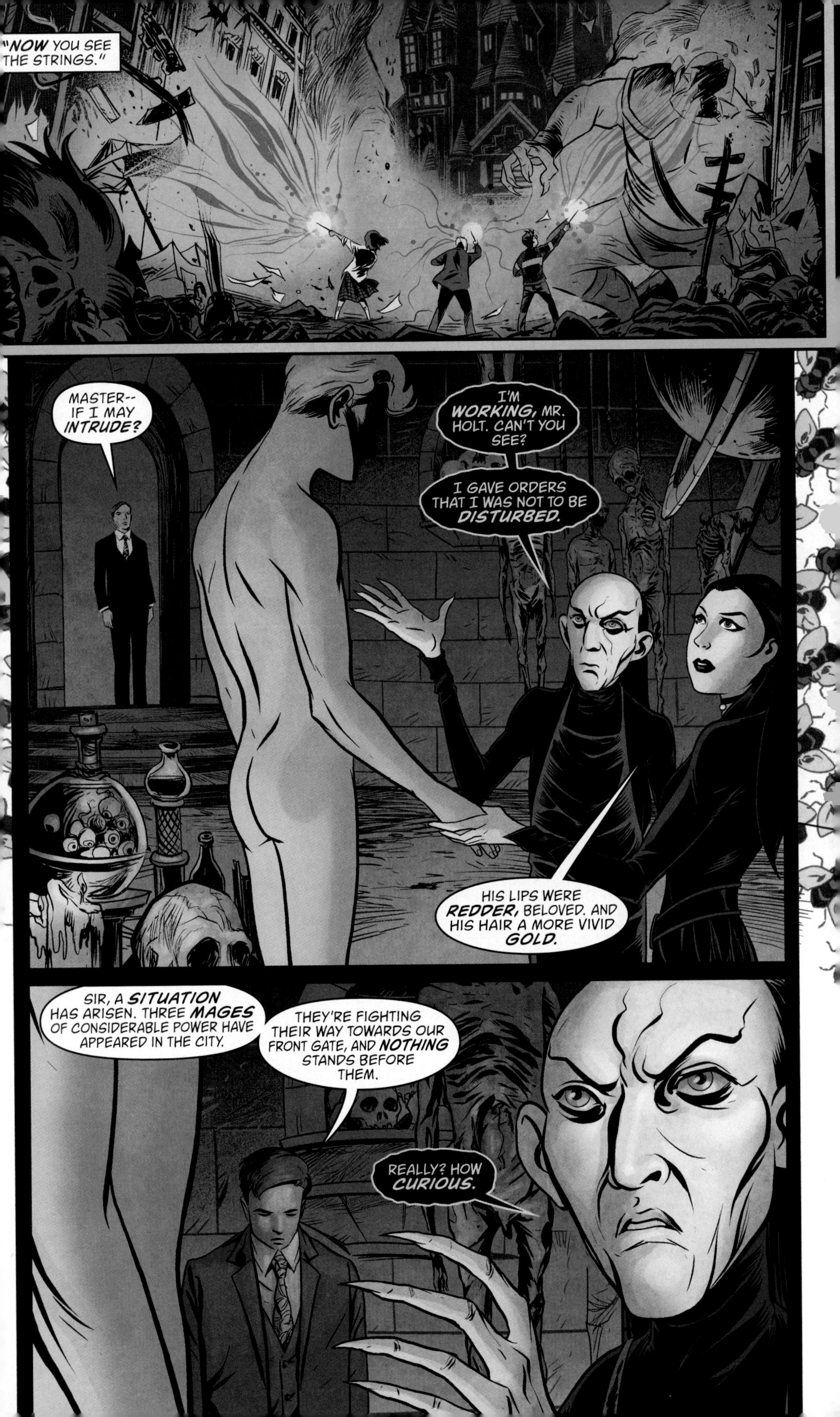
"NOW YOU SEE THE STRINGS."
MASTER-- IF I MAY INTRUDE?
I'M WORKING, MR. HOLT. CAN'T YOU SEE?
I GAVE ORDERS THAT I WAS NOT TO BE DISTURBED.
HIS LIPS WERE REDDER, BELOVED. AND HIS HAIR A MORE VIVID GOLD.
SIR, A SITUATION HAS ARISEN. THREE MAGES OF CONSIDERABLE POWER HAVE APPEARED IN THE CITY.
THEY'RE FIGHTING THEIR WAY TOWARDS OUR FRONT GATE, AND NOTHING STANDS BEFORE THEM.
REALLY? HOW CURIOUS.

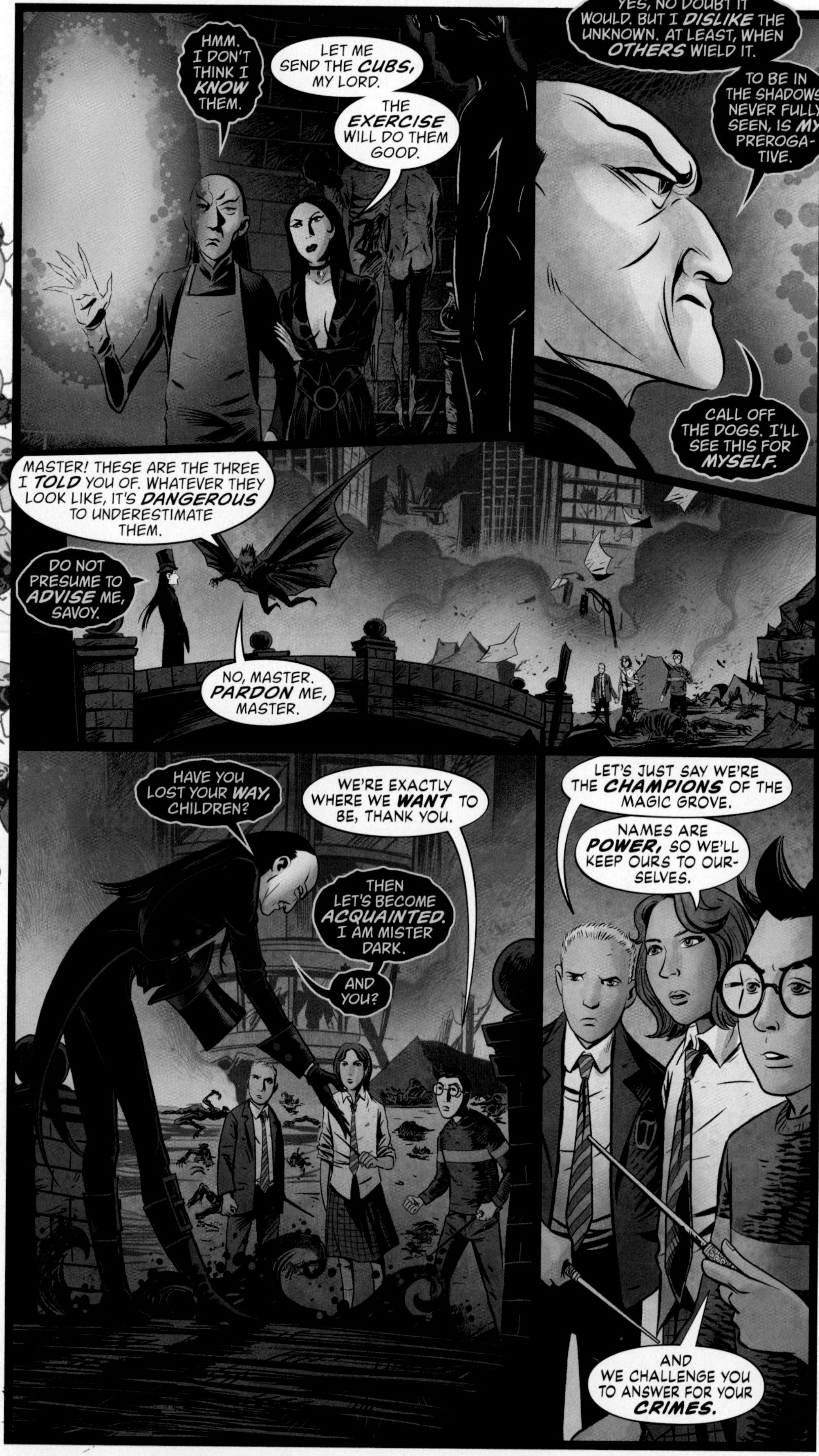
HMM. I DON'T THINK I KNOW THEM.
LET ME SEND THE CUBS, MY LORD.
THE EXERCISE WILL DO THEM GOOD.
YES, NO DOUBT IT WOULD. BUT I DISLIKE THE UNKNOWN. AT LEAST, WHEN OTHERS WIELD IT.
TO BE IN THE SHADOWS, NEVER FULLY SEEN, IS MY PREROGA-TIVE.
CALL OFF THE DOGS. I'LL SEE THIS FOR MYSELF.
MASTER! THESE ARE THE THREE I TOLD YOU OF. WHATEVER THEY LOOK LIKE, IT'S DANGEROUS TO UNDERESTIMATE THEM.
DO NOT PRESUME TO ADVISE ME, SAVOY.
NO, MASTER. PARDON ME, MASTER.
HAVE YOU LOST YOUR WAY, CHILDREN?
WE'RE EXACTLY WHERE WE WANT TO BE, THANK YOU.
THEN LET'S BECOME ACQUAINTED. I AM MISTER DARK.
AND YOU?
LET'S JUST SAY WE'RE THE CHAMPIONS OF THE MAGIC GROVE.
NAMES ARE POWER, SO WE'LL KEEP OURS TO OUR-SELVES.
AND WE CHALLENGE YOU TO ANSWER FOR YOUR CRIMES.

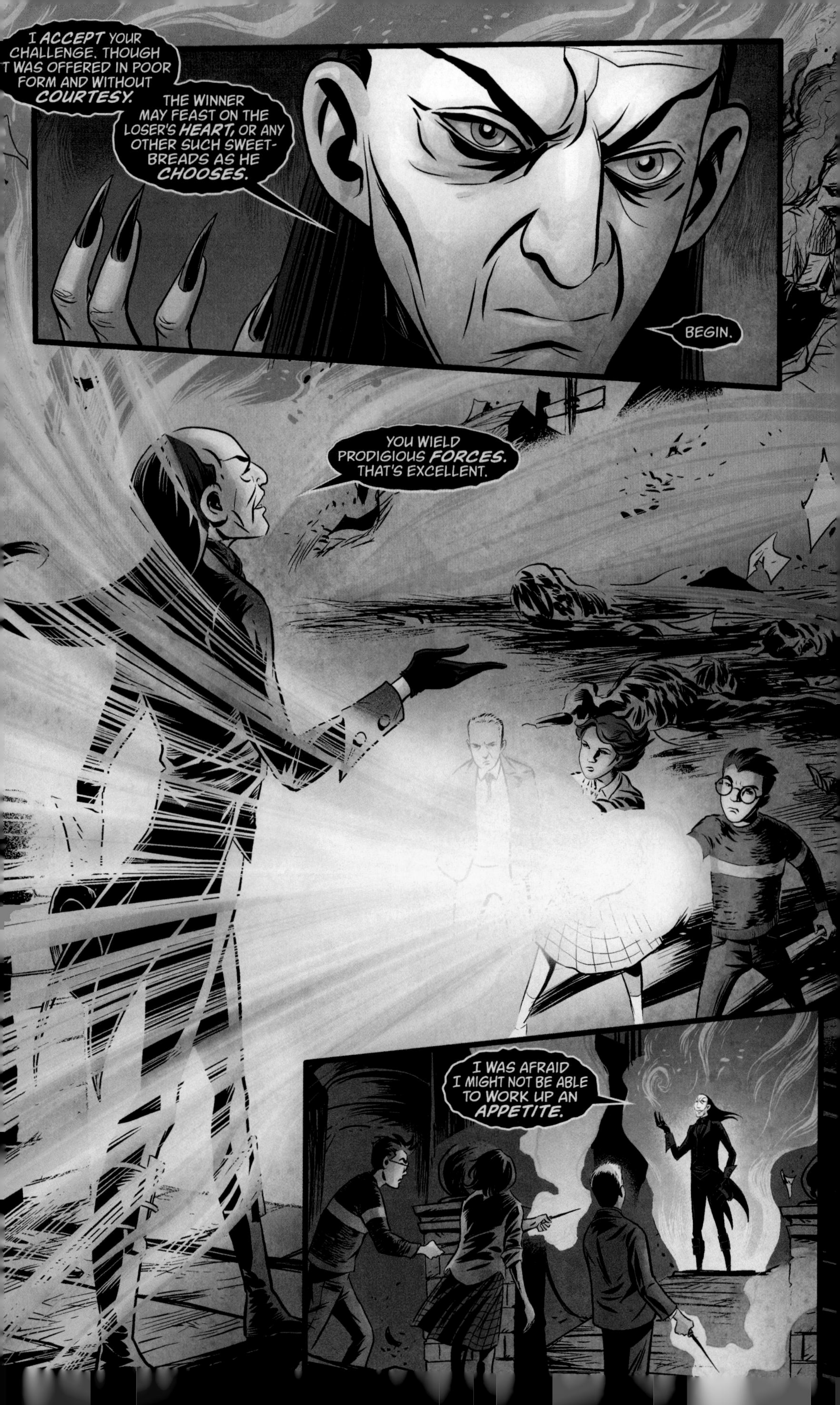
I ACCEPT YOUR CHALLENGE. THOUGH IT WAS OFFERED IN POOR FORM AND WITHOUT COURTESY.
THE WINNER MAY FEAST ON THE LOSER'S HEART, OR ANY OTHER SUCH SWEET-BREADS AS HE CHOOSES.
BEGIN.
YOU WIELD PRODIGIOUS FORCES. THAT'S EXCELLENT.
I WAS AFRAID I MIGHT NOT BE ABLE TO WORK UP AN APPETITE.

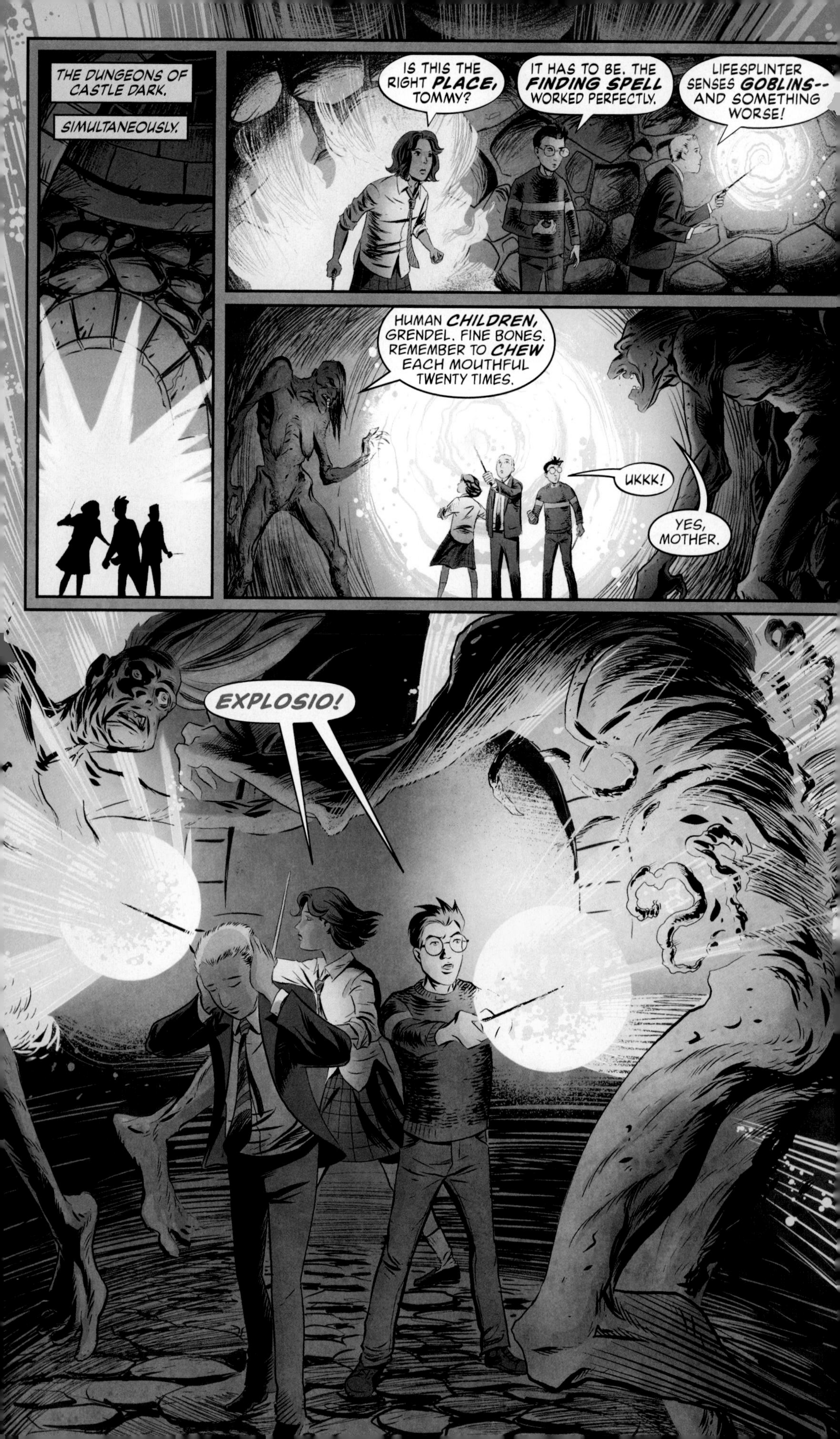

THE DUNGEONS OF CASTLE DARK.
SIMULTANEOUSLY.
IS THIS THE RIGHT PLACE, TOMMY?
IT HAS TO BE. THE FINDING SPELL WORKED PERFECTLY.
LIFESPLINTER SENSES GOBLINS-- AND SOMETHING WORSE!
HUMAN CHILDREN, GRENDEL. FINE BONES. REMEMBER TO CHEW EACH MOUTHFUL TWENTY TIMES.
UKKK!
YES, MOTHER.
EXPLOSIO!

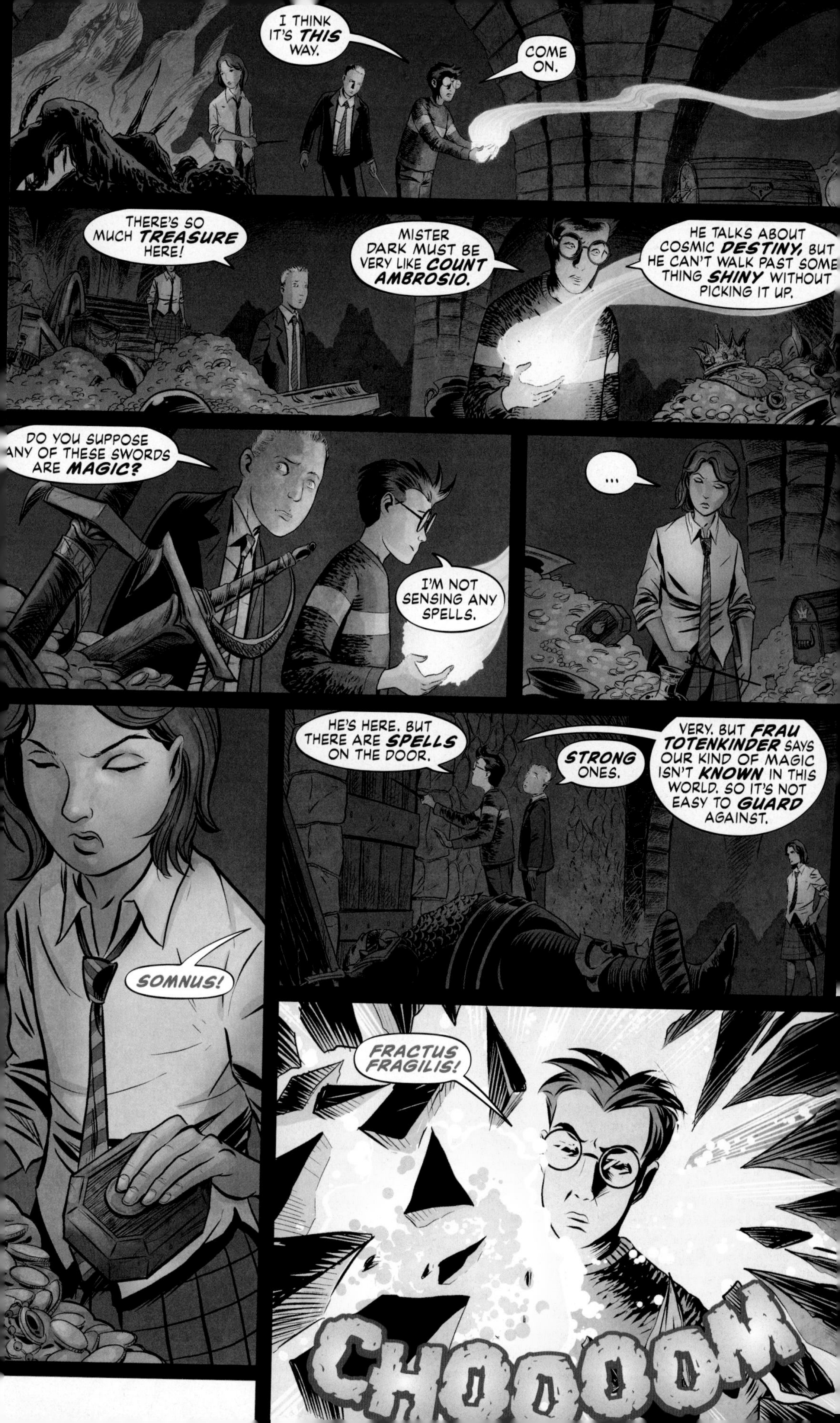

I THINK IT'S THIS WAY.
COME ON.
THERE'S SO MUCH TREASURE HERE!
MISTER DARK MUST BE VERY LIKE COUNT AMBROSIO.
HE TALKS ABOUT COSMIC DESTINY, BUT HE CAN'T WALK PAST SOME THING SHINY WITHOUT PICKING IT UP.
DO YOU SUPPOSE ANY OF THESE SWORDS ARE MAGIC?
I'M NOT SENSING ANY SPELLS.
...
HE'S HERE. BUT THERE ARE SPELLS ON THE DOOR.
STRONG ONES.
VERY. BUT FRAU TOTENKINDER SAYS OUR KIND OF MAGIC ISN'T KNOWN IN THIS WORLD. SO IT'S NOT EASY TO GUARD AGAINST.
SOMNUS!
FRACTUS FRAGILIS!
CHOOOOM

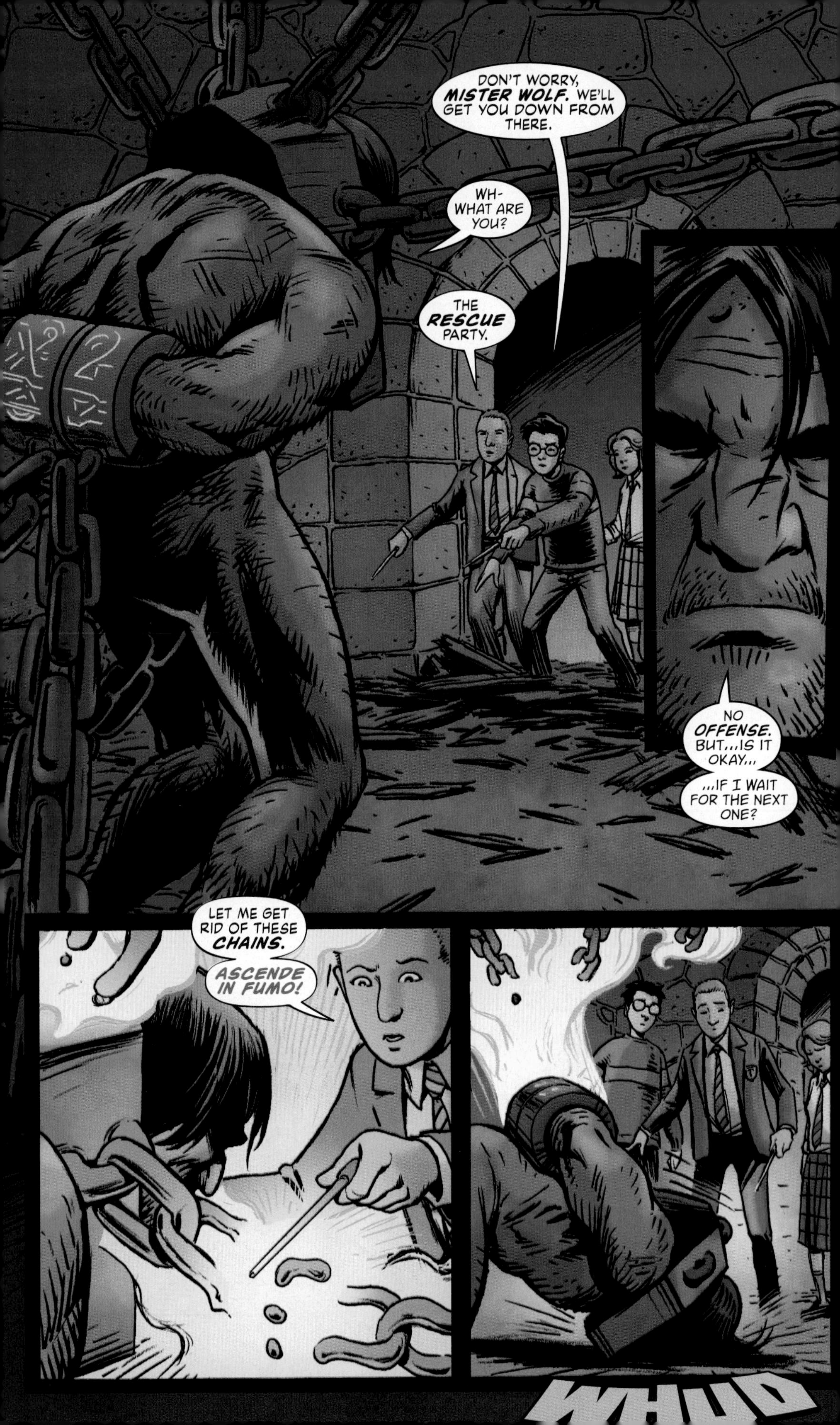
DON'T WORRY, MISTER WOLF. WE'LL GET YOU DOWN FROM THERE.
WH- WHAT ARE YOU?
THE RESCUE PARTY.
NO OFFENSE. BUT...IS IT OKAY...
...IF I WAIT FOR THE NEXT ONE?
LET ME GET RID OF THESE CHAINS.
ASCENDE IN FUMO!
WHUD

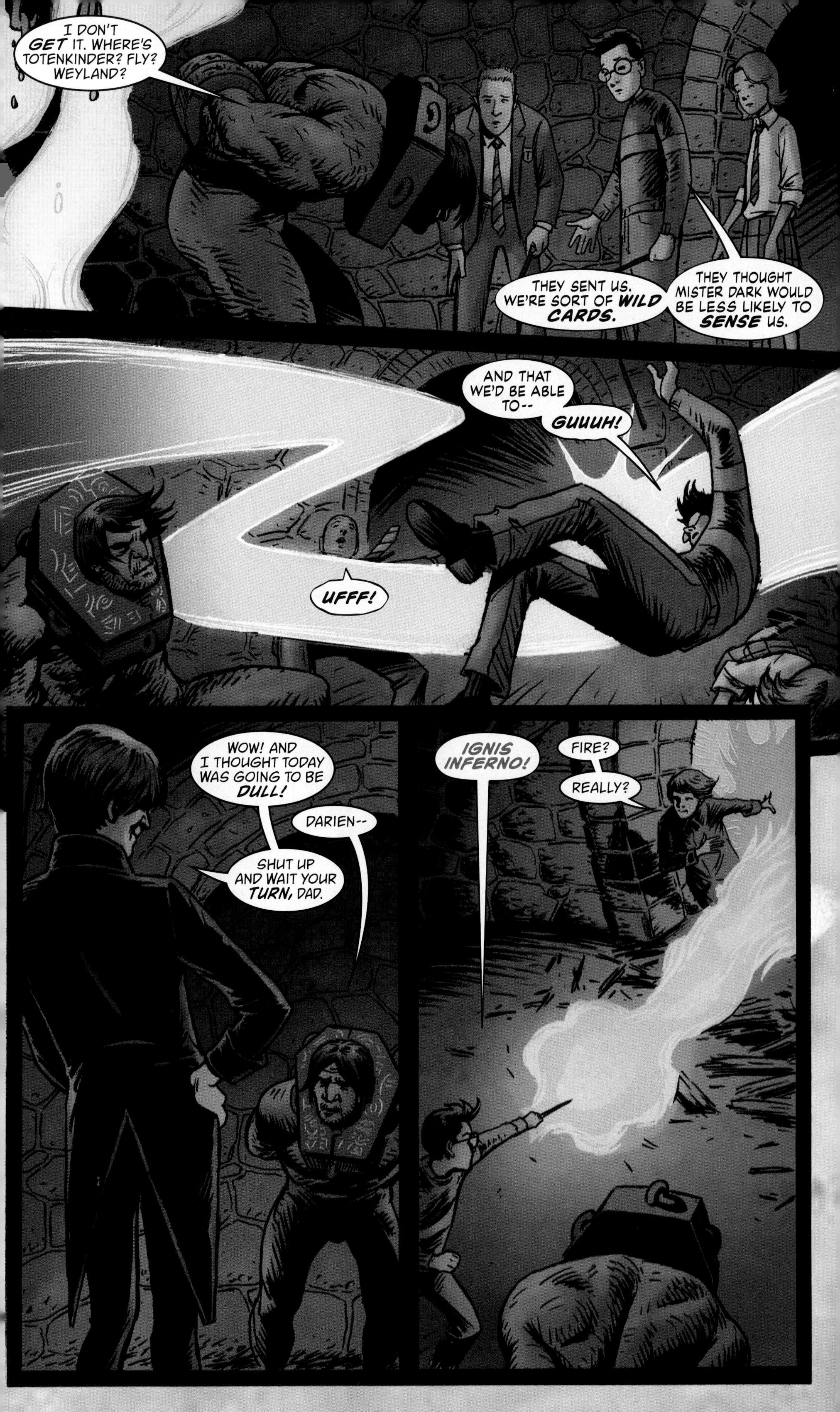

I DON'T GET IT. WHERE'S TOTENKINDER? FLY? WEYLAND?
THEY SENT US. WE'RE SORT OF WILD CARDS.
THEY THOUGHT MISTER DARK WOULD BE LESS LIKELY TO SENSE US.
AND THAT WE'D BE ABLE TO--
GUUUH!
UFFF!
WOW! AND I THOUGHT TODAY WAS GOING TO BE DULL!
DARIEN--
SHUT UP AND WAIT YOUR TURN, DAD.
IGNIS INFERNO!
FIRE?
REALLY?

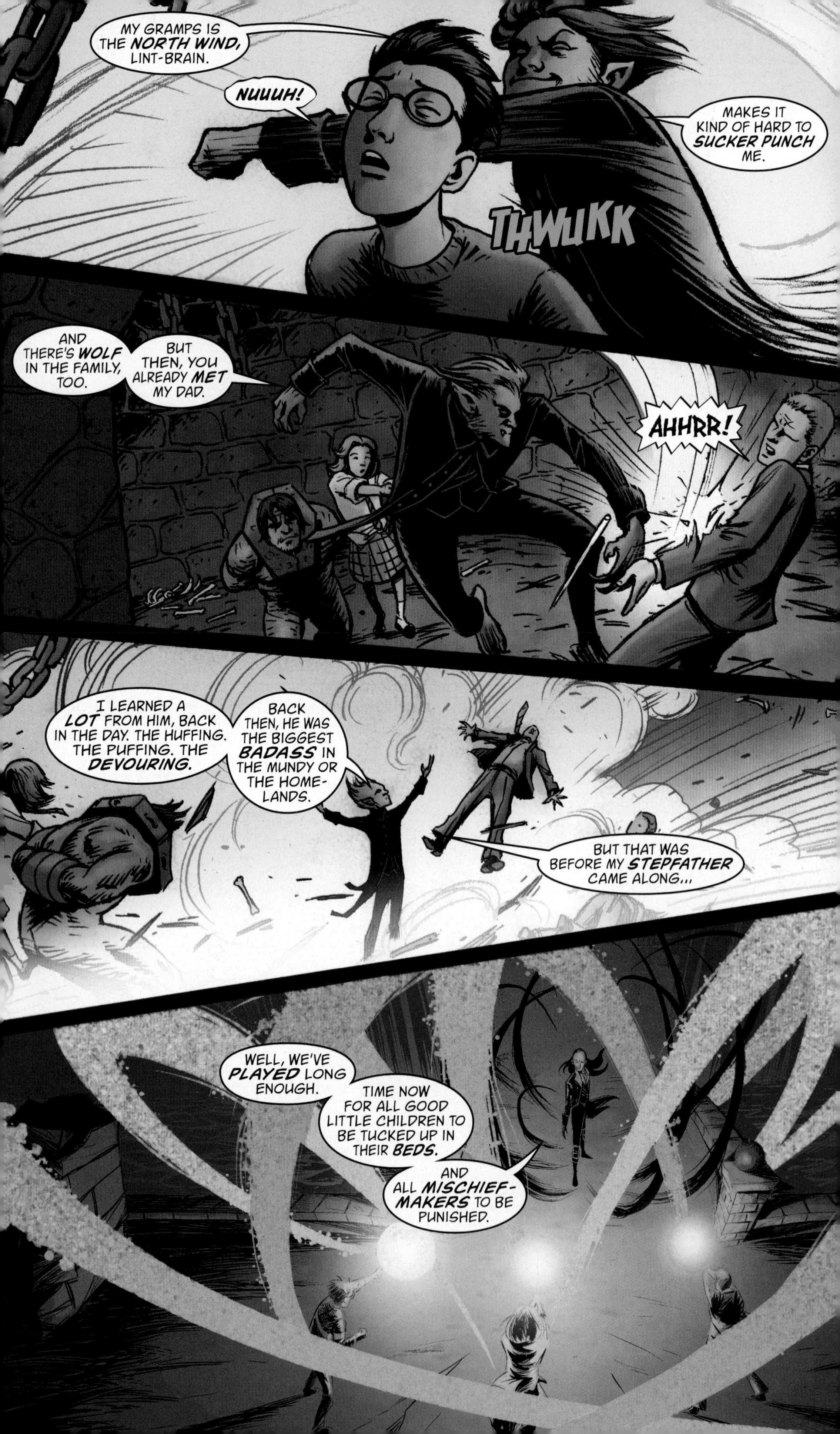

MY GRAMPS IS THE NORTH WIND, LINT-BRAIN.
NUUUH!
MAKES IT KIND OF HARD TO SUCKER PUNCH ME.
THWUKK
AND THERE'S WOLF IN THE FAMILY, TOO.
BUT THEN, YOU ALREADY MET MY DAD.
AHHRR!
I LEARNED A LOT FROM HIM, BACK IN THE DAY. THE HUFFING. THE PUFFING. THE DEVOURING.
BACK THEN, HE WAS THE BIGGEST BADASS IN THE MUNDY OR THE HOME-LANDS.
BUT THAT WAS BEFORE MY STEPFATHER CAME ALONG...
WELL, WE'VE PLAYED LONG ENOUGH.
TIME NOW FOR ALL GOOD LITTLE CHILDREN TO BE TUCKED UP IN THEIR BEDS.
AND ALL MISCHIEF-MAKERS TO BE PUNISHED.

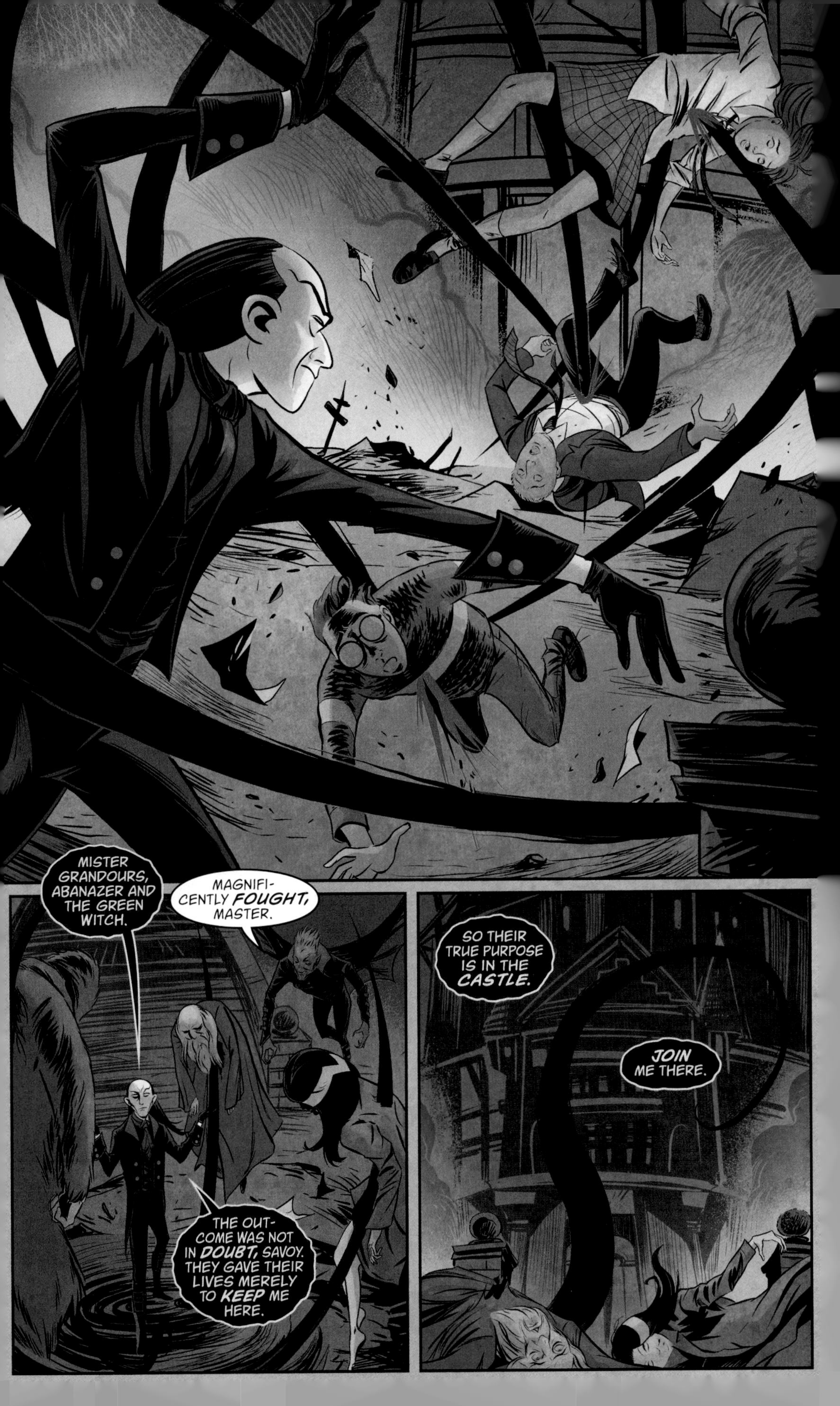
MISTER GRANDOURS, ABANAZER AND THE GREEN WITCH.
MAGNIFI- CENTLY FOUGHT, MASTER.
THE OUT- COME WAS NOT IN DOUBT, SAVOY. THEY GAVE THEIR LIVES MERELY TO KEEP ME HERE.
SO THEIR TRUE PURPOSE IS IN THE CASTLE.
JOIN ME THERE.

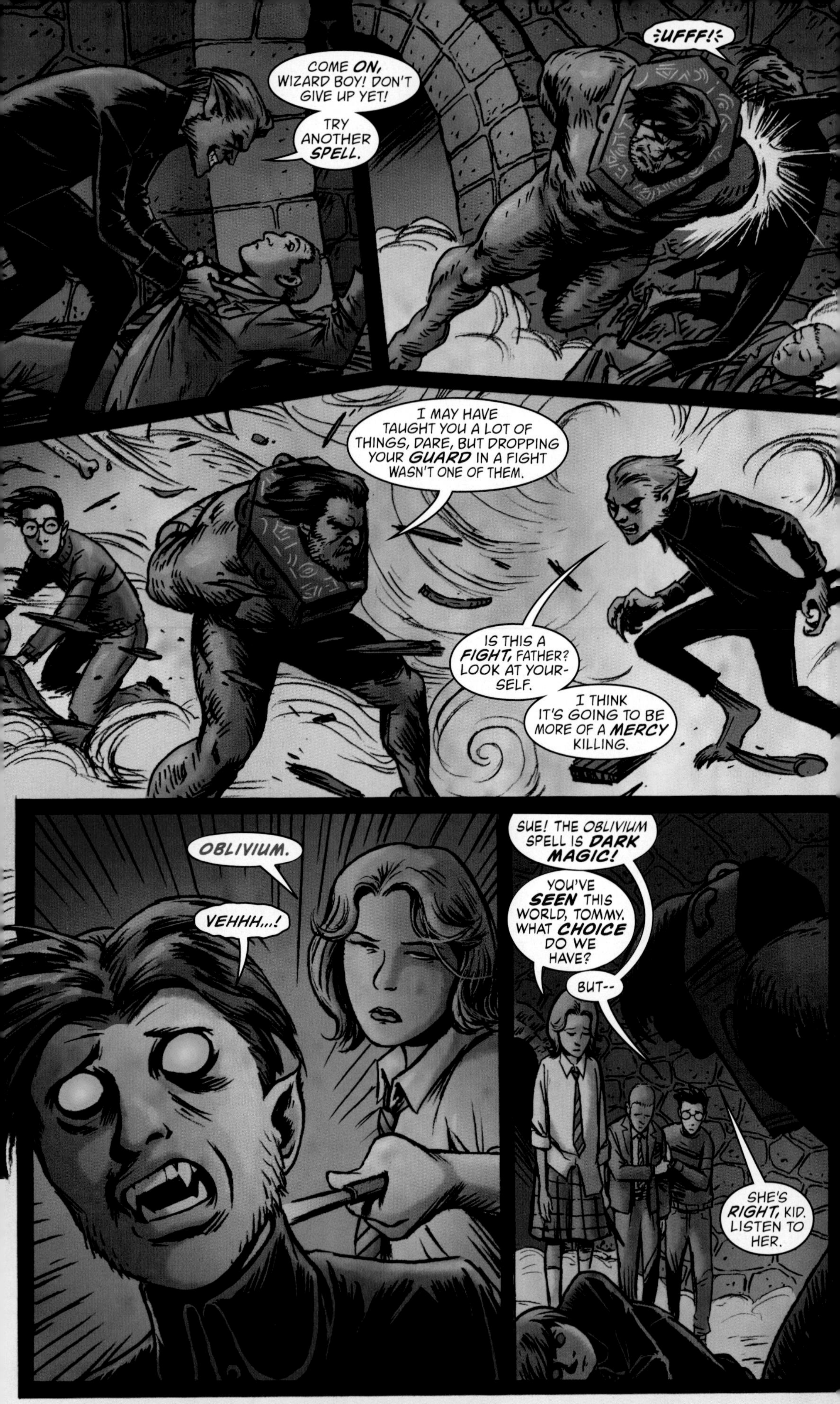
COME ON, WIZARD BOY! DON'T GIVE UP YET!
TRY ANOTHER SPELL.
UFFF!
I MAY HAVE TAUGHT YOU A LOT OF THINGS, DARE, BUT DROPPING YOUR GUARD IN A FIGHT WASN'T ONE OF THEM.
IS THIS A FIGHT, FATHER? LOOK AT YOURSELF.
I THINK IT'S GOING TO BE MORE OF A MERCY KILLING.
OBLIVIUM.
VEHHH...!
SUE! THE OBLIVIUM SPELL IS DARK MAGIC!
YOU'VE SEEN THIS WORLD, TOMMY. WHAT CHOICE DO WE HAVE?
BUT--
SHE'S RIGHT, KID. LISTEN TO HER.

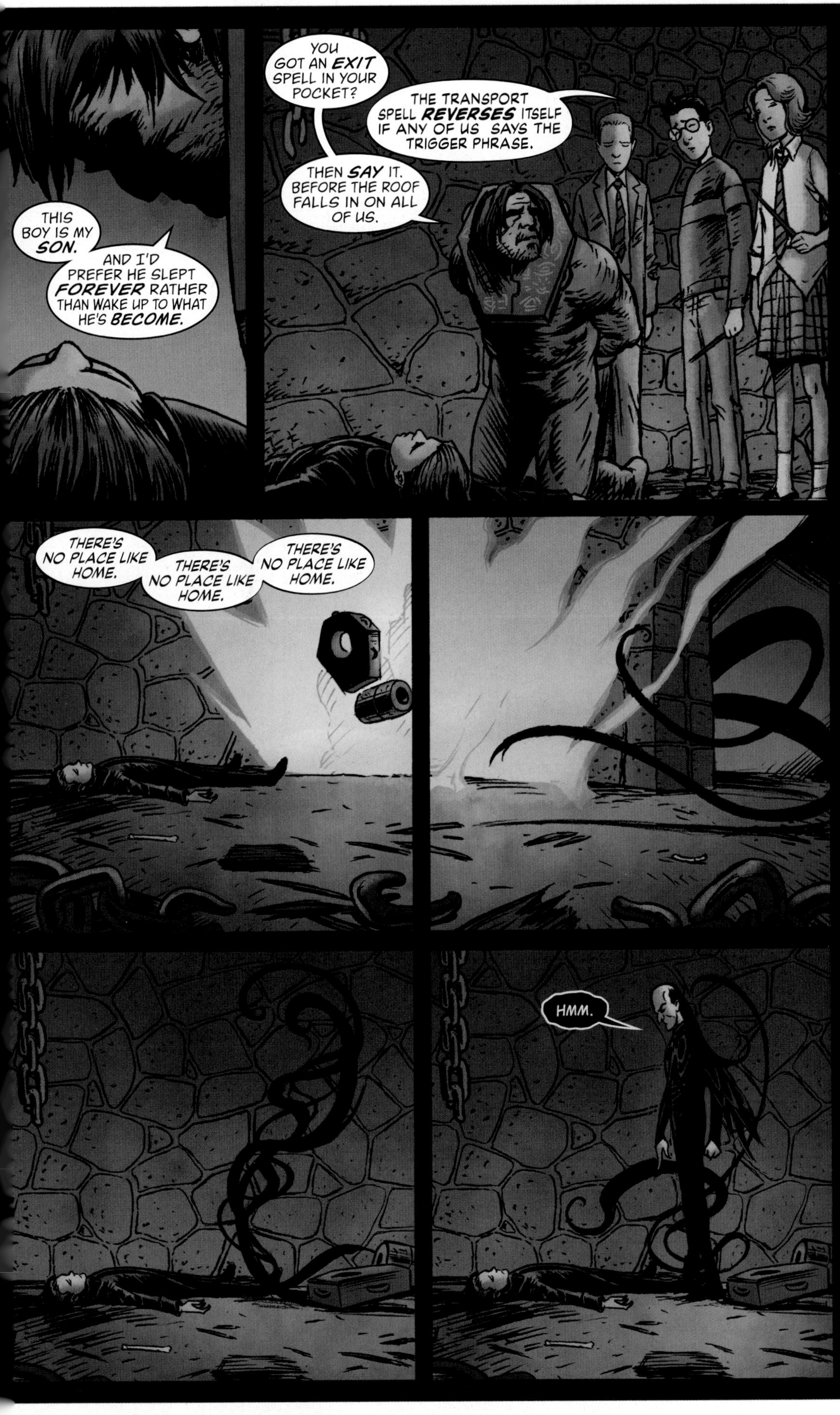
THIS BOY IS MY SON.
AND I'D PREFER HE SLEPT FOREVER RATHER THAN WAKE UP TO WHAT HE'S BECOME.
YOU GOT AN EXIT SPELL IN YOUR POCKET?
THE TRANSPORT SPELL REVERSES ITSELF IF ANY OF US SAYS THE TRIGGER PHRASE.
THEN SAY IT. BEFORE THE ROOF FALLS IN ON ALL OF US.
THERE'S NO PLACE LIKE HOME.
THERE'S NO PLACE LIKE HOME.
THERE'S NO PLACE LIKE HOME.
HMM.

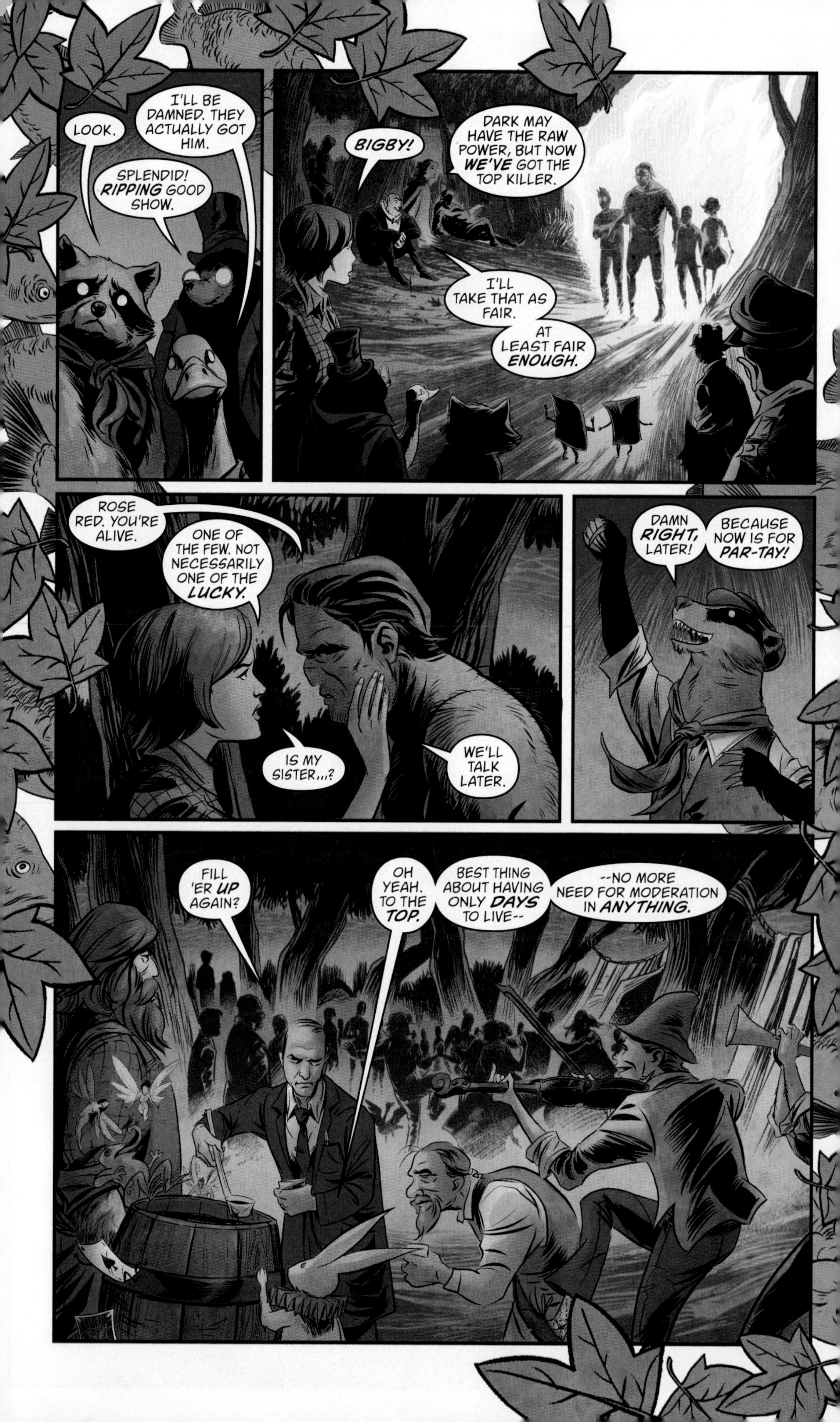
LOOK.
I'LL BE DAMNED. THEY ACTUALLY GOT HIM.
SPLENDID! RIPPING GOOD SHOW.
BIGBY!
DARK MAY HAVE THE RAW POWER, BUT NOW WE'VE GOT THE TOP KILLER.
I'LL TAKE THAT AS FAIR.
AT LEAST FAIR ENOUGH.
ROSE RED. YOU'RE ALIVE.
ONE OF THE FEW. NOT NECESSARILY ONE OF THE LUCKY.
IS MY SISTER...?
WE'LL TALK LATER.
DAMN RIGHT, LATER!
BECAUSE NOW IS FOR PAR-TAY!
FILL 'ER UP AGAIN?
OH YEAH. TO THE TOP.
BEST THING ABOUT HAVING ONLY DAYS TO LIVE--
--NO MORE NEED FOR MODERATION IN ANYTHING.

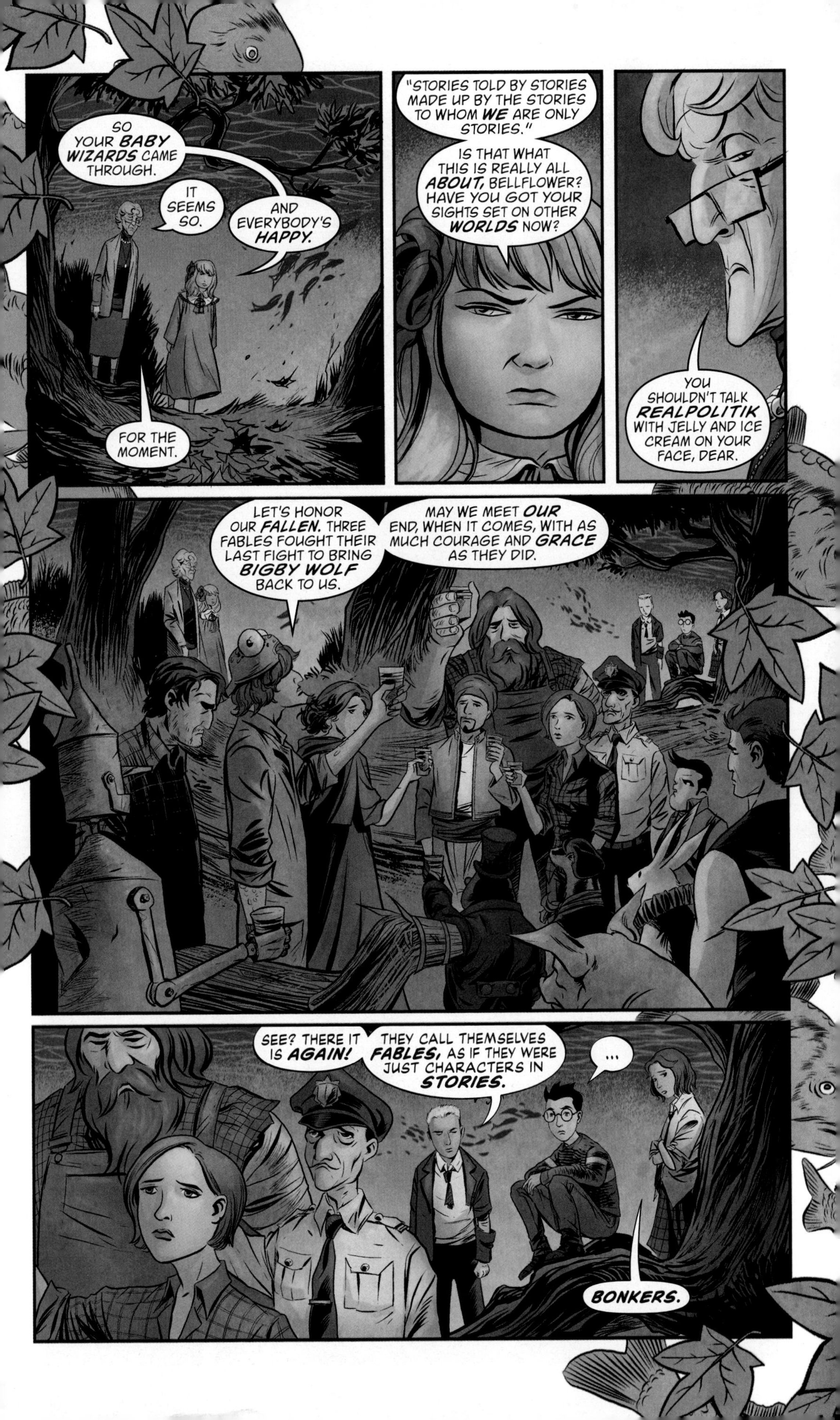
SO YOUR BABY WIZARDS CAME THROUGH.
IT SEEMS SO.
AND EVERYBODY'S HAPPY.
FOR THE MOMENT.
"STORIES TOLD BY STORIES MADE UP BY THE STORIES TO WHOM WE ARE ONLY STORIES."
IS THAT WHAT THIS IS REALLY ALL ABOUT, BELLFLOWER? HAVE YOU GOT YOUR SIGHTS SET ON OTHER WORLDS NOW?
YOU SHOULDN'T TALK REALPOLITIK WITH JELLY AND ICE CREAM ON YOUR FACE, DEAR.
LET'S HONOR OUR FALLEN. THREE FABLES FOUGHT THEIR LAST FIGHT TO BRING BIGBY WOLF BACK TO US.
MAY WE MEET OUR END, WHEN IT COMES, WITH AS MUCH COURAGE AND GRACE AS THEY DID.
SEE? THERE IT IS AGAIN!
THEY CALL THEMSELVES FABLES, AS IF THEY WERE JUST CHARACTERS IN STORIES.
...
BONKERS.

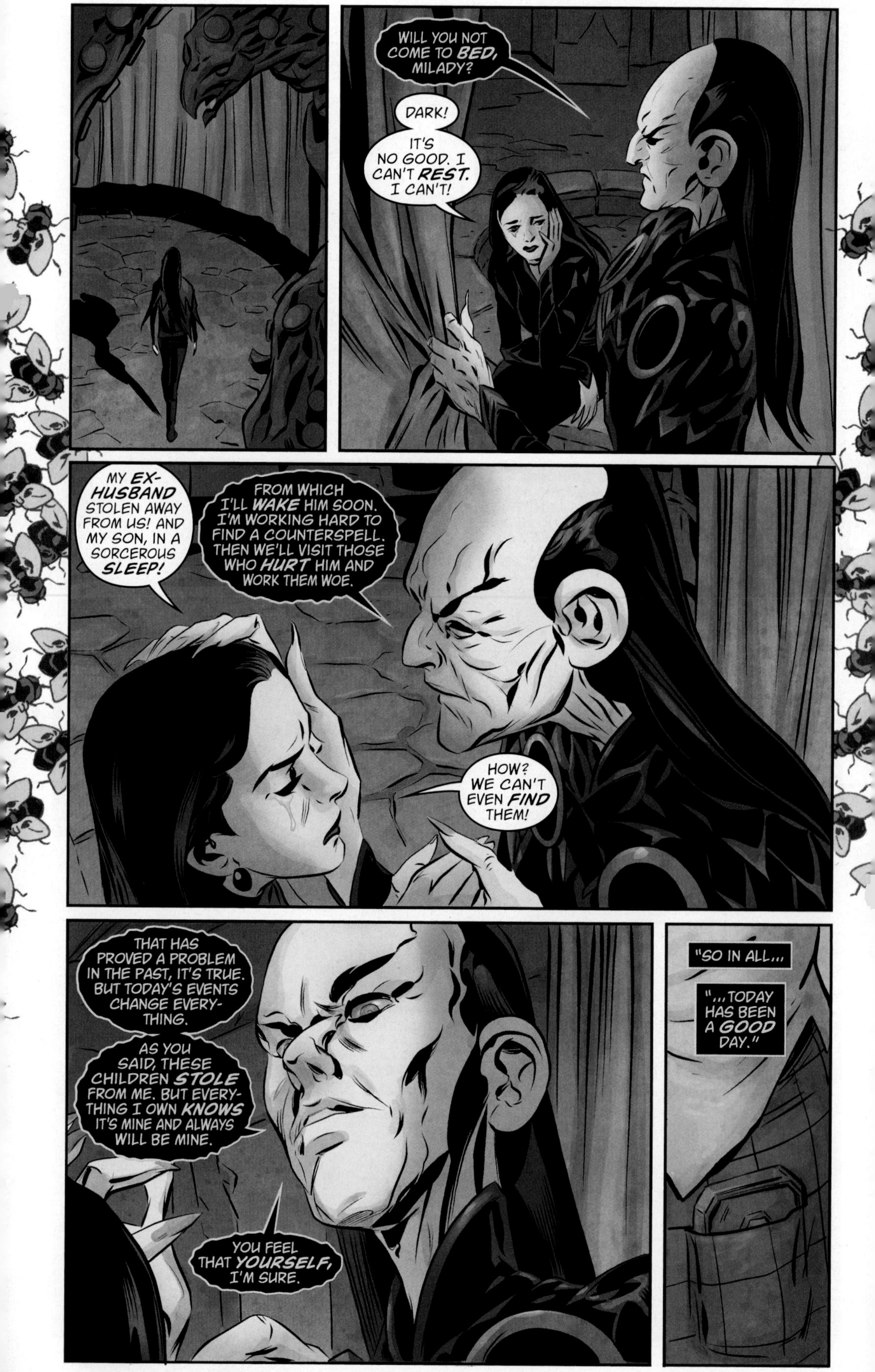
WILL YOU NOT COME TO BED, MILADY?
DARK!
IT'S NO GOOD. I CAN'T REST. I CAN'T!
MY EX-HUSBAND STOLEN AWAY FROM US! AND MY SON, IN A SORCEROUS SLEEP!
FROM WHICH I'LL WAKE HIM SOON. I'M WORKING HARD TO FIND A COUNTERSPELL. THEN WE'LL VISIT THOSE WHO HURT HIM AND WORK THEM WOE.
HOW? WE CAN'T EVEN FIND THEM!
THAT HAS PROVED A PROBLEM IN THE PAST, IT'S TRUE. BUT TODAY'S EVENTS CHANGE EVERY-THING.
AS YOU SAID, THESE CHILDREN STOLE FROM ME. BUT EVERY-THING I OWN KNOWS IT'S MINE AND ALWAYS WILL BE MINE.
YOU FEEL THAT YOURSELF, I'M SURE.
"SO IN ALL...
"...TODAY HAS BEEN A GOOD DAY."

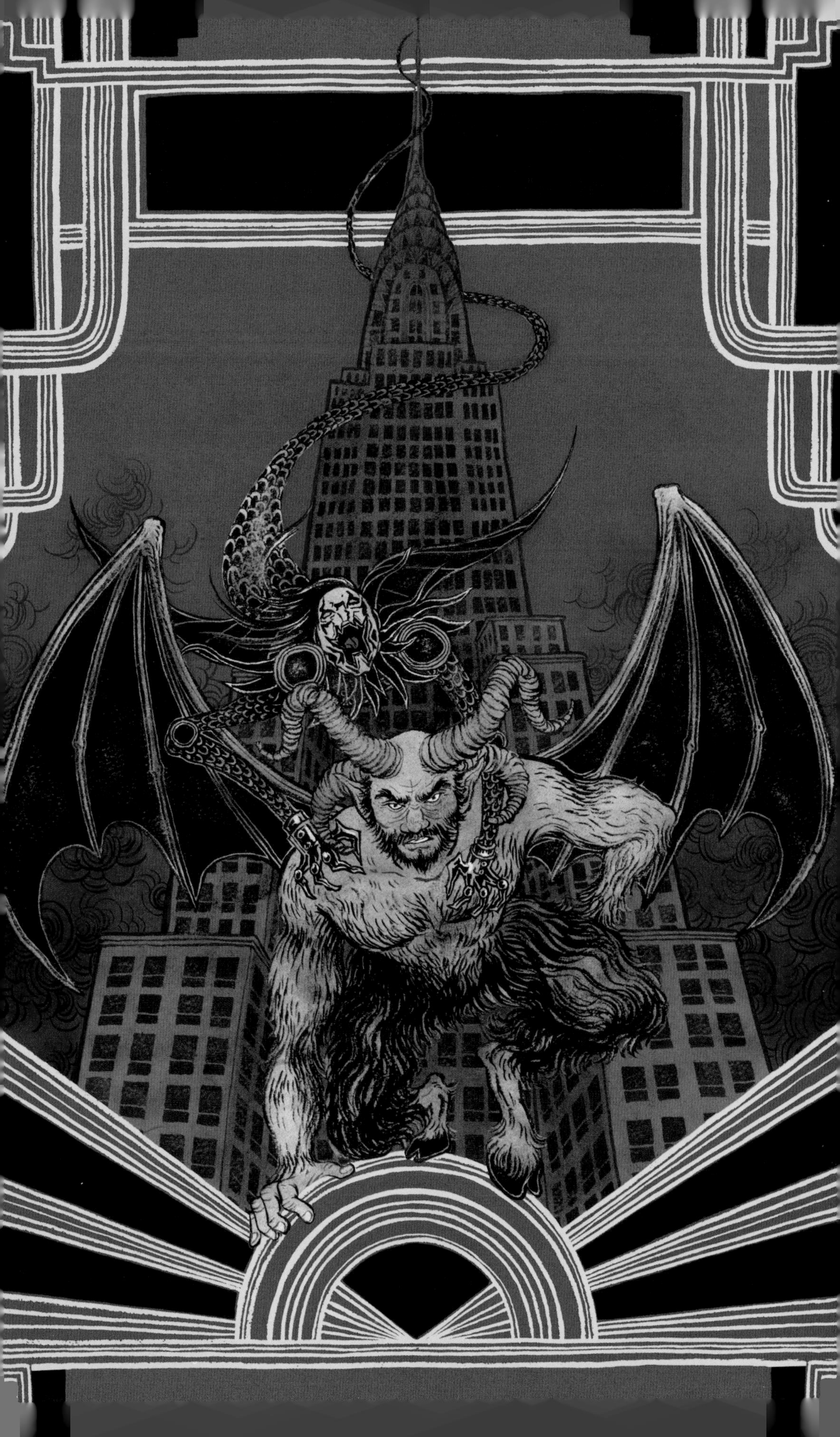

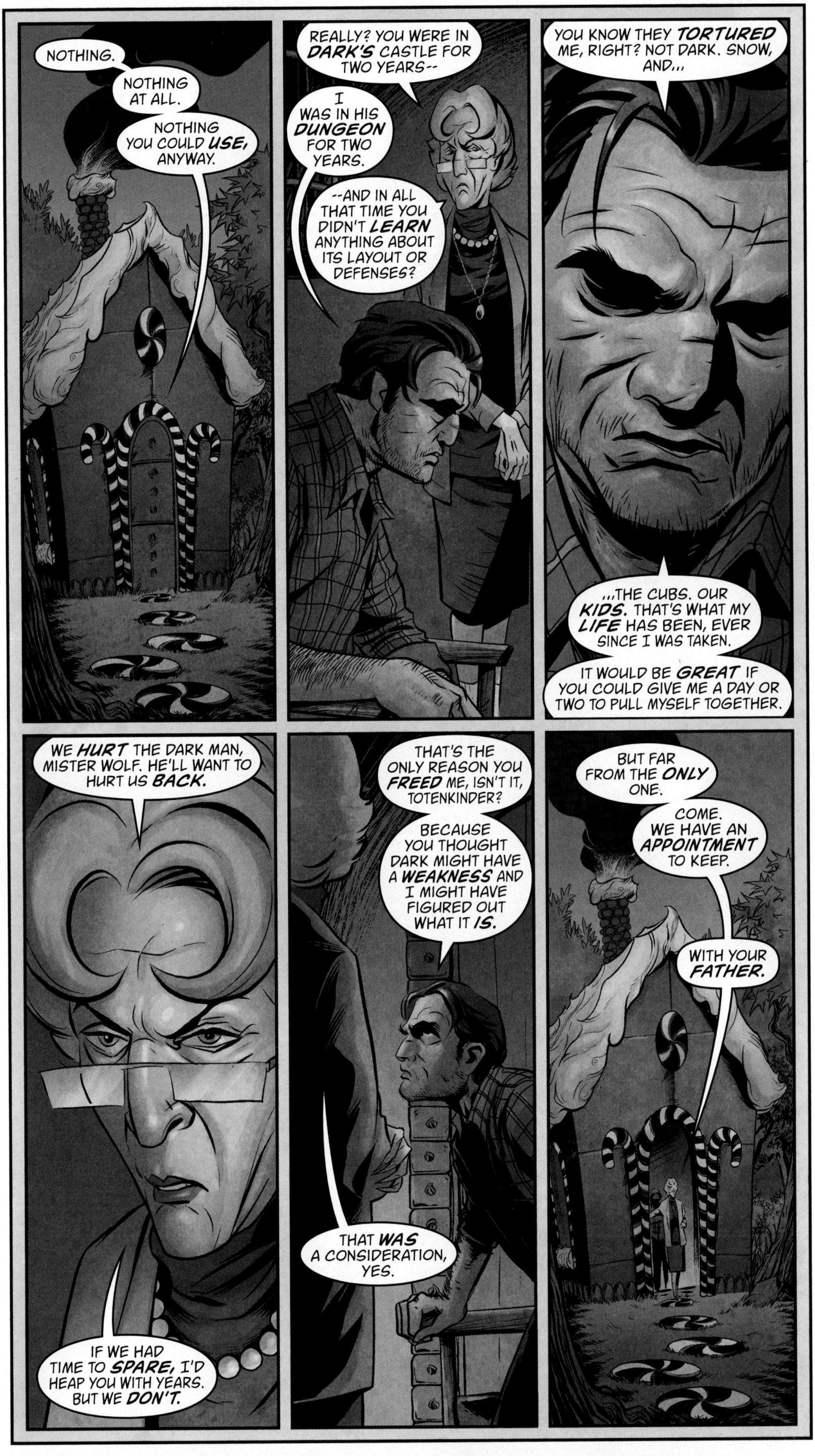
NOTHING.
NOTHING AT ALL.
NOTHING YOU COULD USE, ANYWAY.
REALLY? YOU WERE IN DARK'S CASTLE FOR TWO YEARS--
I WAS IN HIS DUNGEON FOR TWO YEARS.
--AND IN ALL THAT TIME YOU DIDN'T LEARN ANYTHING ABOUT ITS LAYOUT OR DEFENSES?
YOU KNOW THEY TORTURED ME, RIGHT? NOT DARK. SNOW, AND...
...THE CUBS. OUR KIDS. THAT'S WHAT MY LIFE HAS BEEN, EVER SINCE I WAS TAKEN.
IT WOULD BE GREAT IF YOU COULD GIVE ME A DAY OR TWO TO PULL MYSELF TOGETHER.
WE HURT THE DARK MAN, MISTER WOLF. HE'LL WANT TO HURT US BACK.
IF WE HAD TIME TO SPARE, I'D HEAP YOU WITH YEARS. BUT WE DON'T.
THAT'S THE ONLY REASON YOU FREED ME, ISN'T IT, TOTENKINDER?
BECAUSE YOU THOUGHT DARK MIGHT HAVE A WEAKNESS AND I MIGHT HAVE FIGURED OUT WHAT IT IS.
THAT WAS A CONSIDERATION, YES.
BUT FAR FROM THE ONLY ONE.
COME. WE HAVE AN APPOINTMENT TO KEEP.
WITH YOUR FATHER.

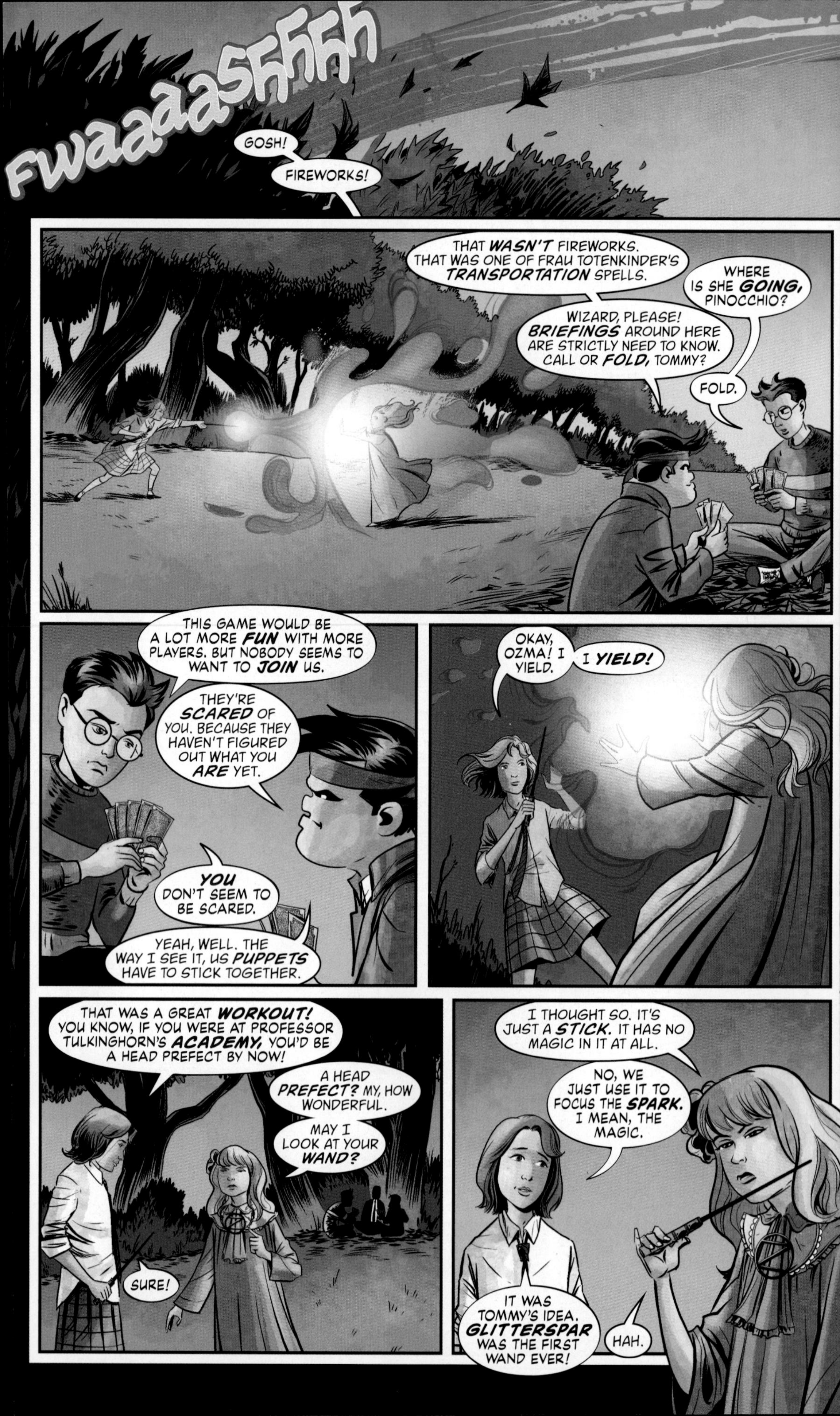
FWAAAASHHHH
GOSH!
FIREWORKS!
THAT WASN'T FIREWORKS. THAT WAS ONE OF FRAU TOTENKINDER'S TRANSPORTATION SPELLS.
WHERE IS SHE GOING, PINOCCHIO?
WIZARD, PLEASE! BRIEFINGS AROUND HERE ARE STRICTLY NEED TO KNOW. CALL OR FOLD, TOMMY?
FOLD.
THIS GAME WOULD BE A LOT MORE FUN WITH MORE PLAYERS. BUT NOBODY SEEMS TO WANT TO JOIN US.
THEY'RE SCARED OF YOU. BECAUSE THEY HAVEN'T FIGURED OUT WHAT YOU ARE YET.
YOU DON'T SEEM TO BE SCARED.
YEAH, WELL. THE WAY I SEE IT, US PUPPETS HAVE TO STICK TOGETHER.
OKAY, OZMA! I YIELD.
I YIELD!
THAT WAS A GREAT WORKOUT! YOU KNOW, IF YOU WERE AT PROFESSOR TULKINGHORN'S ACADEMY, YOU'D BE A HEAD PREFECT BY NOW!
A HEAD PREFECT? MY, HOW WONDERFUL.
MAY I LOOK AT YOUR WAND?
SURE!
I THOUGHT SO. IT'S JUST A STICK. IT HAS NO MAGIC IN IT AT ALL.
NO, WE JUST USE IT TO FOCUS THE SPARK. I MEAN, THE MAGIC.
IT WAS TOMMY'S IDEA. GLITTERSPAR WAS THE FIRST WAND EVER!
HAH.

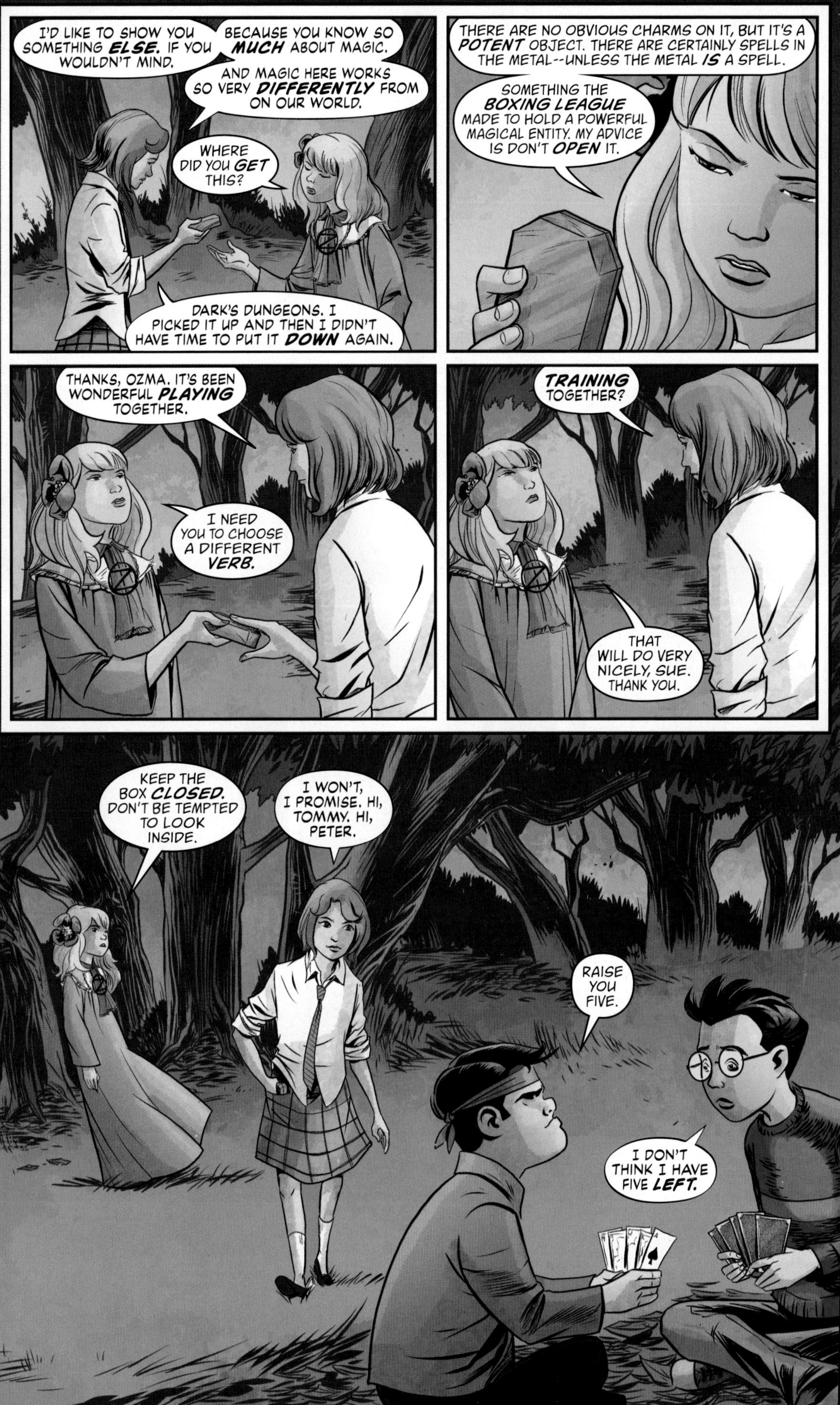
I'D LIKE TO SHOW YOU SOMETHING ELSE. IF YOU WOULDN'T MIND.
BECAUSE YOU KNOW SO MUCH ABOUT MAGIC.
AND MAGIC HERE WORKS SO VERY DIFFERENTLY FROM ON OUR WORLD.
WHERE DID YOU GET THIS?
DARK'S DUNGEONS. I PICKED IT UP AND THEN I DIDN'T HAVE TIME TO PUT IT DOWN AGAIN.
THERE ARE NO OBVIOUS CHARMS ON IT, BUT IT'S A POTENT OBJECT. THERE ARE CERTAINLY SPELLS IN THE METAL--UNLESS THE METAL IS A SPELL.
SOMETHING THE BOXING LEAGUE MADE TO HOLD A POWERFUL MAGICAL ENTITY. MY ADVICE IS DON'T OPEN IT.
THANKS, OZMA. IT'S BEEN WONDERFUL PLAYING TOGETHER.
I NEED YOU TO CHOOSE A DIFFERENT VERB.
TRAINING TOGETHER?
THAT WILL DO VERY NICELY, SUE. THANK YOU.
KEEP THE BOX CLOSED. DON'T BE TEMPTED TO LOOK INSIDE.
I WON'T, I PROMISE. HI, TOMMY. HI, PETER.
RAISE YOU FIVE.
I DON'T THINK I HAVE FIVE LEFT.

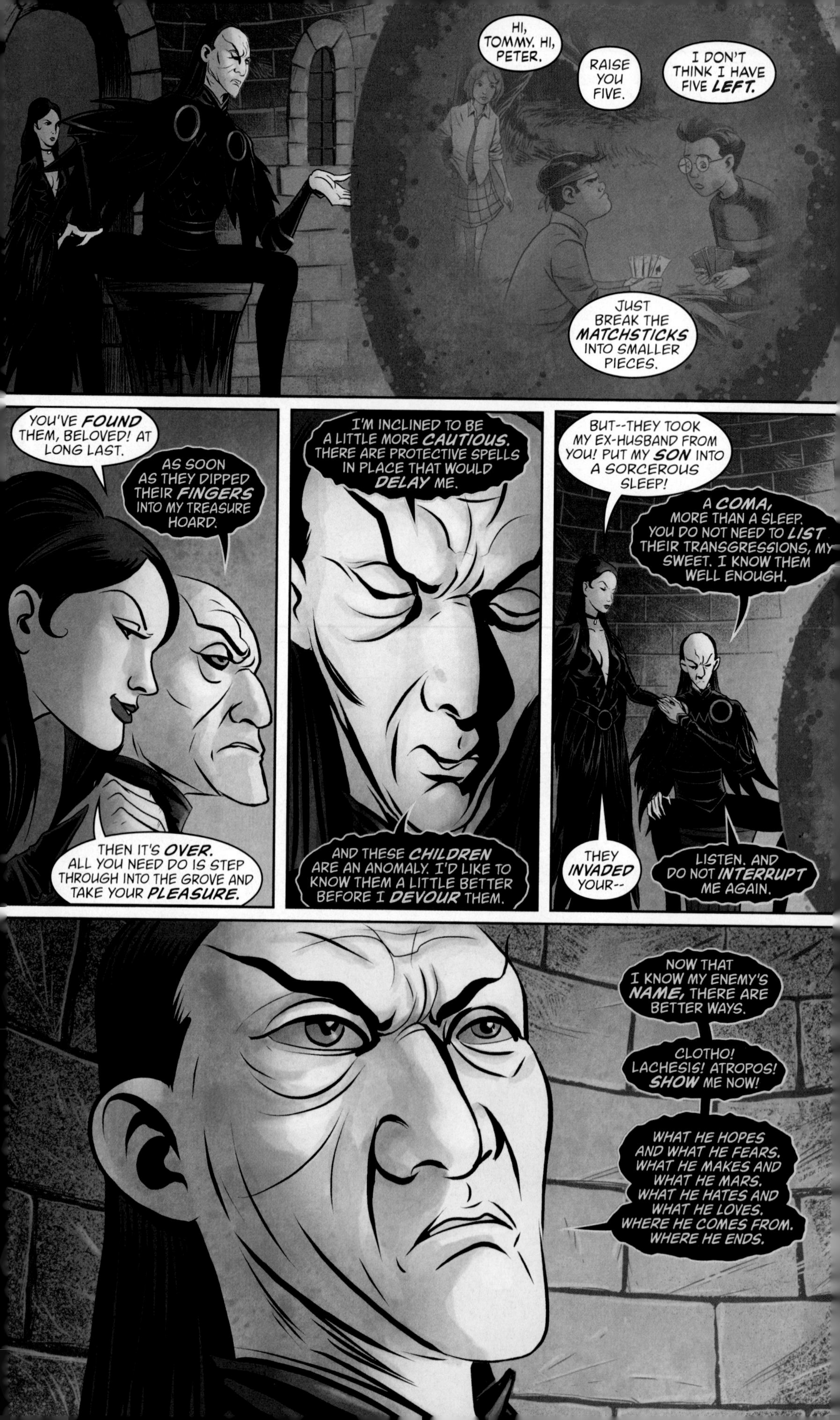
HI, TOMMY. HI, PETER.
RAISE YOU FIVE.
I DON'T THINK I HAVE FIVE LEFT.
JUST BREAK THE MATCHSTICKS INTO SMALLER PIECES.
YOU'VE FOUND THEM, BELOVED! AT LONG LAST.
AS SOON AS THEY DIPPED THEIR FINGERS INTO MY TREASURE HOARD.
THEN IT'S OVER. ALL YOU NEED DO IS STEP THROUGH INTO THE GROVE AND TAKE YOUR PLEASURE.
I'M INCLINED TO BE A LITTLE MORE CAUTIOUS. THERE ARE PROTECTIVE SPELLS IN PLACE THAT WOULD DELAY ME.
AND THESE CHILDREN ARE AN ANOMALY. I'D LIKE TO KNOW THEM A LITTLE BETTER BEFORE I DEVOUR THEM.
BUT--THEY TOOK MY EX-HUSBAND FROM YOU! PUT MY SON INTO A SORCEROUS SLEEP!
A COMA, MORE THAN A SLEEP. YOU DO NOT NEED TO LIST THEIR TRANSGRESSIONS, MY SWEET. I KNOW THEM WELL ENOUGH.
THEY INVADED YOUR--
LISTEN. AND DO NOT INTERRUPT ME AGAIN.
NOW THAT I KNOW MY ENEMY'S NAME, THERE ARE BETTER WAYS.
CLOTHO! LACHESIS! ATROPOS! SHOW ME NOW!
WHAT HE HOPES AND WHAT HE FEARS. WHAT HE MAKES AND WHAT HE MARS. WHAT HE HATES AND WHAT HE LOVES. WHERE HE COMES FROM. WHERE HE ENDS.

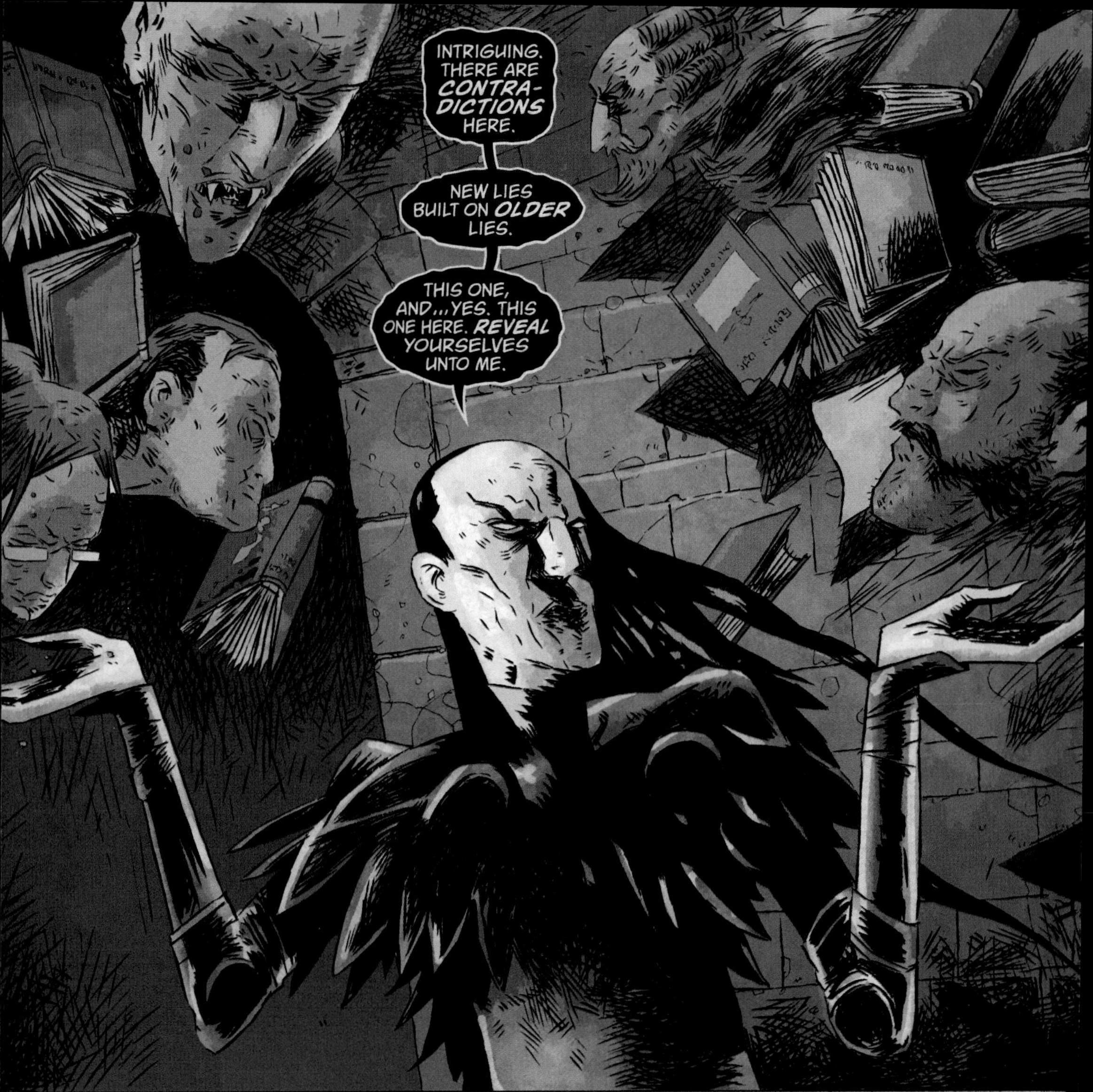
INTRIGUING. THERE ARE CONTRADICTIONS HERE.
NEW LIES BUILT ON OLDER LIES.
THIS ONE, AND...YES. THIS ONE HERE. REVEAL YOURSELVES UNTO ME.

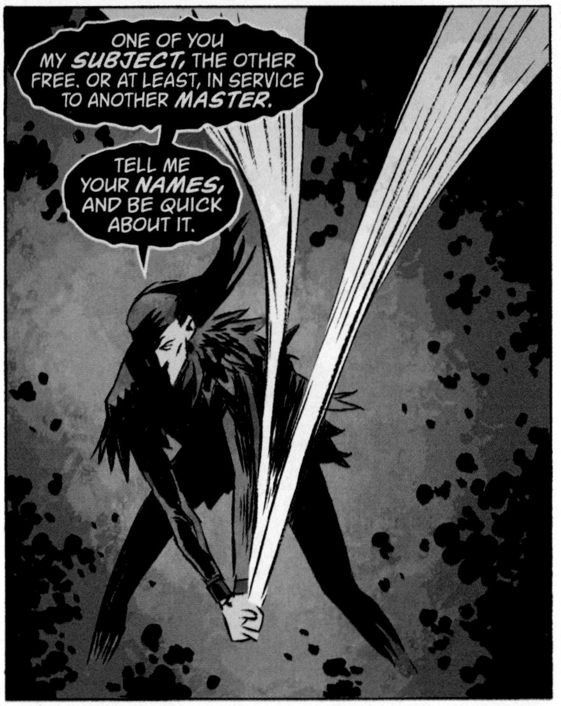
ONE OF YOU MY SUBJECT, THE OTHER FREE. OR AT LEAST, IN SERVICE TO ANOTHER MASTER.
TELL ME YOUR NAMES, AND BE QUICK ABOUT IT.

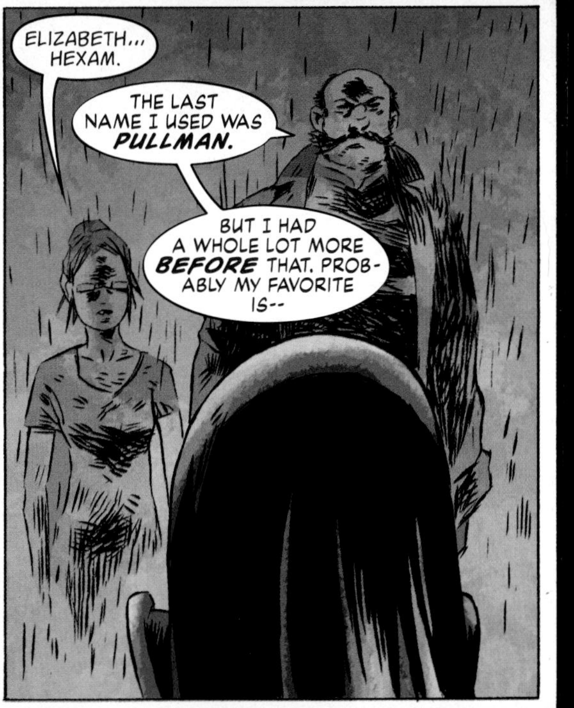
ELIZABETH... HEXAM.
THE LAST NAME I USED WAS PULLMAN.
BUT I HAD A WHOLE LOT MORE BEFORE THAT. PROBABLY MY FAVORITE IS--

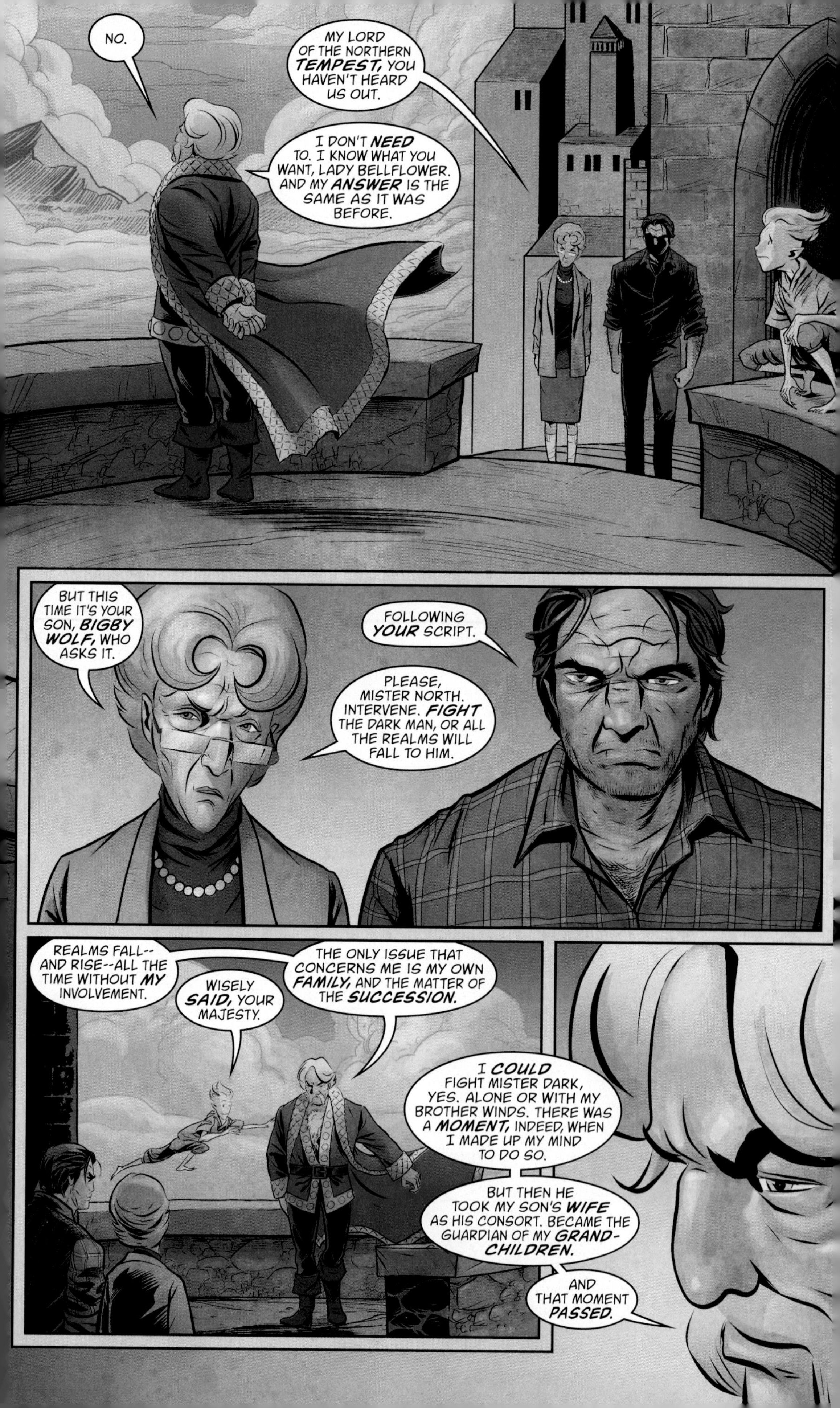
NO.
MY LORD OF THE NORTHERN TEMPEST, YOU HAVEN'T HEARD US OUT.
I DON'T NEED TO. I KNOW WHAT YOU WANT, LADY BELLFLOWER. AND MY ANSWER IS THE SAME AS IT WAS BEFORE.
BUT THIS TIME IT'S YOUR SON, BIGBY WOLF, WHO ASKS IT.
FOLLOWING YOUR SCRIPT.
PLEASE, MISTER NORTH. INTERVENE. FIGHT THE DARK MAN, OR ALL THE REALMS WILL FALL TO HIM.
REALMS FALL--AND RISE--ALL THE TIME WITHOUT MY INVOLVEMENT.
THE ONLY ISSUE THAT CONCERNS ME IS MY OWN FAMILY, AND THE MATTER OF THE SUCCESSION.
WISELY SAID, YOUR MAJESTY.
I COULD FIGHT MISTER DARK, YES. ALONE OR WITH MY BROTHER WINDS. THERE WAS A MOMENT, INDEED, WHEN I MADE UP MY MIND TO DO SO.
BUT THEN HE TOOK MY SON'S WIFE AS HIS CONSORT. BECAME THE GUARDIAN OF MY GRAND-CHILDREN.
AND THAT MOMENT PASSED.

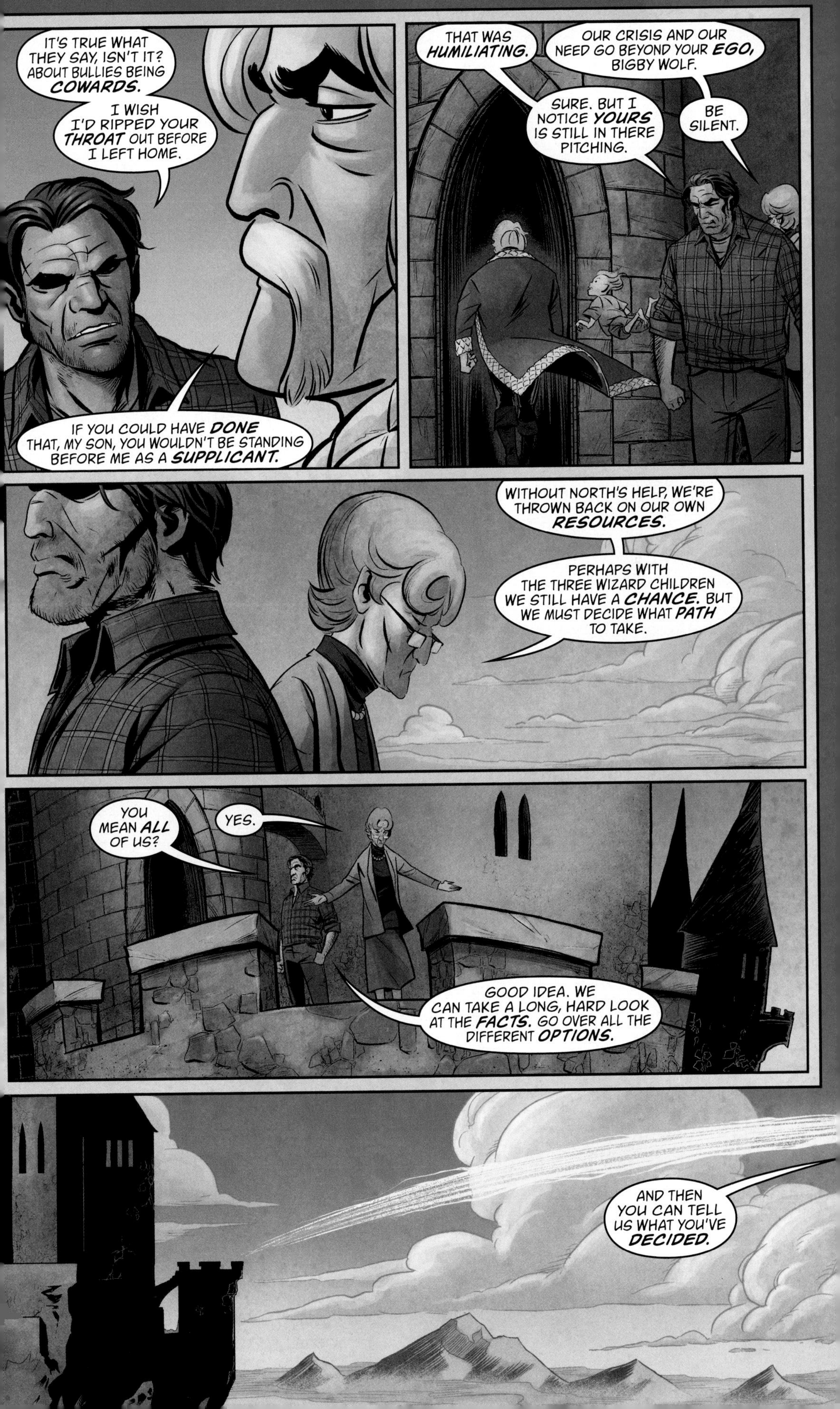
IT'S TRUE WHAT THEY SAY, ISN'T IT? ABOUT BULLIES BEING COWARDS.
I WISH I'D RIPPED YOUR THROAT OUT BEFORE I LEFT HOME.
IF YOU COULD HAVE DONE THAT, MY SON, YOU WOULDN'T BE STANDING BEFORE ME AS A SUPPLICANT.
THAT WAS HUMILIATING.
OUR CRISIS AND OUR NEED GO BEYOND YOUR EGO, BIGBY WOLF.
SURE. BUT I NOTICE YOURS IS STILL IN THERE PITCHING.
BE SILENT.
WITHOUT NORTH'S HELP, WE'RE THROWN BACK ON OUR OWN RESOURCES.
PERHAPS WITH THE THREE WIZARD CHILDREN WE STILL HAVE A CHANCE. BUT WE MUST DECIDE WHAT PATH TO TAKE.
YOU MEAN ALL OF US?
YES.
GOOD IDEA. WE CAN TAKE A LONG, HARD LOOK AT THE FACTS. GO OVER ALL THE DIFFERENT OPTIONS.
AND THEN YOU CAN TELL US WHAT YOU'VE DECIDED.

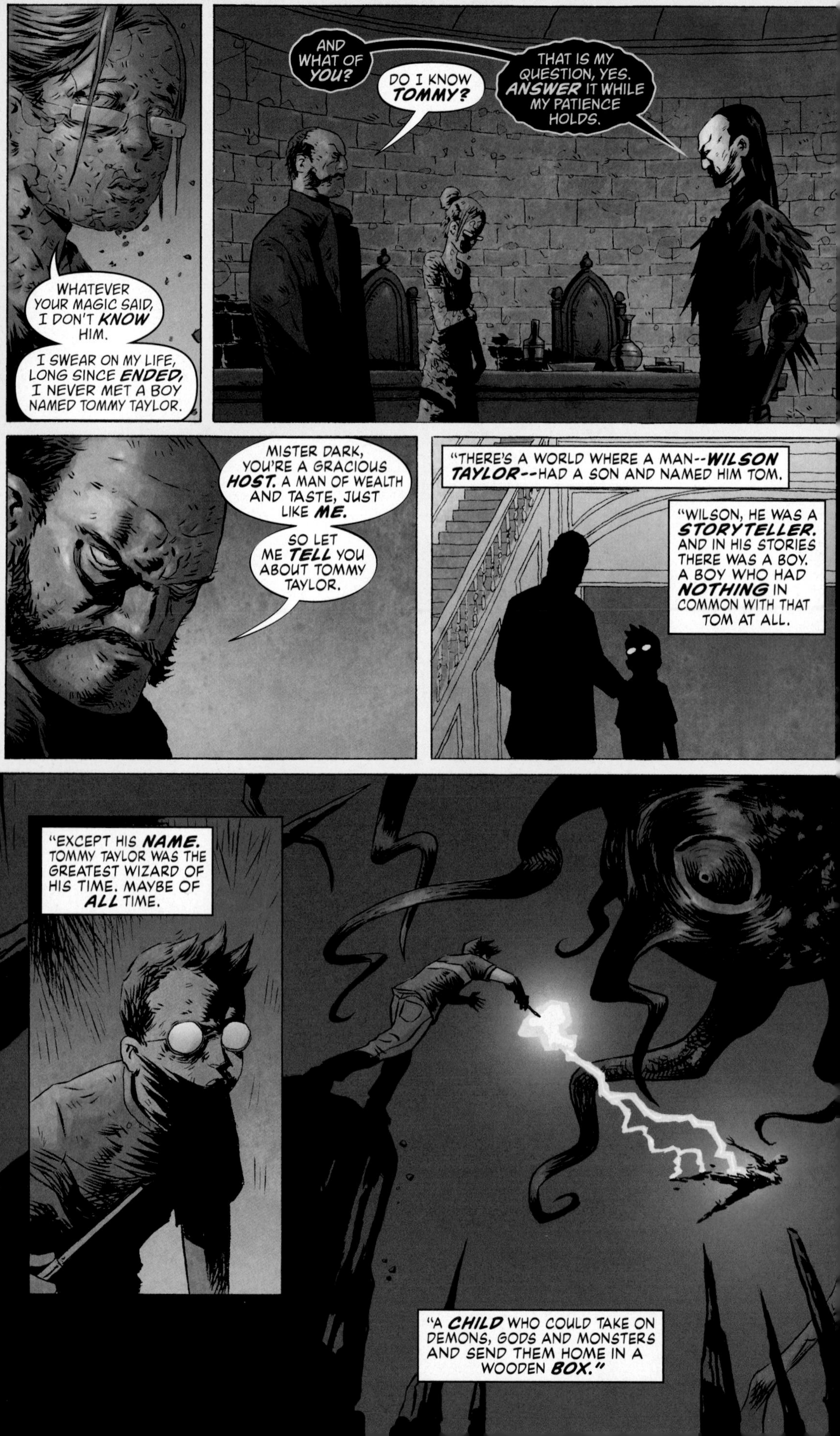
WHATEVER YOUR MAGIC SAID, I DON'T KNOW HIM.
I SWEAR ON MY LIFE, LONG SINCE ENDED, I NEVER MET A BOY NAMED TOMMY TAYLOR.
AND WHAT OF YOU?
DO I KNOW TOMMY?
THAT IS MY QUESTION, YES. ANSWER IT WHILE MY PATIENCE HOLDS.
MISTER DARK, YOU'RE A GRACIOUS HOST. A MAN OF WEALTH AND TASTE, JUST LIKE ME.
SO LET ME TELL YOU ABOUT TOMMY TAYLOR.
"THERE'S A WORLD WHERE A MAN--WILSON TAYLOR--HAD A SON AND NAMED HIM TOM.
"WILSON, HE WAS A STORYTELLER. AND IN HIS STORIES THERE WAS A BOY. A BOY WHO HAD NOTHING IN COMMON WITH THAT TOM AT ALL.
"EXCEPT HIS NAME. TOMMY TAYLOR WAS THE GREATEST WIZARD OF HIS TIME. MAYBE OF ALL TIME.
"A CHILD WHO COULD TAKE ON DEMONS, GODS AND MONSTERS AND SEND THEM HOME IN A WOODEN BOX."

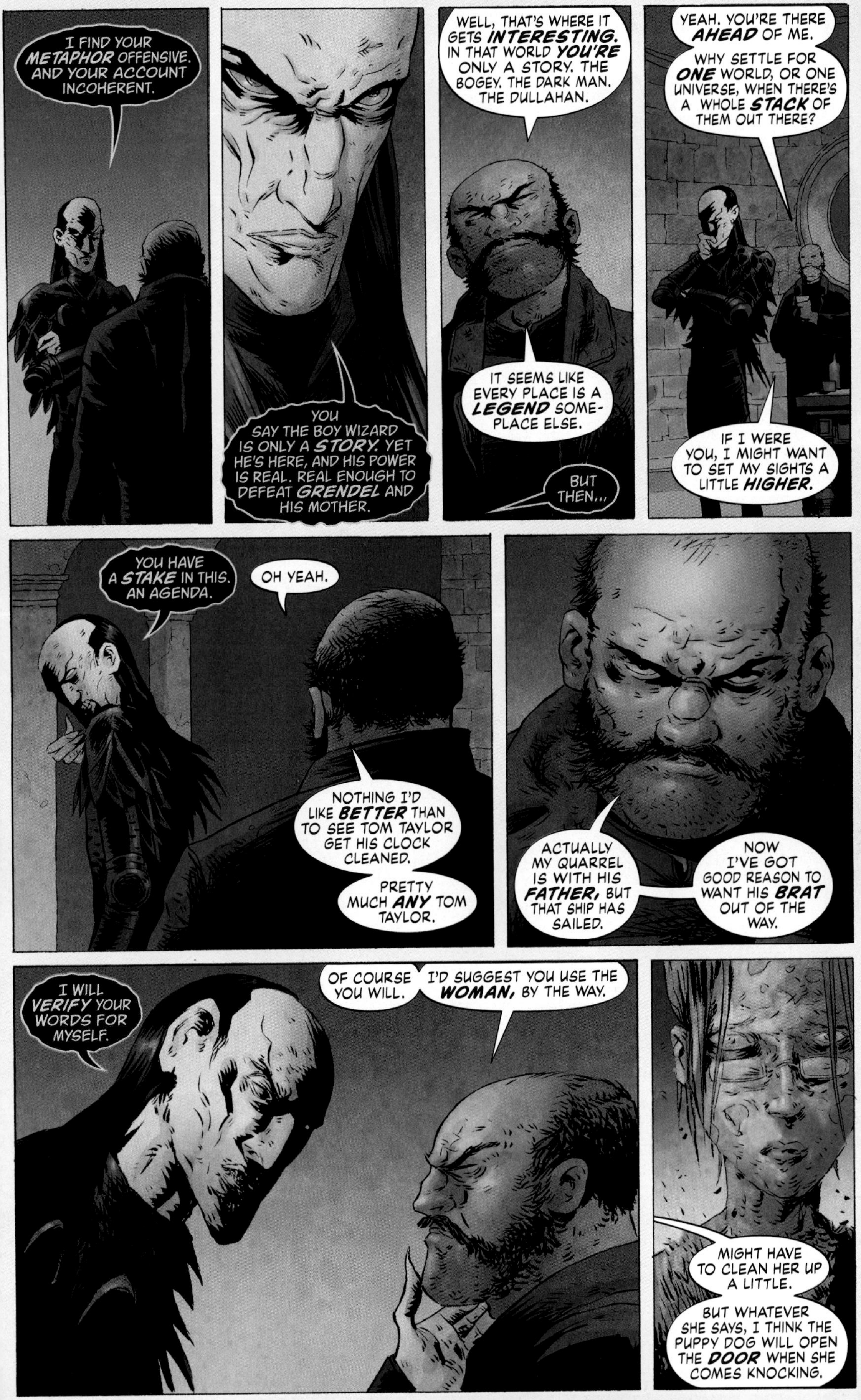
I FIND YOUR METAPHOR OFFENSIVE. AND YOUR ACCOUNT INCOHERENT.
YOU SAY THE BOY WIZARD IS ONLY A STORY. YET HE'S HERE, AND HIS POWER IS REAL. REAL ENOUGH TO DEFEAT GRENDEL AND HIS MOTHER.
WELL, THAT'S WHERE IT GETS INTERESTING. IN THAT WORLD YOU'RE ONLY A STORY. THE BOGEY. THE DARK MAN. THE DULLAHAN.
IT SEEMS LIKE EVERY PLACE IS A LEGEND SOME-PLACE ELSE.
BUT THEN...
YEAH. YOU'RE THERE AHEAD OF ME.
WHY SETTLE FOR ONE WORLD, OR ONE UNIVERSE, WHEN THERE'S A WHOLE STACK OF THEM OUT THERE?
IF I WERE YOU, I MIGHT WANT TO SET MY SIGHTS A LITTLE HIGHER.
YOU HAVE A STAKE IN THIS. AN AGENDA.
OH YEAH.
NOTHING I'D LIKE BETTER THAN TO SEE TOM TAYLOR GET HIS CLOCK CLEANED.
PRETTY MUCH ANY TOM TAYLOR.
ACTUALLY MY QUARREL IS WITH HIS FATHER, BUT THAT SHIP HAS SAILED.
NOW I'VE GOT GOOD REASON TO WANT HIS BRAT OUT OF THE WAY.
I WILL VERIFY YOUR WORDS FOR MYSELF.
OF COURSE YOU WILL.
I'D SUGGEST YOU USE THE WOMAN, BY THE WAY.
MIGHT HAVE TO CLEAN HER UP A LITTLE.
BUT WHATEVER SHE SAYS, I THINK THE PUPPY DOG WILL OPEN THE DOOR WHEN SHE COMES KNOCKING.

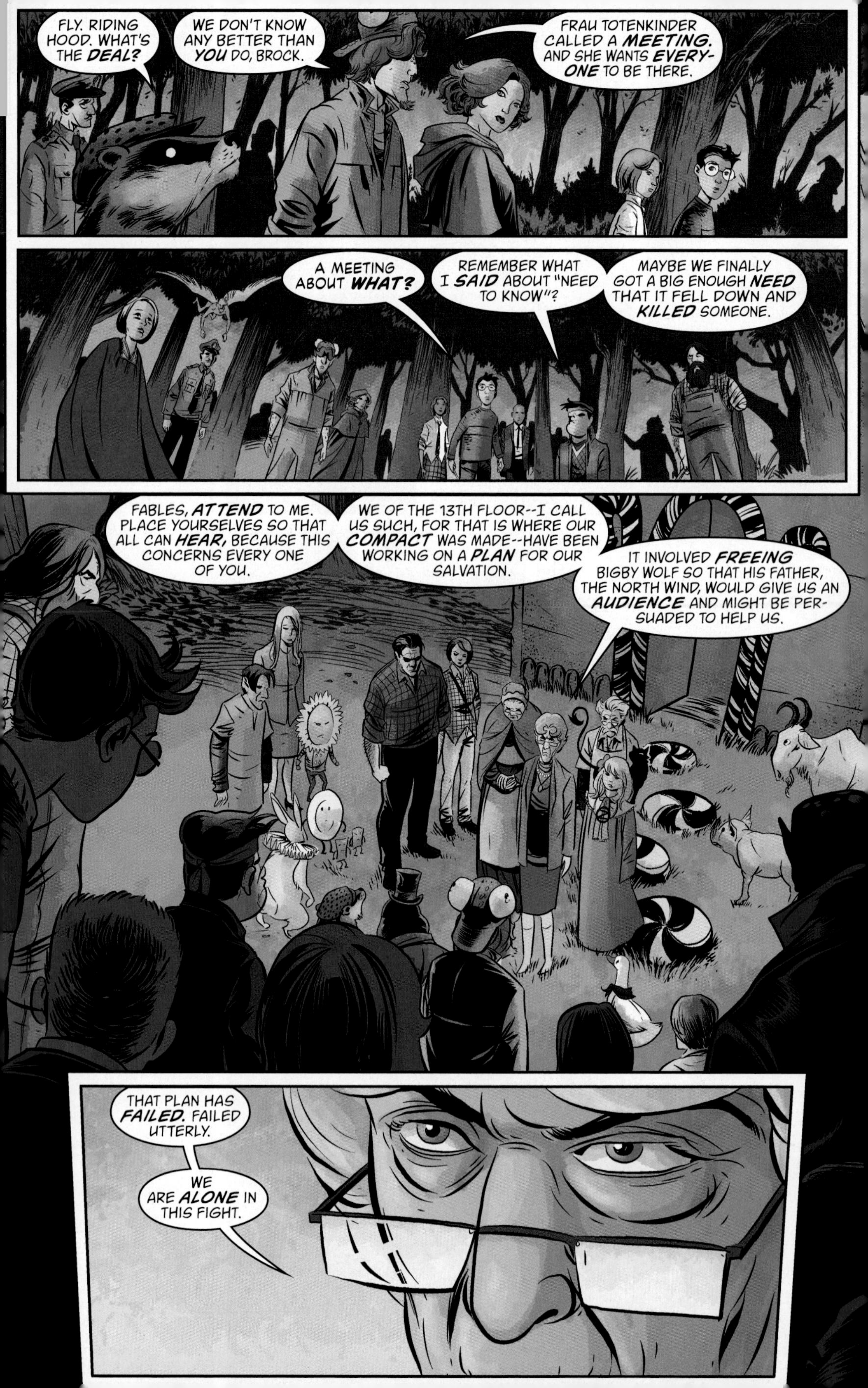
FLY. RIDING HOOD. WHAT'S THE *DEAL?*
WE DON'T KNOW ANY BETTER THAN *YOU* DO, BROCK.
FRAU TOTENKINDER CALLED A *MEETING.* AND SHE WANTS *EVERY-ONE* TO BE THERE.
A MEETING ABOUT *WHAT?*
REMEMBER WHAT I *SAID* ABOUT "NEED TO KNOW"?
MAYBE WE FINALLY GOT A BIG ENOUGH *NEED* THAT IT FELL DOWN AND *KILLED* SOMEONE.
FABLES, *ATTEND* TO ME. PLACE YOURSELVES SO THAT ALL CAN *HEAR,* BECAUSE THIS CONCERNS EVERY ONE OF YOU.
WE OF THE 13TH FLOOR--I CALL US SUCH, FOR THAT IS WHERE OUR *COMPACT* WAS MADE--HAVE BEEN WORKING ON A *PLAN* FOR OUR SALVATION.
IT INVOLVED *FREEING* BIGBY WOLF SO THAT HIS FATHER, THE NORTH WIND, WOULD GIVE US AN *AUDIENCE* AND MIGHT BE PER-SUADED TO HELP US.
THAT PLAN HAS *FAILED.* FAILED UTTERLY.
WE ARE *ALONE* IN THIS FIGHT.

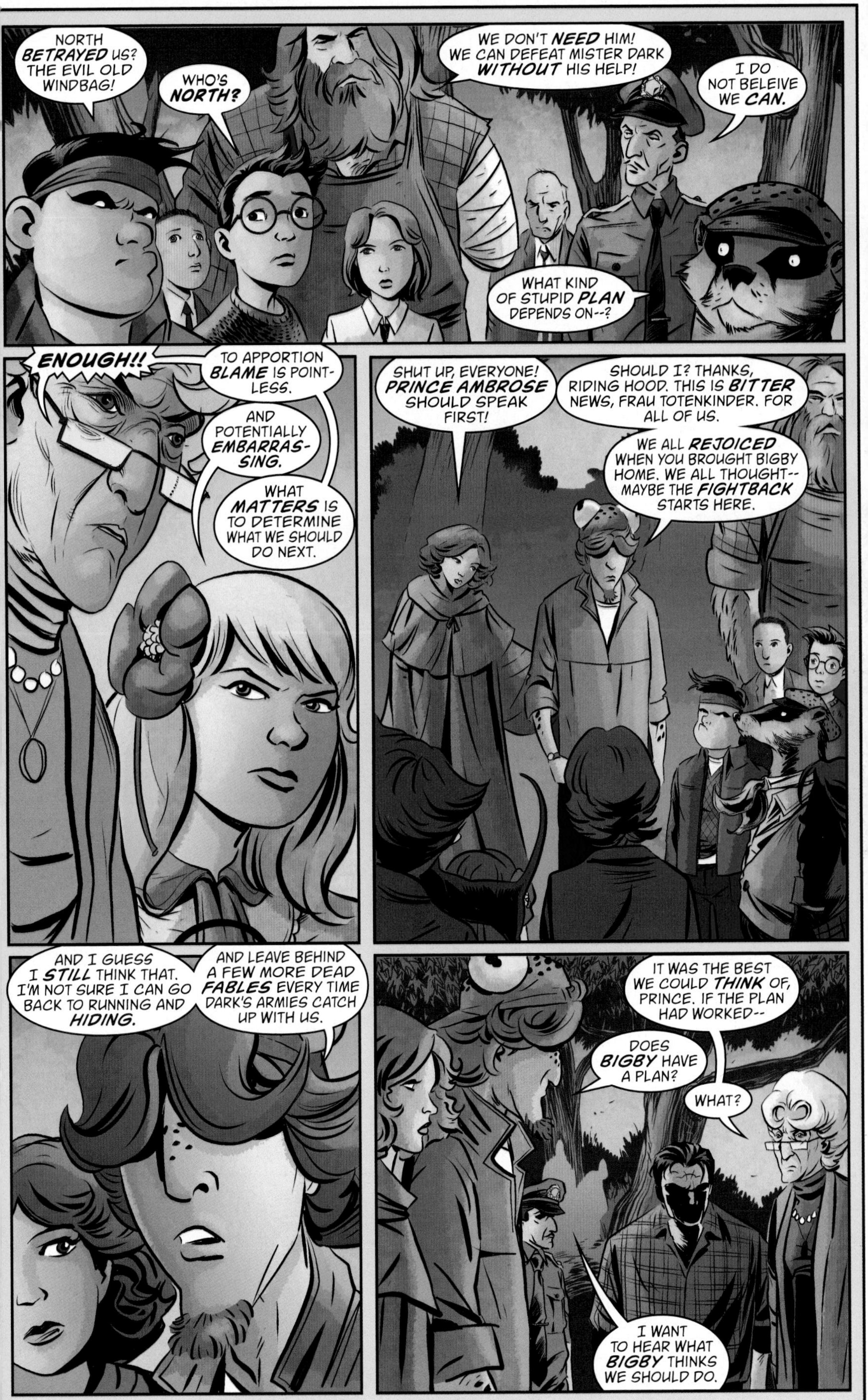
NORTH BETRAYED US? THE EVIL OLD WINDBAG!
WHO'S NORTH?
WE DON'T NEED HIM! WE CAN DEFEAT MISTER DARK WITHOUT HIS HELP!
I DO NOT BELEIVE WE CAN.
WHAT KIND OF STUPID PLAN DEPENDS ON--?
ENOUGH!!
TO APPORTION BLAME IS POINTLESS.
AND POTENTIALLY EMBARRASSING.
WHAT MATTERS IS TO DETERMINE WHAT WE SHOULD DO NEXT.
SHUT UP, EVERYONE! PRINCE AMBROSE SHOULD SPEAK FIRST!
SHOULD I? THANKS, RIDING HOOD. THIS IS BITTER NEWS, FRAU TOTENKINDER. FOR ALL OF US.
WE ALL REJOICED WHEN YOU BROUGHT BIGBY HOME. WE ALL THOUGHT--MAYBE THE FIGHTBACK STARTS HERE.
AND I GUESS I STILL THINK THAT. I'M NOT SURE I CAN GO BACK TO RUNNING AND HIDING.
AND LEAVE BEHIND A FEW MORE DEAD FABLES EVERY TIME DARK'S ARMIES CATCH UP WITH US.
IT WAS THE BEST WE COULD THINK OF, PRINCE. IF THE PLAN HAD WORKED--
DOES BIGBY HAVE A PLAN?
WHAT?
I WANT TO HEAR WHAT BIGBY THINKS WE SHOULD DO.

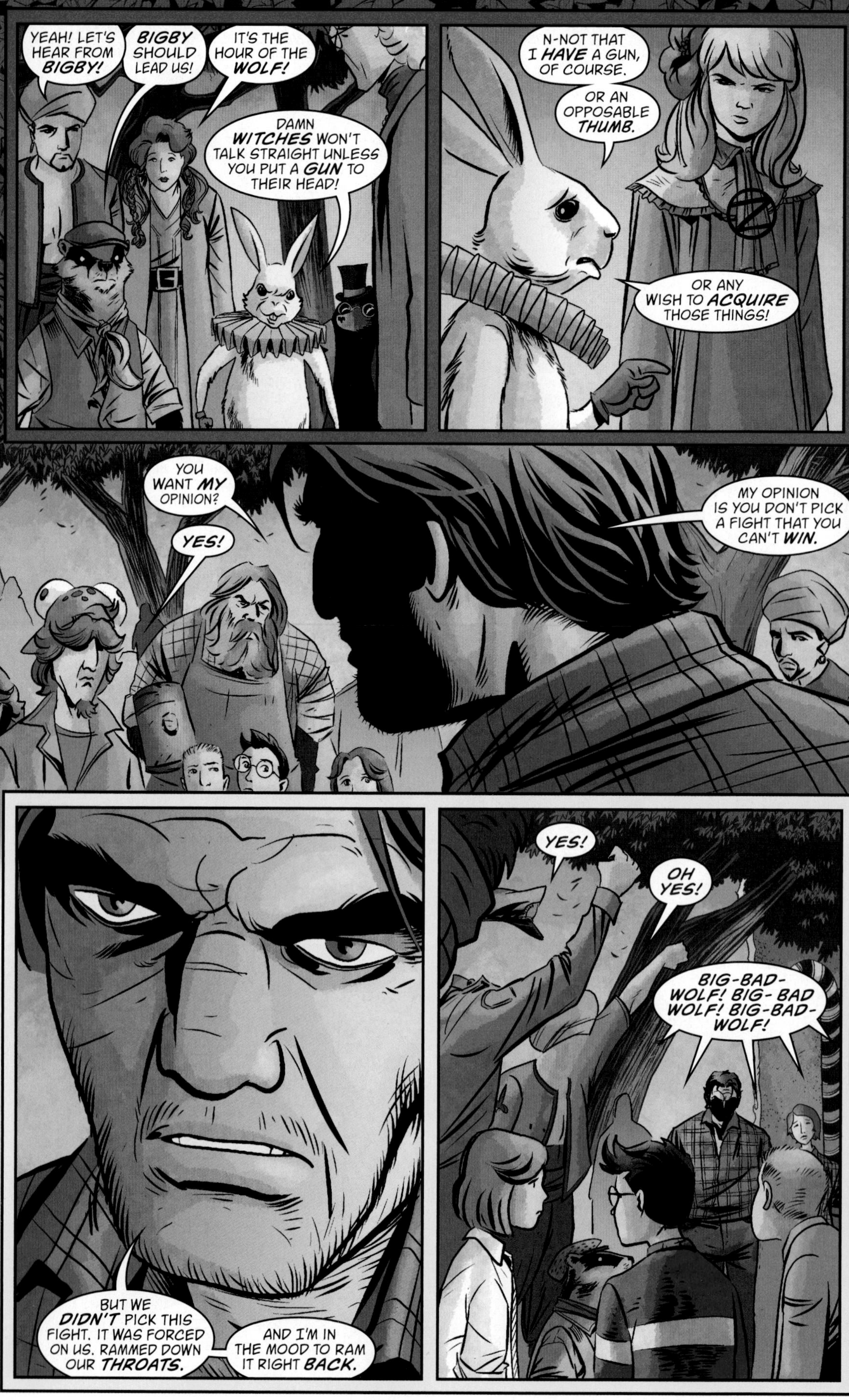

YEAH! LET'S HEAR FROM BIGBY!
BIGBY SHOULD LEAD US!
IT'S THE HOUR OF THE WOLF!
DAMN WITCHES WON'T TALK STRAIGHT UNLESS YOU PUT A GUN TO THEIR HEAD!
N-NOT THAT I HAVE A GUN, OF COURSE.
OR AN OPPOSABLE THUMB.
OR ANY WISH TO ACQUIRE THOSE THINGS!
YOU WANT MY OPINION?
YES!
MY OPINION IS YOU DON'T PICK A FIGHT THAT YOU CAN'T WIN.
BUT WE DIDN'T PICK THIS FIGHT. IT WAS FORCED ON US. RAMMED DOWN OUR THROATS.
AND I'M IN THE MOOD TO RAM IT RIGHT BACK.
YES!
OH YES!
BIG-BAD-WOLF! BIG-BAD WOLF! BIG-BAD-WOLF!

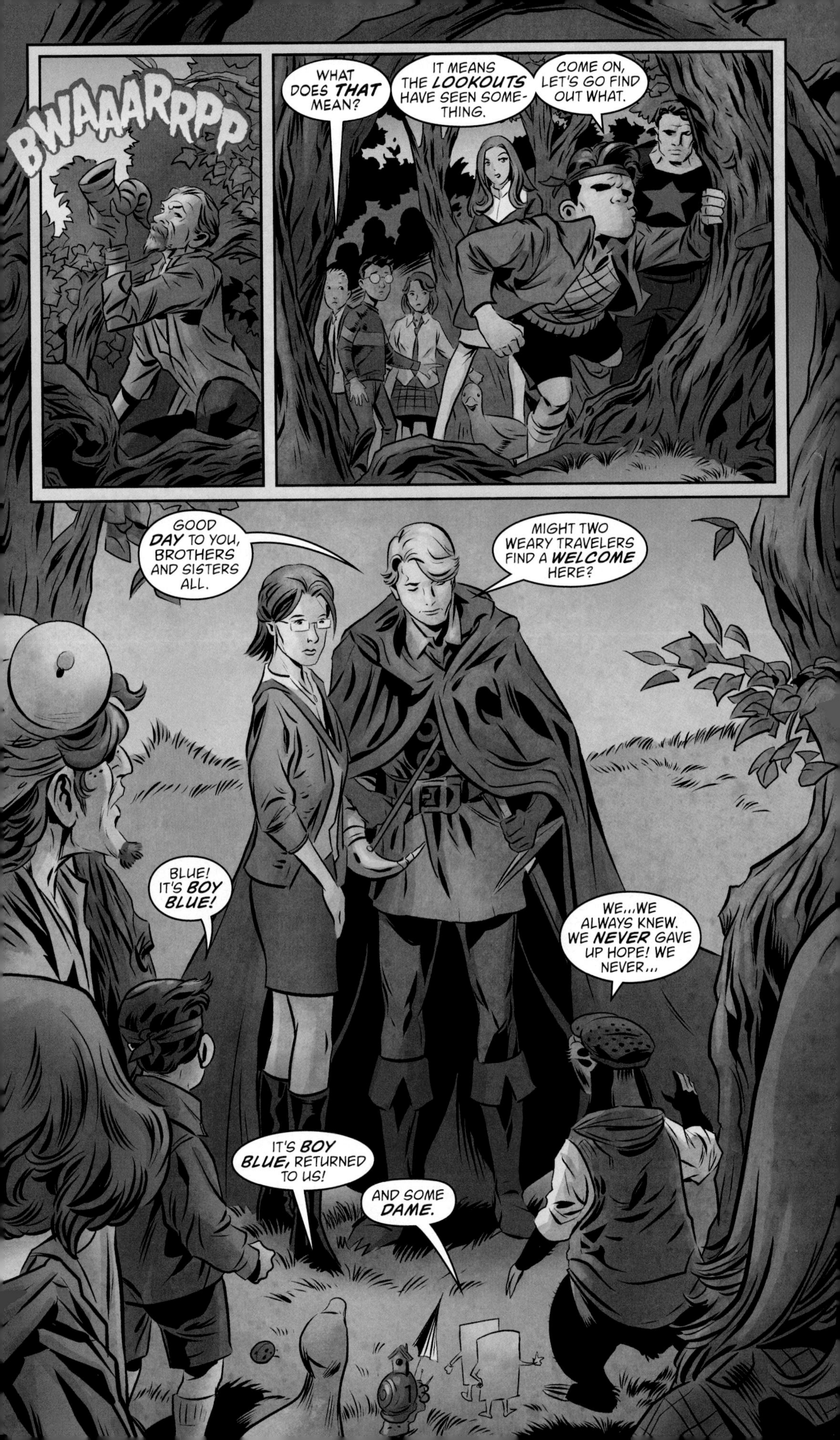
BWAAARRPP
WHAT DOES **THAT** MEAN?
IT MEANS THE **LOOKOUTS** HAVE SEEN SOMETHING.
COME ON, LET'S GO FIND OUT WHAT.
GOOD **DAY** TO YOU, BROTHERS AND SISTERS ALL.
MIGHT TWO WEARY TRAVELERS FIND A **WELCOME** HERE?
BLUE! IT'S **BOY BLUE!**
WE...WE ALWAYS KNEW. WE **NEVER** GAVE UP HOPE! WE NEVER...
IT'S **BOY BLUE,** RETURNED TO US!
AND SOME **DAME.**

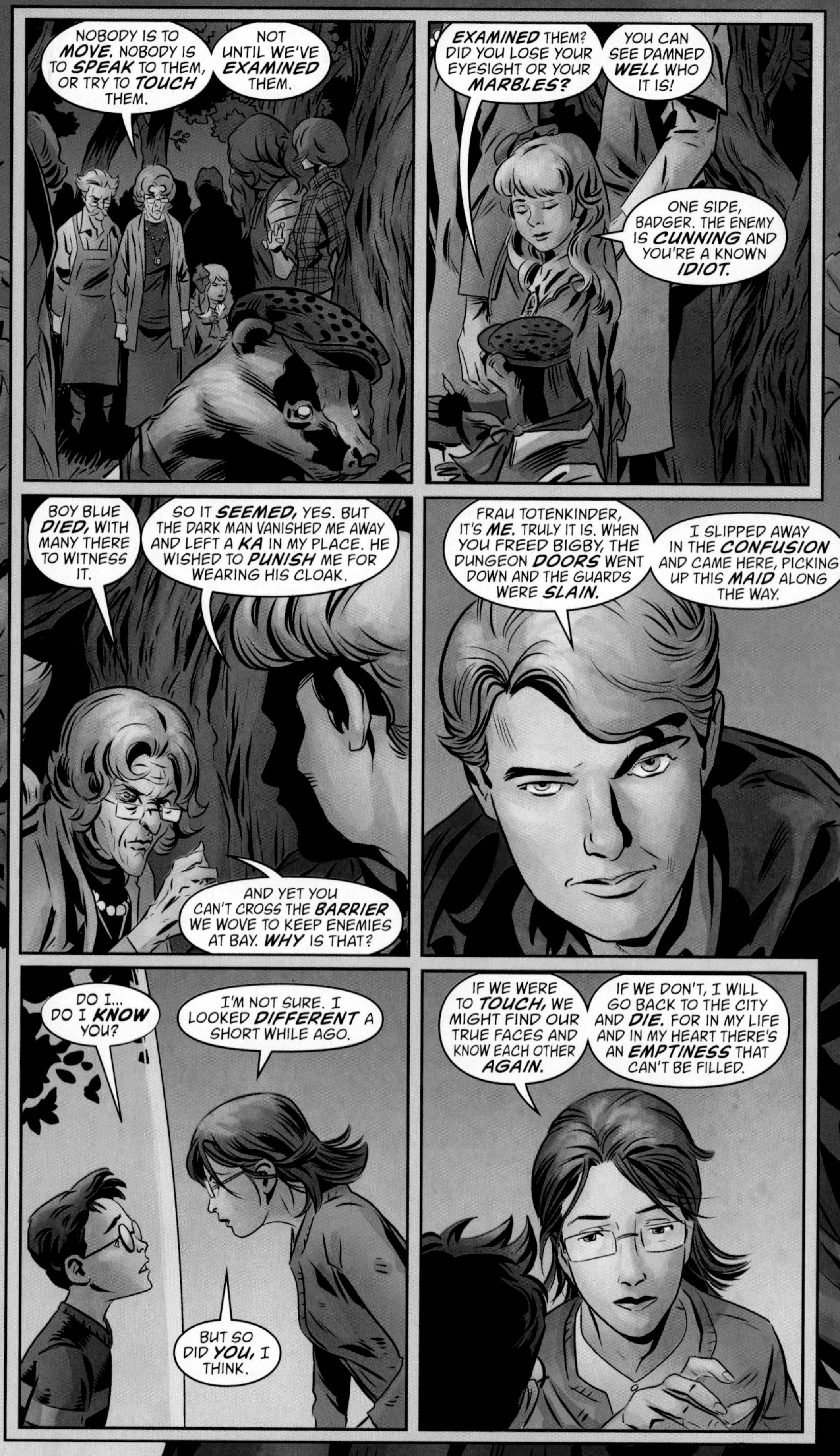
NOBODY IS TO MOVE. NOBODY IS TO SPEAK TO THEM, OR TRY TO TOUCH THEM.
NOT UNTIL WE'VE EXAMINED THEM.
EXAMINED THEM? DID YOU LOSE YOUR EYESIGHT OR YOUR MARBLES?
YOU CAN SEE DAMNED WELL WHO IT IS!
ONE SIDE, BADGER. THE ENEMY IS CUNNING AND YOU'RE A KNOWN IDIOT.
BOY BLUE DIED, WITH MANY THERE TO WITNESS IT.
SO IT SEEMED, YES. BUT THE DARK MAN VANISHED ME AWAY AND LEFT A KA IN MY PLACE. HE WISHED TO PUNISH ME FOR WEARING HIS CLOAK.
AND YET YOU CAN'T CROSS THE BARRIER WE WOVE TO KEEP ENEMIES AT BAY. WHY IS THAT?
FRAU TOTENKINDER, IT'S ME. TRULY IT IS. WHEN YOU FREED BIGBY, THE DUNGEON DOORS WENT DOWN AND THE GUARDS WERE SLAIN.
I SLIPPED AWAY IN THE CONFUSION AND CAME HERE, PICKING UP THIS MAID ALONG THE WAY.
DO I... DO I KNOW YOU?
I'M NOT SURE. I LOOKED DIFFERENT A SHORT WHILE AGO.
BUT SO DID YOU, I THINK.
IF WE WERE TO TOUCH, WE MIGHT FIND OUR TRUE FACES AND KNOW EACH OTHER AGAIN.
IF WE DON'T, I WILL GO BACK TO THE CITY AND DIE. FOR IN MY LIFE AND IN MY HEART THERE'S AN EMPTINESS THAT CAN'T BE FILLED.

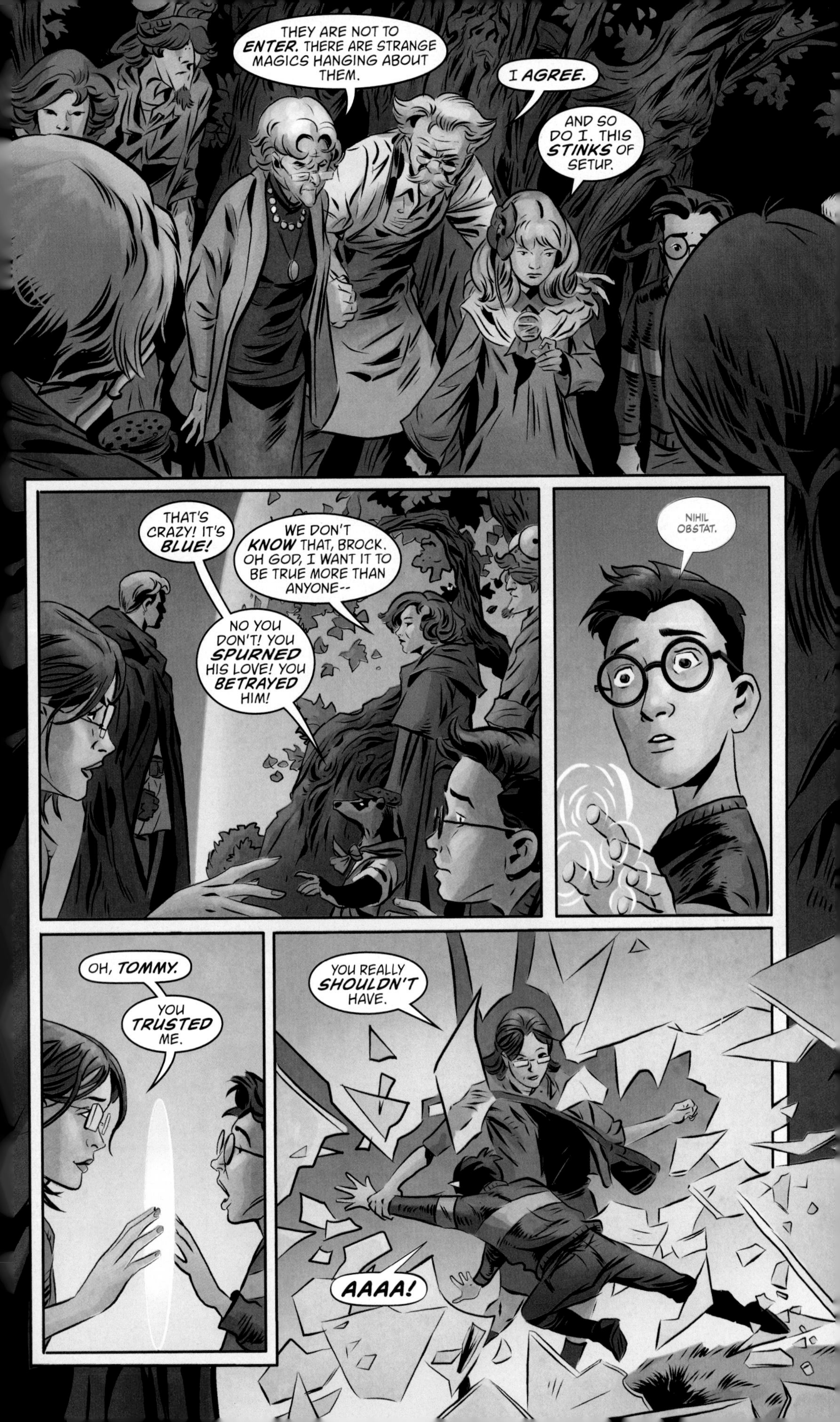
THEY ARE NOT TO ENTER. THERE ARE STRANGE MAGICS HANGING ABOUT THEM.
I AGREE.
AND SO DO I. THIS STINKS OF SETUP.
THAT'S CRAZY! IT'S BLUE!
WE DON'T KNOW THAT, BROCK. OH GOD, I WANT IT TO BE TRUE MORE THAN ANYONE--
NO YOU DON'T! YOU SPURNED HIS LOVE! YOU BETRAYED HIM!
NIHIL OBSTAT.
OH, TOMMY.
YOU TRUSTED ME.
YOU REALLY SHOULDN'T HAVE.
AAAA!

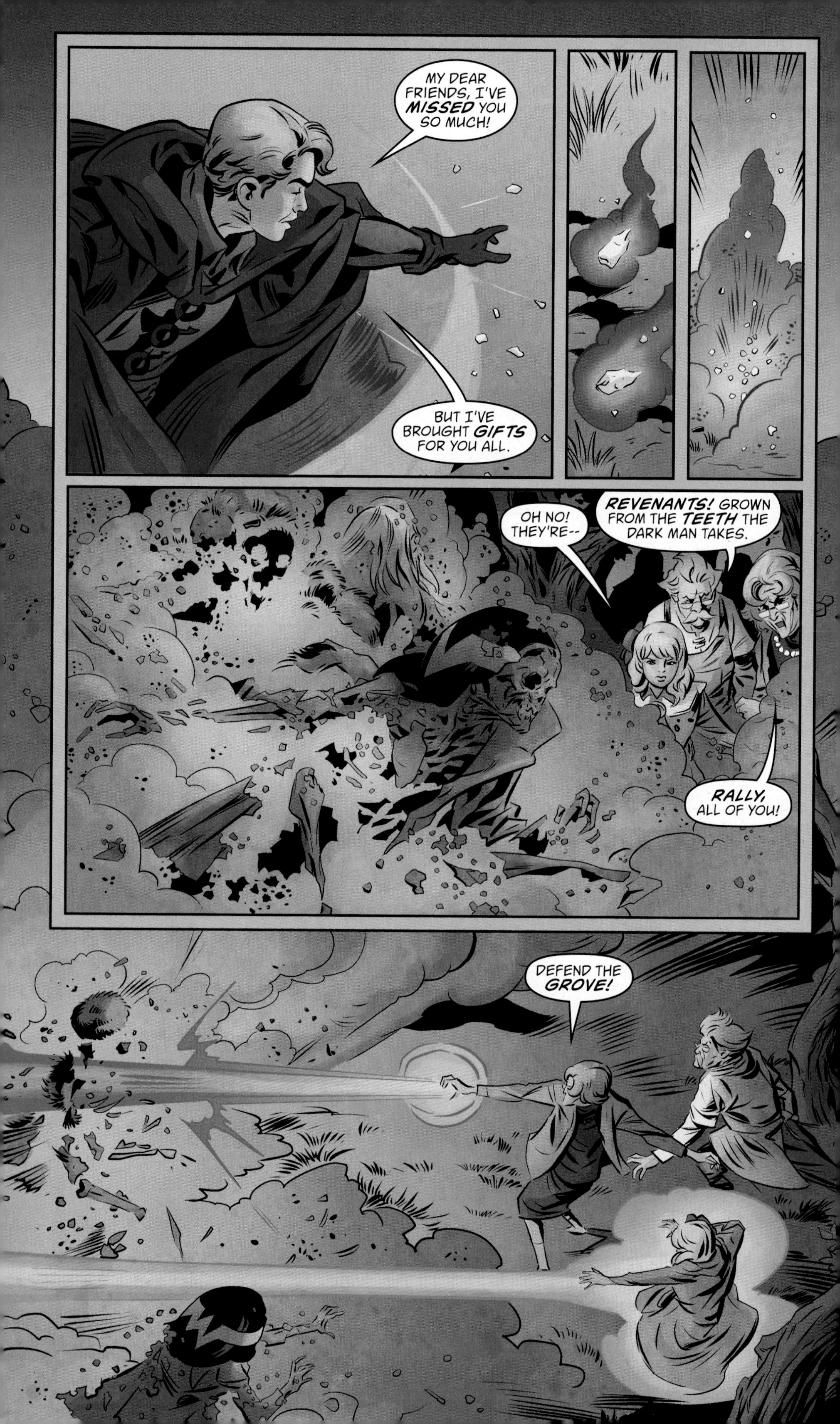
MY DEAR FRIENDS, I'VE MISSED YOU SO MUCH!
BUT I'VE BROUGHT GIFTS FOR YOU ALL.
OH NO! THEY'RE--
REVENANTS! GROWN FROM THE TEETH THE DARK MAN TAKES.
RALLY, ALL OF YOU!
DEFEND THE GROVE!

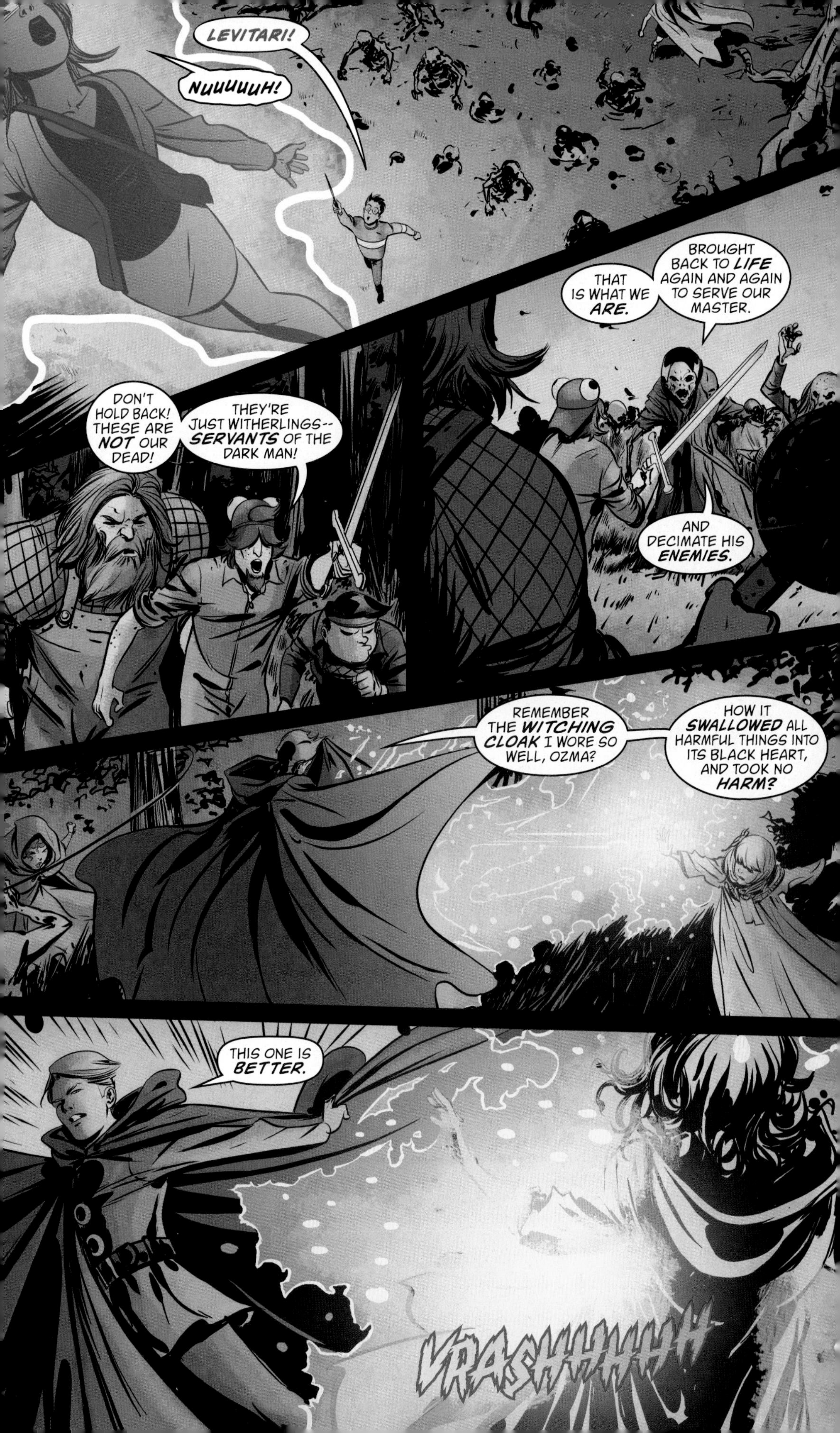
LEVITARI!
NUUUUUH!
DON'T HOLD BACK! THESE ARE NOT OUR DEAD!
THEY'RE JUST WITHERLINGS-- SERVANTS OF THE DARK MAN!
THAT IS WHAT WE ARE.
BROUGHT BACK TO LIFE AGAIN AND AGAIN TO SERVE OUR MASTER.
AND DECIMATE HIS ENEMIES.
REMEMBER THE WITCHING CLOAK I WORE SO WELL, OZMA?
HOW IT SWALLOWED ALL HARMFUL THINGS INTO ITS BLACK HEART, AND TOOK NO HARM?
THIS ONE IS BETTER.
VRASHHHHH

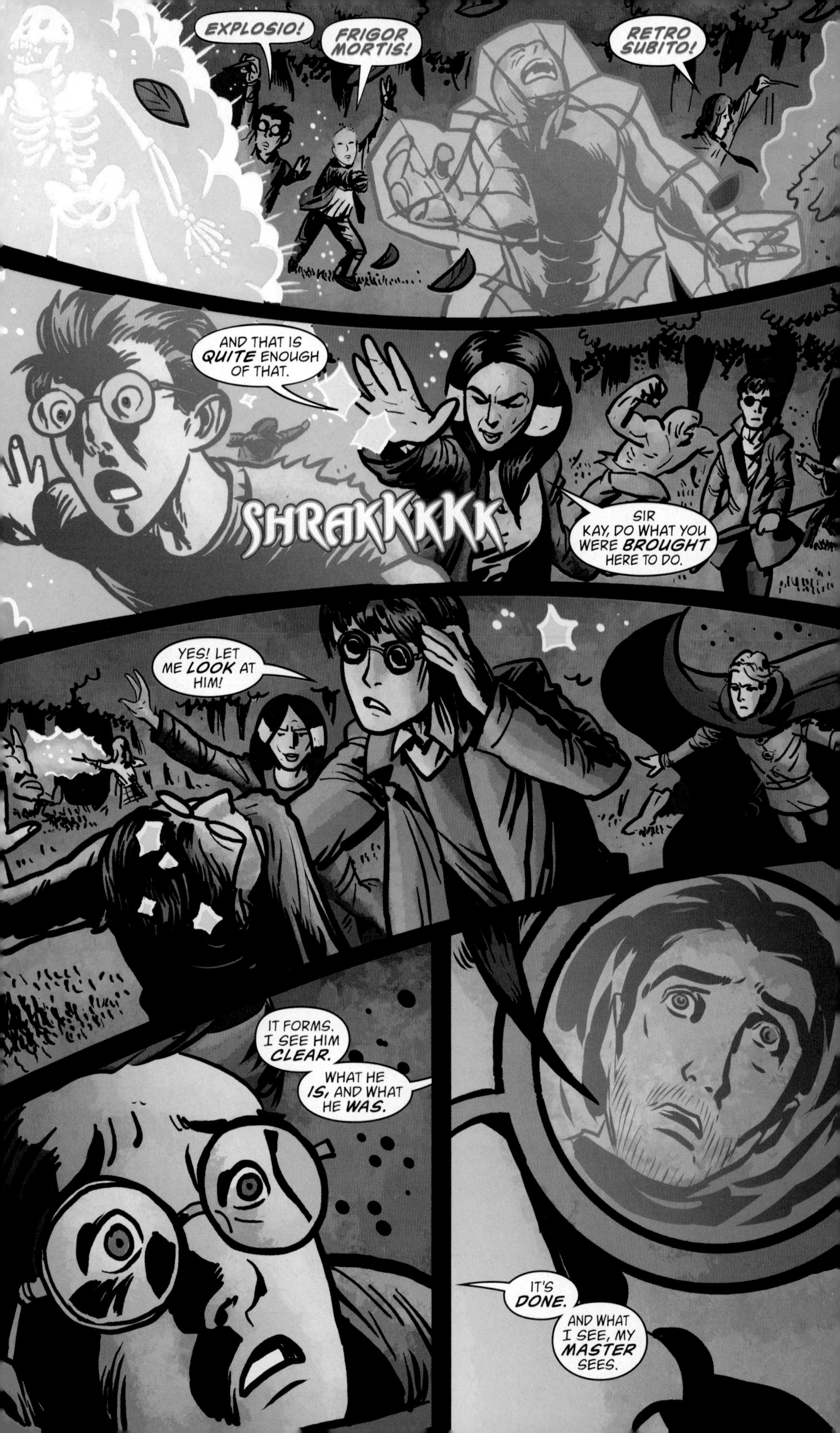
EXPLOSIO!
FRIGOR MORTIS!
RETRO SUBITO!
AND THAT IS QUITE ENOUGH OF THAT.
SHRAKKKKK
SIR KAY, DO WHAT YOU WERE BROUGHT HERE TO DO.
YES! LET ME LOOK AT HIM!
IT FORMS. I SEE HIM CLEAR.
WHAT HE IS, AND WHAT HE WAS.
IT'S DONE.
AND WHAT I SEE, MY MASTER SEES.

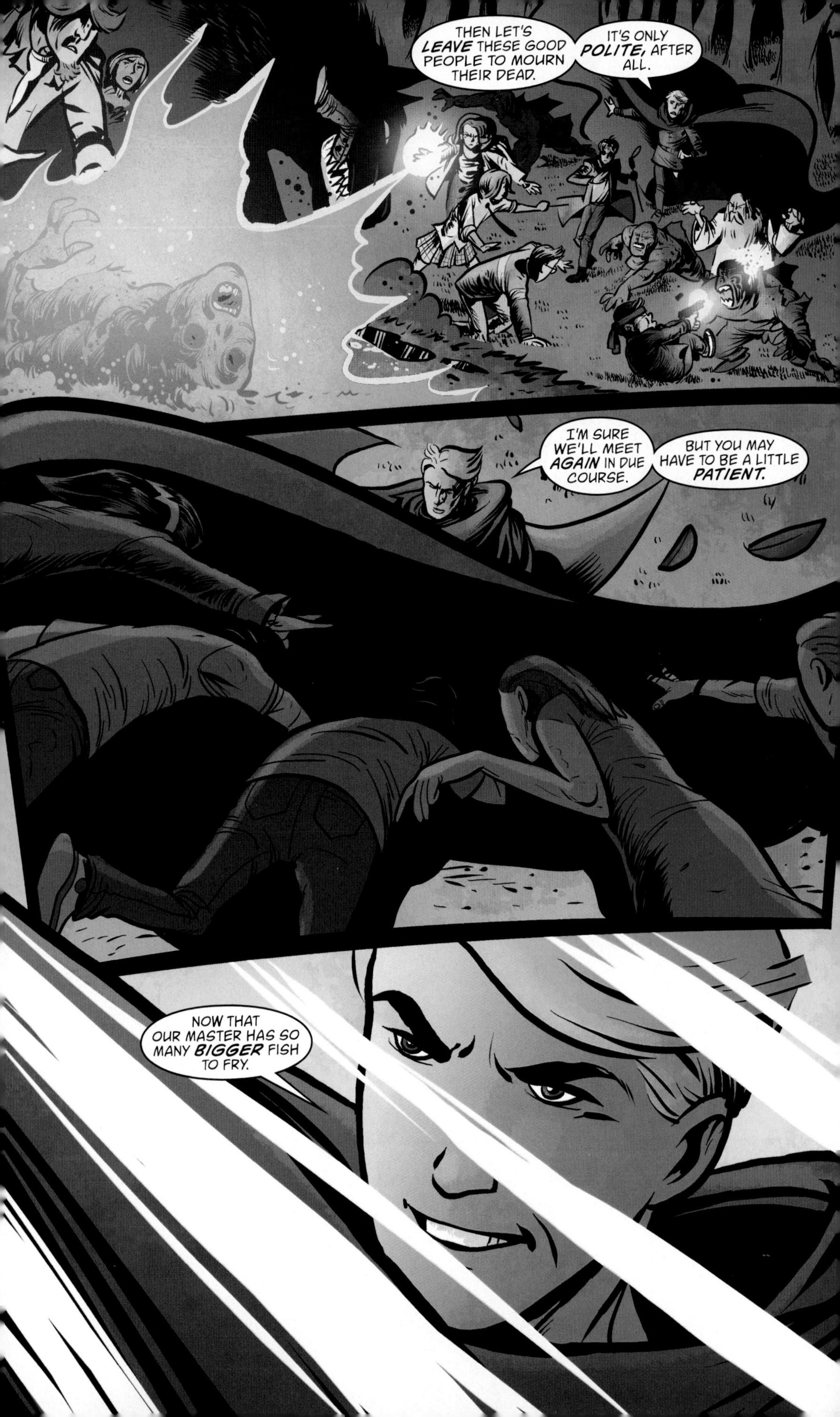
THEN LET'S LEAVE THESE GOOD PEOPLE TO MOURN THEIR DEAD.
IT'S ONLY POLITE, AFTER ALL.
I'M SURE WE'LL MEET AGAIN IN DUE COURSE.
BUT YOU MAY HAVE TO BE A LITTLE PATIENT.
NOW THAT OUR MASTER HAS SO MANY BIGGER FISH TO FRY.

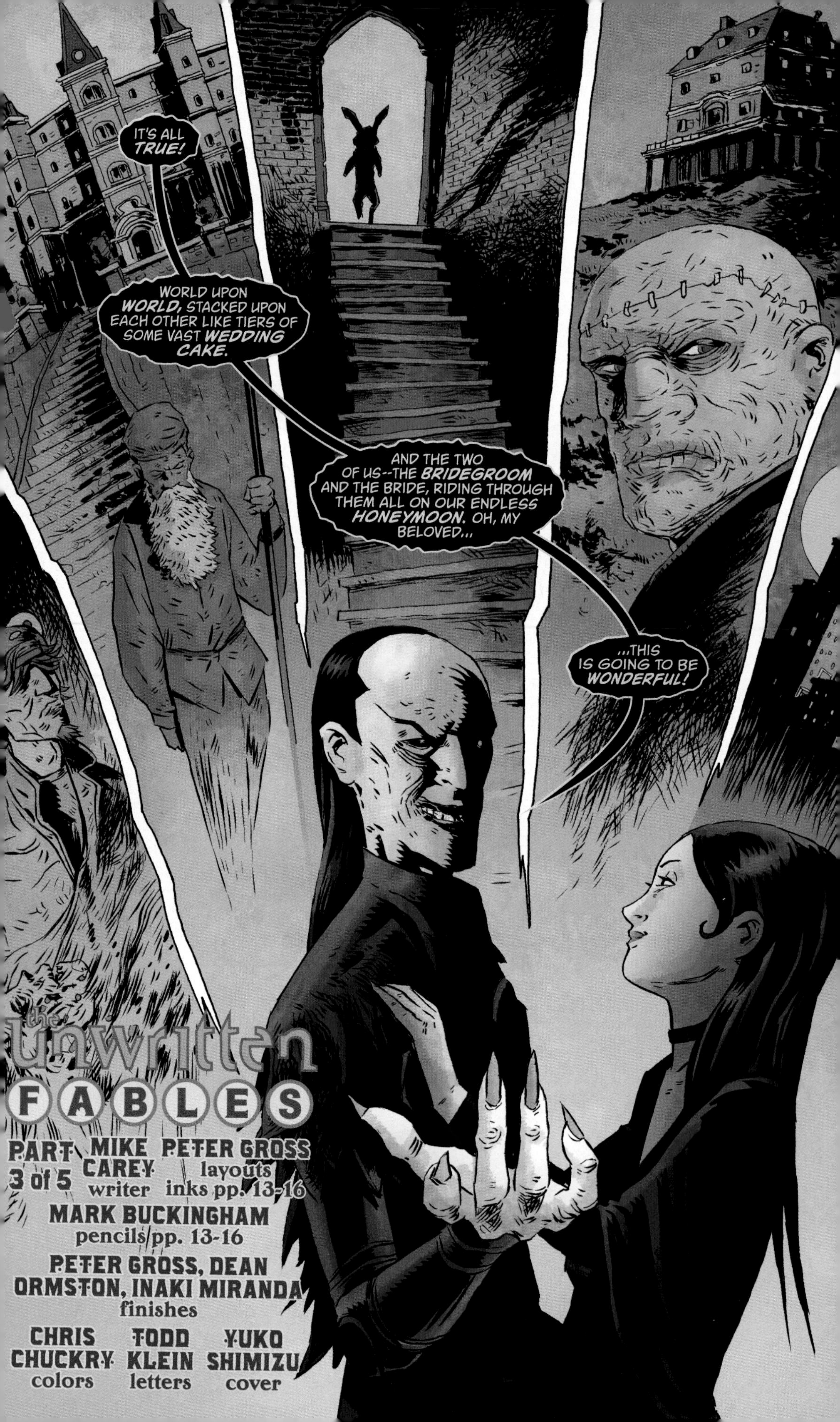
IT'S ALL TRUE!
WORLD UPON WORLD, STACKED UPON EACH OTHER LIKE TIERS OF SOME VAST WEDDING CAKE.
AND THE TWO OF US--THE BRIDEGROOM AND THE BRIDE, RIDING THROUGH THEM ALL ON OUR ENDLESS HONEYMOON. OH, MY BELOVED...
...THIS IS GOING TO BE WONDERFUL!
the unwritten
FABLES
PART 3 of 5
MIKE CAREY writer
PETER GROSS layouts inks pp. 13-16
MARK BUCKINGHAM pencils pp. 13-16
PETER GROSS, DEAN ORMSTON, INAKI MIRANDA finishes
CHRIS CHUCKRY colors
TODD KLEIN letters
YUKO SHIMIZU cover

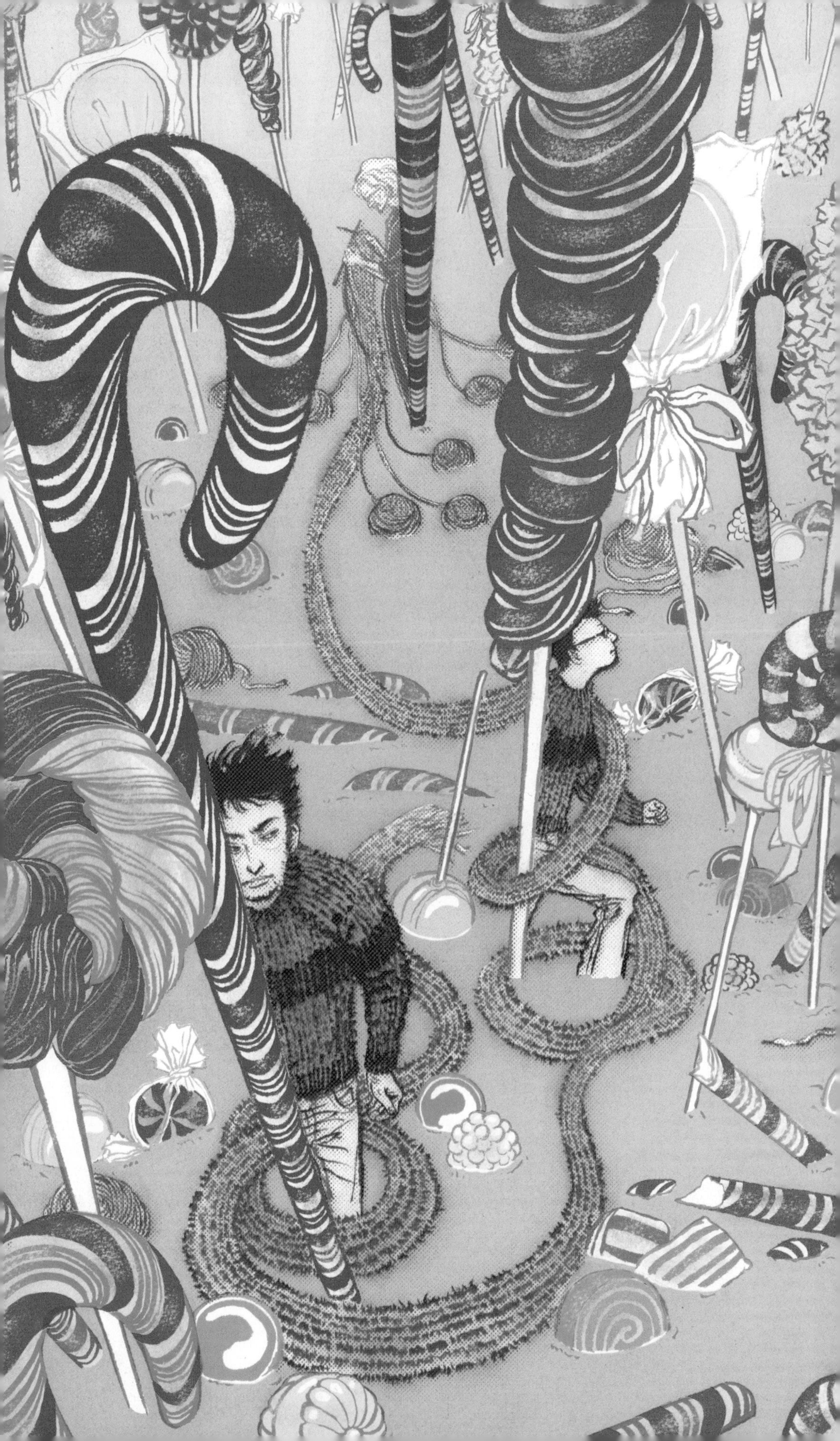

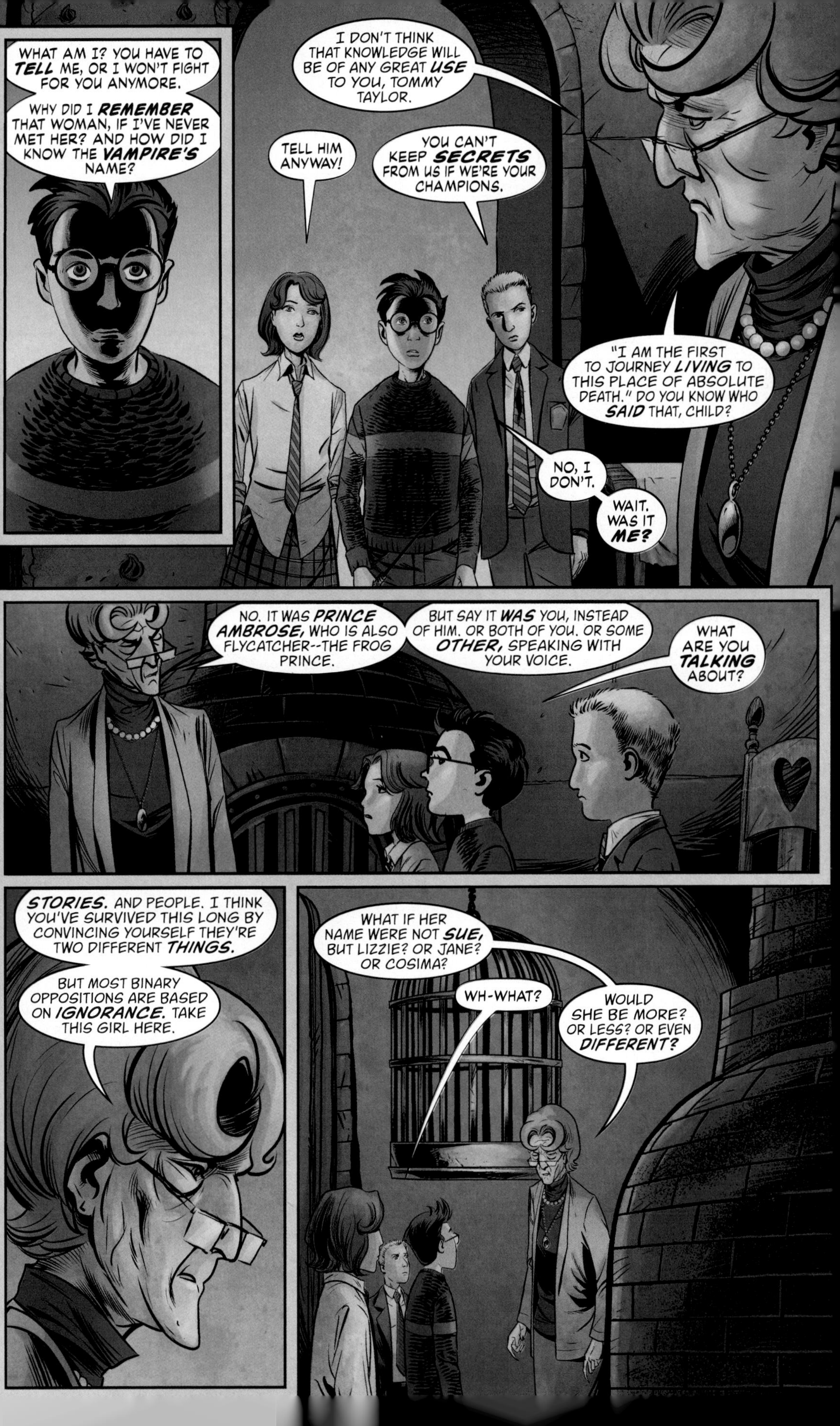

WHAT AM I? YOU HAVE TO TELL ME, OR I WON'T FIGHT FOR YOU ANYMORE.
WHY DID I REMEMBER THAT WOMAN, IF I'VE NEVER MET HER? AND HOW DID I KNOW THE VAMPIRE'S NAME?
I DON'T THINK THAT KNOWLEDGE WILL BE OF ANY GREAT USE TO YOU, TOMMY TAYLOR.
TELL HIM ANYWAY!
YOU CAN'T KEEP SECRETS FROM US IF WE'RE YOUR CHAMPIONS.
"I AM THE FIRST TO JOURNEY LIVING TO THIS PLACE OF ABSOLUTE DEATH." DO YOU KNOW WHO SAID THAT, CHILD?
NO, I DON'T.
WAIT. WAS IT ME?
NO. IT WAS PRINCE AMBROSE, WHO IS ALSO FLYCATCHER--THE FROG PRINCE.
BUT SAY IT WAS YOU, INSTEAD OF HIM. OR BOTH OF YOU. OR SOME OTHER, SPEAKING WITH YOUR VOICE.
WHAT ARE YOU TALKING ABOUT?
STORIES. AND PEOPLE. I THINK YOU'VE SURVIVED THIS LONG BY CONVINCING YOURSELF THEY'RE TWO DIFFERENT THINGS.
BUT MOST BINARY OPPOSITIONS ARE BASED ON IGNORANCE. TAKE THIS GIRL HERE.
WHAT IF HER NAME WERE NOT SUE, BUT LIZZIE? OR JANE? OR COSIMA?
WH-WHAT?
WOULD SHE BE MORE? OR LESS? OR EVEN DIFFERENT?

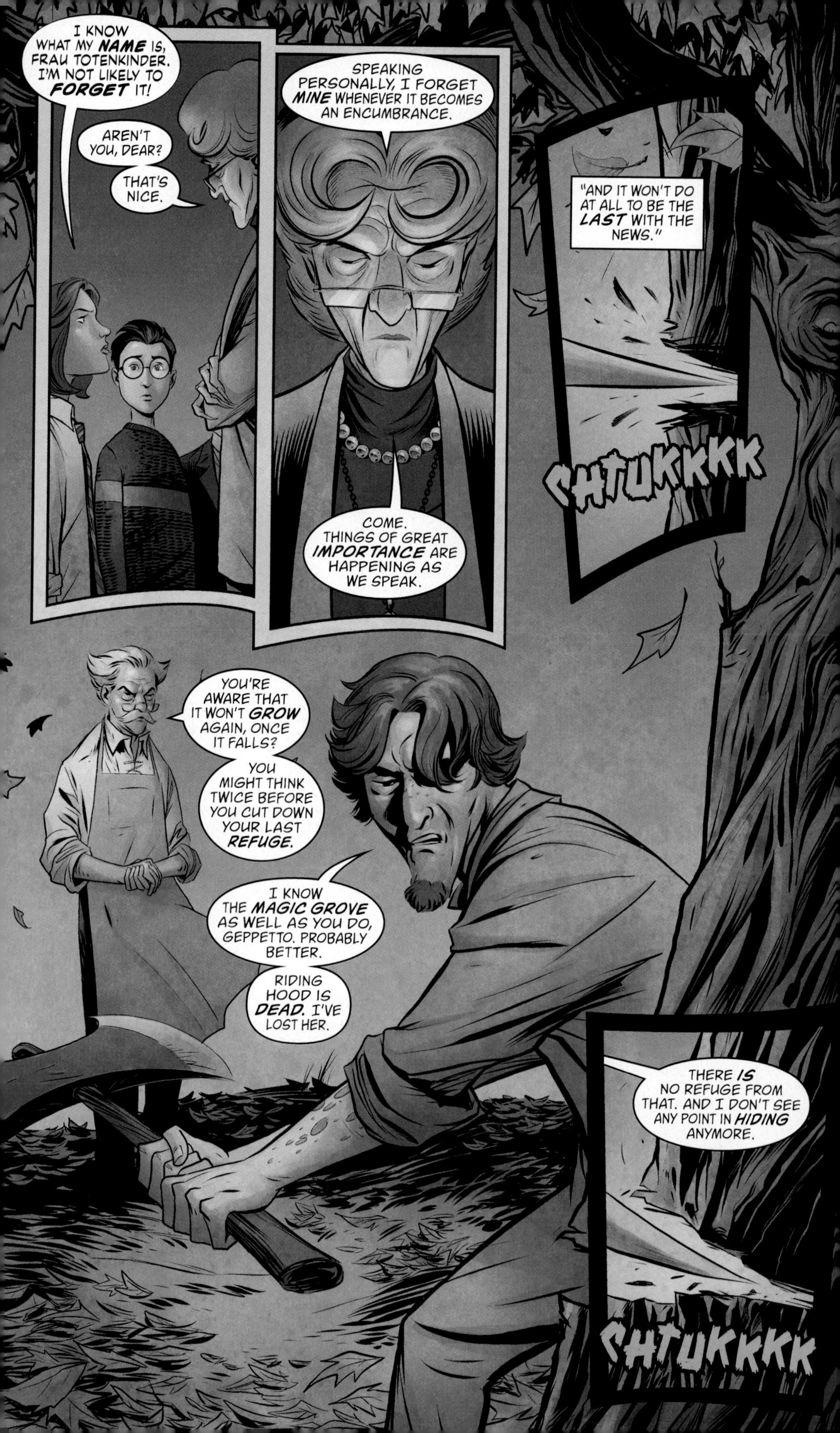
I KNOW WHAT MY NAME IS, FRAU TOTENKINDER. I'M NOT LIKELY TO FORGET IT!
AREN'T YOU, DEAR?
THAT'S NICE.
SPEAKING PERSONALLY, I FORGET MINE WHENEVER IT BECOMES AN ENCUMBRANCE.
COME. THINGS OF GREAT IMPORTANCE ARE HAPPENING AS WE SPEAK.
"AND IT WON'T DO AT ALL TO BE THE LAST WITH THE NEWS."
CHTUKKKK
YOU'RE AWARE THAT IT WON'T GROW AGAIN, ONCE IT FALLS?
YOU MIGHT THINK TWICE BEFORE YOU CUT DOWN YOUR LAST REFUGE.
I KNOW THE MAGIC GROVE AS WELL AS YOU DO, GEPPETTO. PROBABLY BETTER.
RIDING HOOD IS DEAD. I'VE LOST HER.
THERE IS NO REFUGE FROM THAT. AND I DON'T SEE ANY POINT IN HIDING ANYMORE.
CHTUKKKK

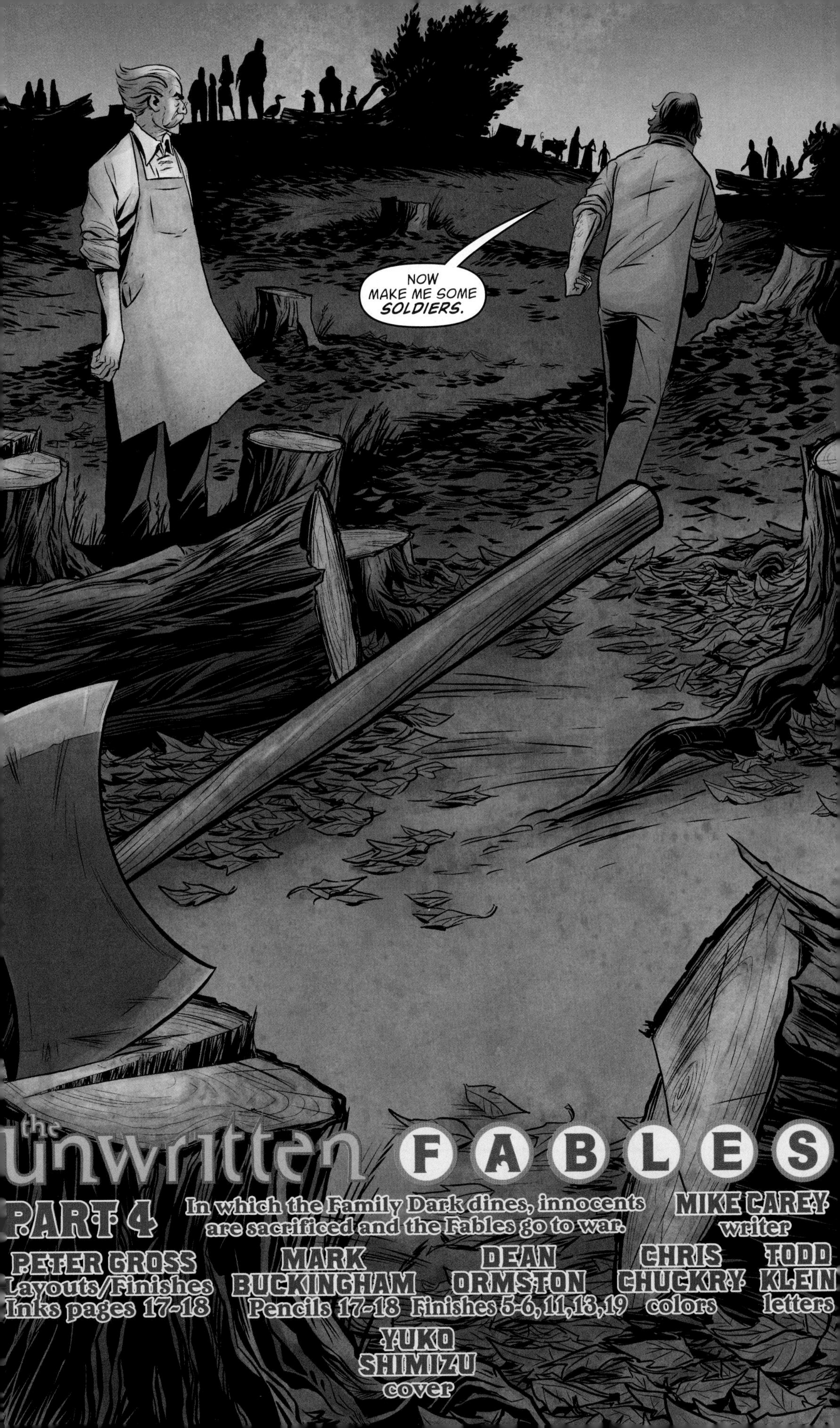

NOW MAKE ME SOME SOLDIERS.
the Unwritten FABLES
PART 4
In which the Family Dark dines, innocents are sacrificed and the Fables go to war.
MIKE CAREY writer
PETER GROSS Layouts/Finishes Inks pages 17-18
MARK BUCKINGHAM Pencils 17-18
DEAN ORMSTON Finishes 5-6, 11, 13, 19
CHRIS CHUCKRY colors
TODD KLEIN letters
YUKO SHIMIZU cover

SO WE'RE GOING TO WAR?

WAY PAST TIME, EYE-EM-AITCH-OH.

BUT SHOULDN'T IT HAVE BEEN A *JOINT* DECISION?

PERHAPS IT SHOULD. BUT *AMBROSE* IS THE KING IN THE GROVE.

HE'S TURNING IT INTO A GOLDEN *ARMY* TO BRING AGAINST MISTER DARK--FOR THE SAKE OF *RIDING HOOD,* WHO DIED.

WELL, AS FAR AS *THAT* GOES, I DON'T SEE THAT WE'VE GOT TOO MANY OTHER *OPTIONS.*

IF I'M GETTING THIS *RIGHT,* YOU BROUGHT THESE KIDS HERE FROM ANOTHER WORLD TO BE YOUR *SHOCK TROOPS?*

THAT'S ESSENTIALLY CORRECT, MISTER WOLF.

AND NOW MISTER DARK KNOWS THEIR *HOME ADDRESS?*

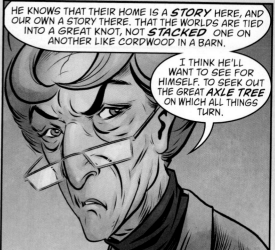

HE KNOWS THAT THEIR HOME IS A *STORY* HERE, AND OUR OWN A STORY THERE. THAT THE WORLDS ARE TIED INTO A GREAT KNOT, NOT *STACKED* ONE ON ANOTHER LIKE CORDWOOD IN A BARN.

I THINK HE'LL WANT TO SEE FOR HIMSELF. TO SEEK OUT THE GREAT *AXLE TREE* ON WHICH ALL THINGS TURN.

AND IF HE GETS HIS *HANDS* ON THAT? YOU THINK HE'LL GO AWAY AND LEAVE US *ALONE?*

NO.

NO. I DON'T THINK SO *EITHER.*

I THINK HE'LL *OOZE* INTO EVERY DAMN CORNER OF THE UNIVERSE, AND THE ONLY STORY *ANYONE* TELLS WILL BE HIS.

SO LET'S DO THIS. WHILE WE STILL *CAN.*

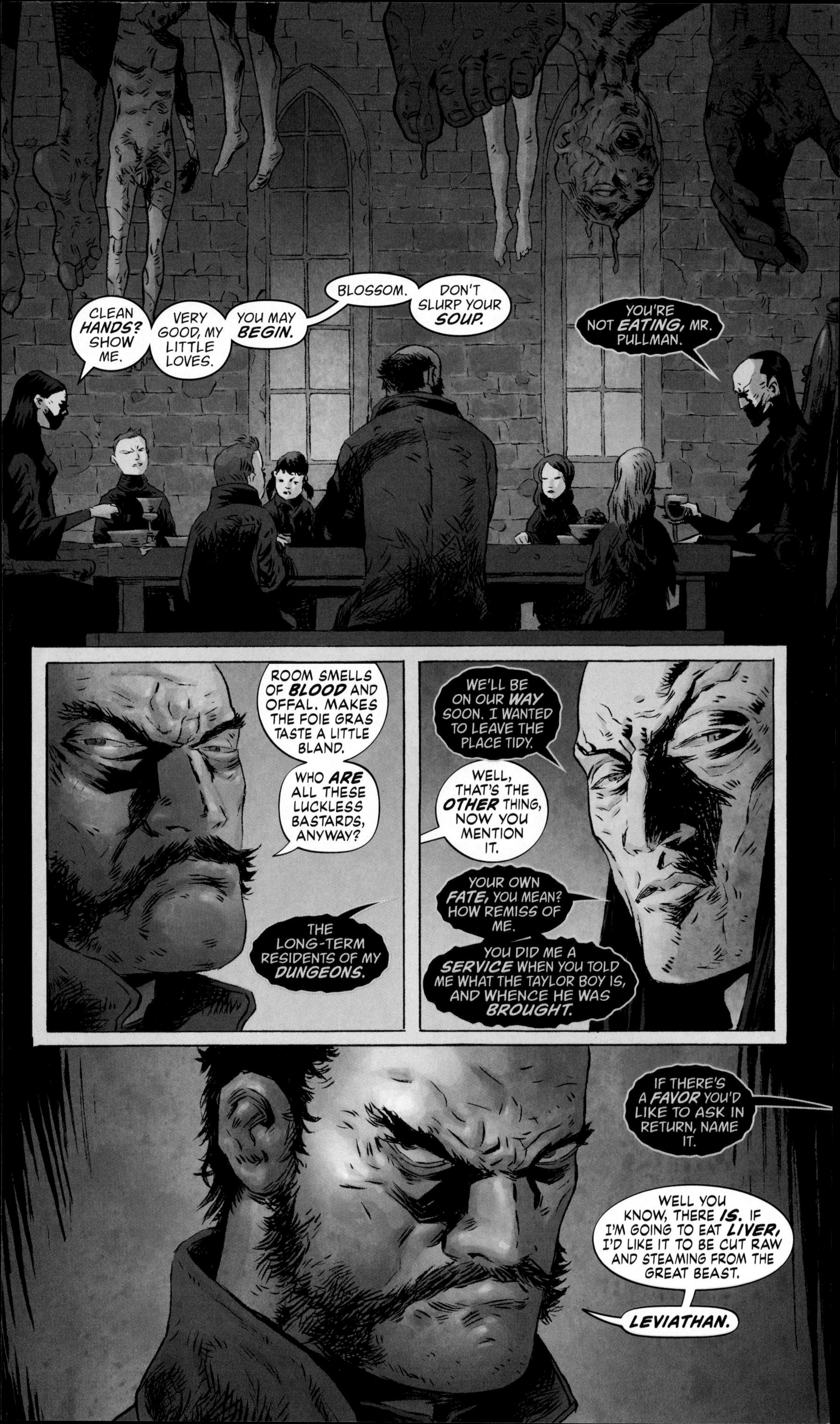
CLEAN HANDS? SHOW ME.
VERY GOOD, MY LITTLE LOVES.
YOU MAY BEGIN.
BLOSSOM.
DON'T SLURP YOUR SOUP.
YOU'RE NOT EATING, MR. PULLMAN.
ROOM SMELLS OF BLOOD AND OFFAL. MAKES THE FOIE GRAS TASTE A LITTLE BLAND.
WHO ARE ALL THESE LUCKLESS BASTARDS, ANYWAY?
THE LONG-TERM RESIDENTS OF MY DUNGEONS.
WE'LL BE ON OUR WAY SOON. I WANTED TO LEAVE THE PLACE TIDY.
WELL, THAT'S THE OTHER THING, NOW YOU MENTION IT.
YOUR OWN FATE, YOU MEAN? HOW REMISS OF ME.
YOU DID ME A SERVICE WHEN YOU TOLD ME WHAT THE TAYLOR BOY IS, AND WHENCE HE WAS BROUGHT.
IF THERE'S A FAVOR YOU'D LIKE TO ASK IN RETURN, NAME IT.
WELL YOU KNOW, THERE IS. IF I'M GOING TO EAT LIVER, I'D LIKE IT TO BE CUT RAW AND STEAMING FROM THE GREAT BEAST.
LEVIATHAN.

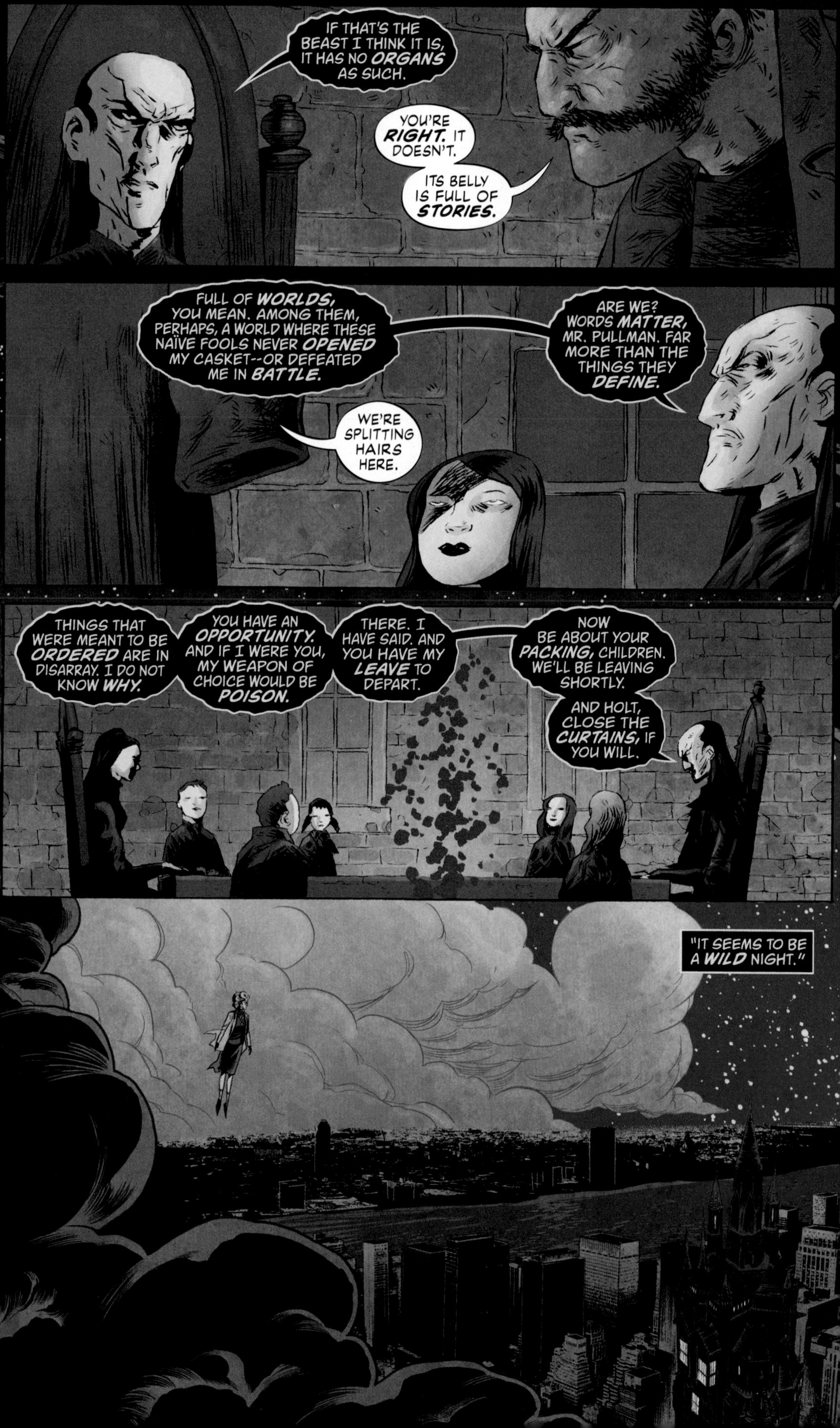
IF THAT'S THE BEAST I THINK IT IS, IT HAS NO ORGANS AS SUCH.
YOU'RE RIGHT. IT DOESN'T.
ITS BELLY IS FULL OF STORIES.
FULL OF WORLDS, YOU MEAN. AMONG THEM, PERHAPS, A WORLD WHERE THESE NAÏVE FOOLS NEVER OPENED MY CASKET--OR DEFEATED ME IN BATTLE.
ARE WE? WORDS MATTER, MR. PULLMAN. FAR MORE THAN THE THINGS THEY DEFINE.
WE'RE SPLITTING HAIRS HERE.
THINGS THAT WERE MEANT TO BE ORDERED ARE IN DISARRAY. I DO NOT KNOW WHY.
YOU HAVE AN OPPORTUNITY. AND IF I WERE YOU, MY WEAPON OF CHOICE WOULD BE POISON.
THERE. I HAVE SAID. AND YOU HAVE MY LEAVE TO DEPART.
NOW BE ABOUT YOUR PACKING, CHILDREN. WE'LL BE LEAVING SHORTLY.
AND HOLT, CLOSE THE CURTAINS, IF YOU WILL.
"IT SEEMS TO BE A WILD NIGHT."

I'D RATHER BE ALONE FOR THIS, IF YOU'D BE SO KIND.
I'M NOT EVEN SURE WHY YOU'RE HERE.
REALLY? YOU DISTURBED THE WINDS, MADAM.
SO THE WINDS' GUARDIANS WERE THE FIRST TO KNOW ABOUT IT.
AND WHAT OF THAT? OUR FIGHT NO LONGER CONCERNS YOU, MISTER NORTH.
TRUE. I'VE STEPPED ASIDE FROM IT. AND I'M NOT PLANNING TO REVISIT THAT DECISION.
BUT WHAT YOU'RE ABOUT TO DO CANNOT BE UNDONE.
ARE YOU SURE YOU CAN LIVE WITH IT, FRAU TOTENKINDER?
MEDITATE ON MY NAME.
YOU MAY FIND YOUR QUESTION HAS ALREADY BEEN ANSWERED.

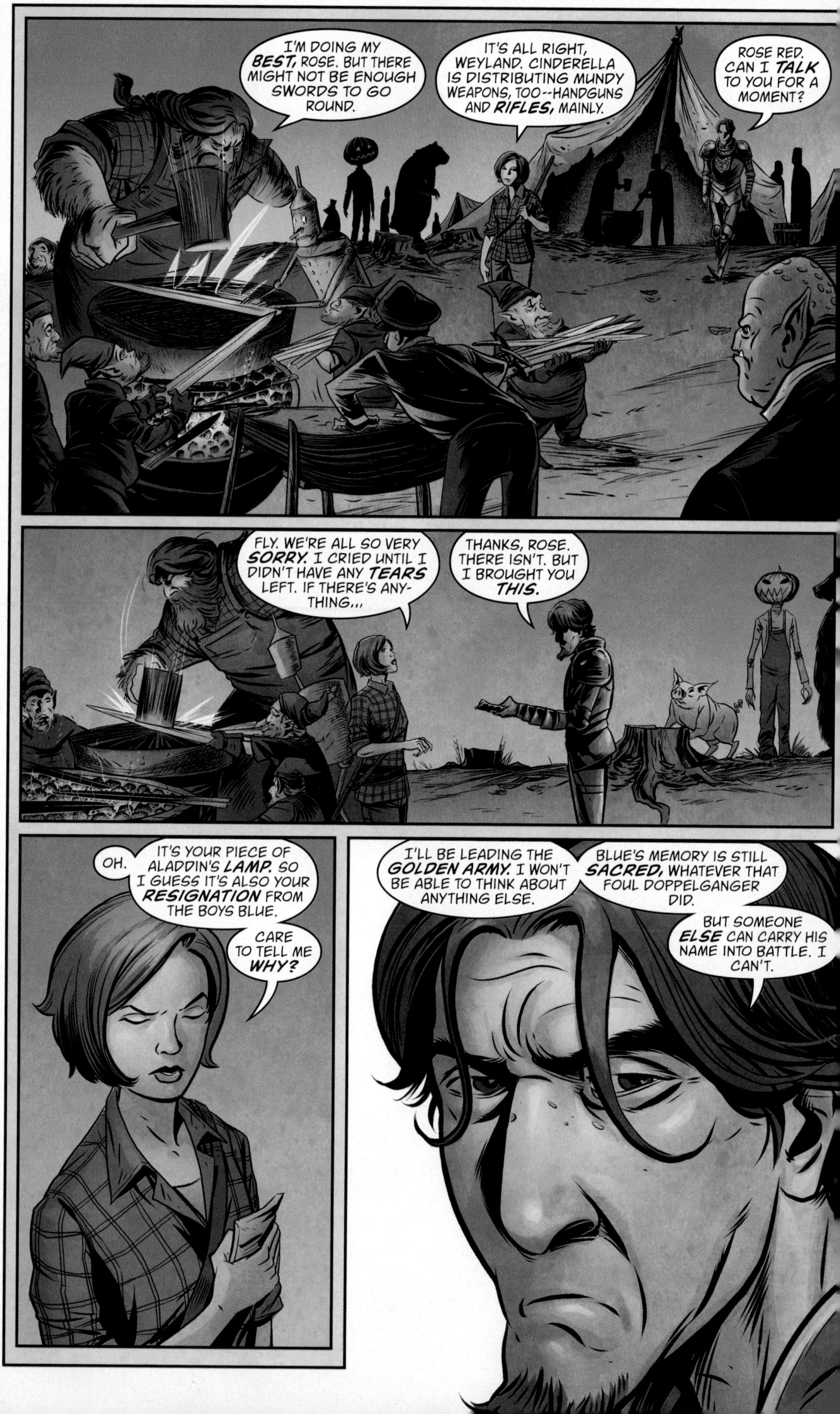
I'M DOING MY BEST, ROSE. BUT THERE MIGHT NOT BE ENOUGH SWORDS TO GO ROUND.
IT'S ALL RIGHT, WEYLAND. CINDERELLA IS DISTRIBUTING MUNDY WEAPONS, TOO--HANDGUNS AND RIFLES, MAINLY.
ROSE RED. CAN I TALK TO YOU FOR A MOMENT?
FLY. WE'RE ALL SO VERY SORRY. I CRIED UNTIL I DIDN'T HAVE ANY TEARS LEFT. IF THERE'S ANY-THING...
THANKS, ROSE. THERE ISN'T. BUT I BROUGHT YOU THIS.
OH.
IT'S YOUR PIECE OF ALADDIN'S LAMP. SO I GUESS IT'S ALSO YOUR RESIGNATION FROM THE BOYS BLUE.
CARE TO TELL ME WHY?
I'LL BE LEADING THE GOLDEN ARMY. I WON'T BE ABLE TO THINK ABOUT ANYTHING ELSE.
BLUE'S MEMORY IS STILL SACRED, WHATEVER THAT FOUL DOPPELGANGER DID.
BUT SOMEONE ELSE CAN CARRY HIS NAME INTO BATTLE. I CAN'T.

I KNOW YOU'RE *THERE*, CHILD. YOUR EYES ARE BORING A HOLE IN MY BACK.

NO NEED TO BE *SHY.* COME ALONG IN.

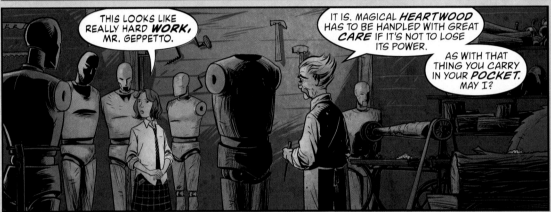

THIS LOOKS LIKE REALLY HARD *WORK*, MR. GEPPETTO.

IT IS. MAGICAL *HEARTWOOD* HAS TO BE HANDLED WITH GREAT *CARE* IF IT'S NOT TO LOSE ITS POWER.

AS WITH THAT THING YOU CARRY IN YOUR *POCKET.* MAY I?

THIS? I DON'T EVEN KNOW WHAT IT *IS.*

BUT OZMA SAID THERE'S POWERFUL *MAGIC* IN IT--AND I CAN FEEL THAT TOO.

WAIT! OZMA SAID I WASN'T TO *OPEN* IT!

WELL, WELL. SHE DOESN'T NEED TO *KNOW,* DOES SHE?

AH YES. AS I *THOUGHT.* FLINT. STEEL. CLOTH SOAKED IN WAX AND TURPENTINE.

IT'S BEEN A LONG TIME SINCE I SAW AN ACTUAL *TINDERBOX.*

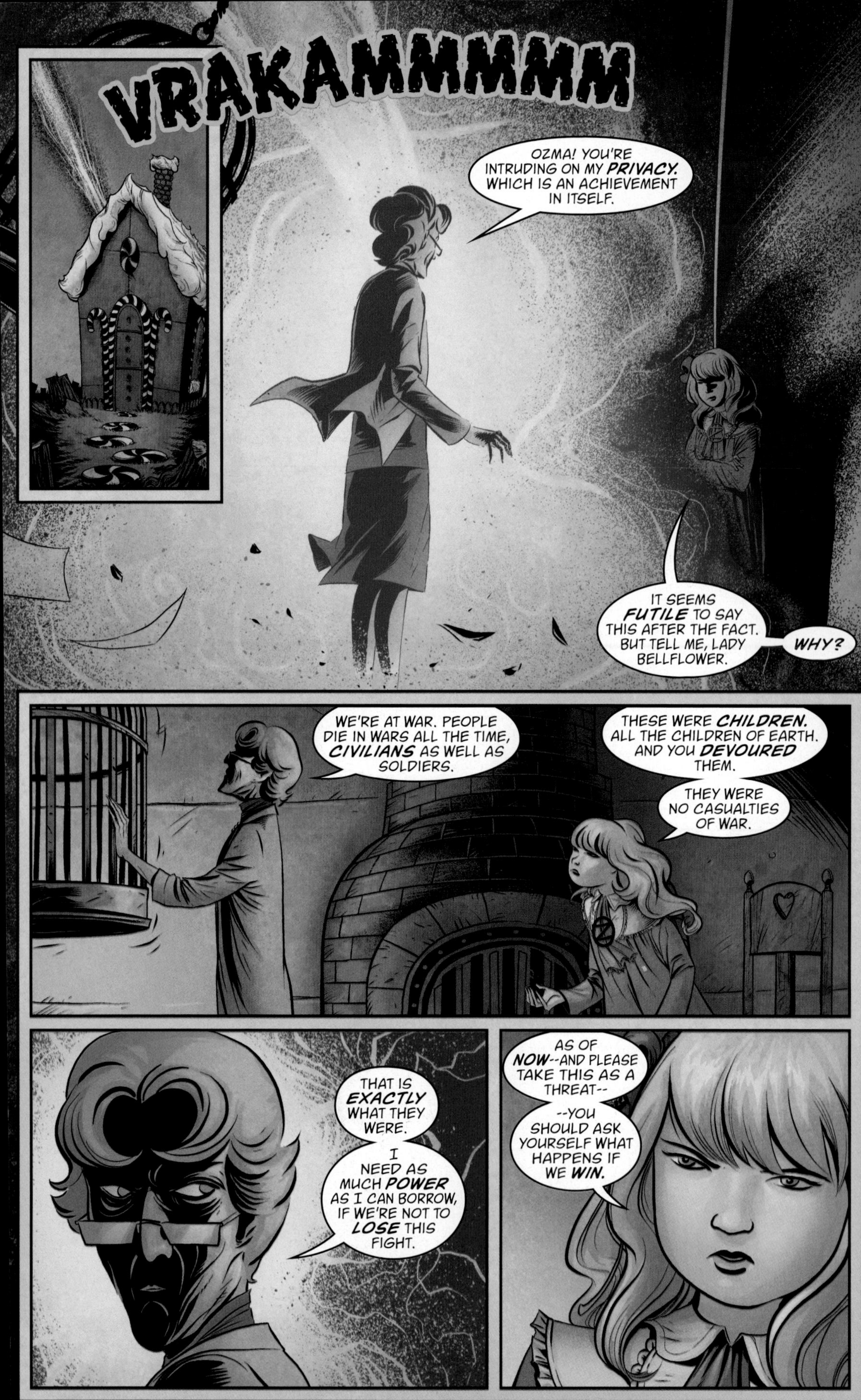

VRAKAMMMMMM
OZMA! YOU'RE INTRUDING ON MY PRIVACY. WHICH IS AN ACHIEVEMENT IN ITSELF.
IT SEEMS FUTILE TO SAY THIS AFTER THE FACT. BUT TELL ME, LADY BELLFLOWER.
WHY?
WE'RE AT WAR. PEOPLE DIE IN WARS ALL THE TIME, CIVILIANS AS WELL AS SOLDIERS.
THESE WERE CHILDREN. ALL THE CHILDREN OF EARTH. AND YOU DEVOURED THEM.
THEY WERE NO CASUALTIES OF WAR.
THAT IS EXACTLY WHAT THEY WERE.
I NEED AS MUCH POWER AS I CAN BORROW, IF WE'RE NOT TO LOSE THIS FIGHT.
AS OF NOW--AND PLEASE TAKE THIS AS A THREAT--
--YOU SHOULD ASK YOURSELF WHAT HAPPENS IF WE WIN.

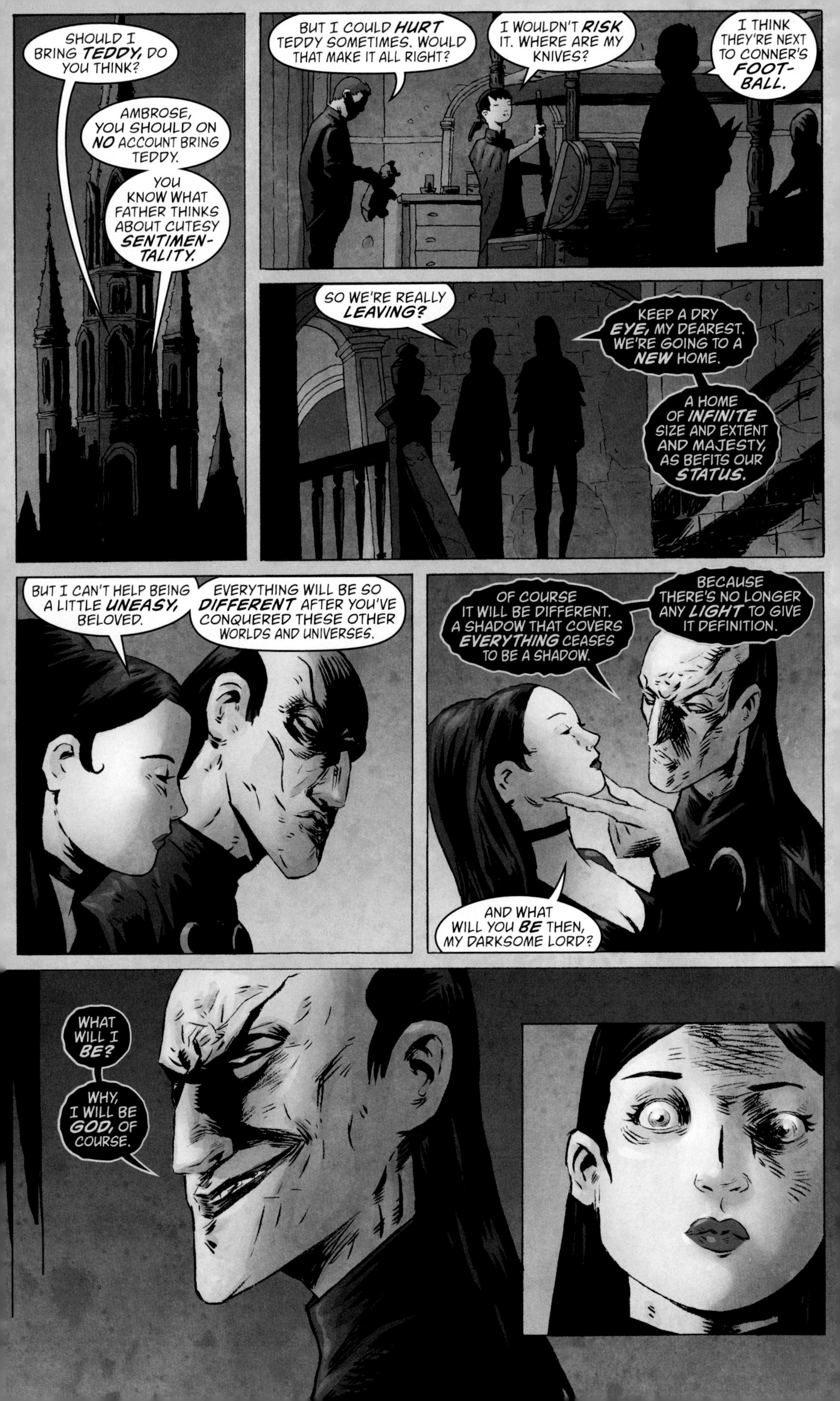
SHOULD I BRING TEDDY, DO YOU THINK?
AMBROSE, YOU SHOULD ON NO ACCOUNT BRING TEDDY.
YOU KNOW WHAT FATHER THINKS ABOUT CUTESY SENTIMEN-TALITY.
BUT I COULD HURT TEDDY SOMETIMES. WOULD THAT MAKE IT ALL RIGHT?
I WOULDN'T RISK IT. WHERE ARE MY KNIVES?
I THINK THEY'RE NEXT TO CONNER'S FOOT-BALL.
SO WE'RE REALLY LEAVING?
KEEP A DRY EYE, MY DEAREST. WE'RE GOING TO A NEW HOME.
A HOME OF INFINITE SIZE AND EXTENT AND MAJESTY, AS BEFITS OUR STATUS.
BUT I CAN'T HELP BEING A LITTLE UNEASY, BELOVED.
EVERYTHING WILL BE SO DIFFERENT AFTER YOU'VE CONQUERED THESE OTHER WORLDS AND UNIVERSES.
OF COURSE IT WILL BE DIFFERENT. A SHADOW THAT COVERS EVERYTHING CEASES TO BE A SHADOW.
BECAUSE THERE'S NO LONGER ANY LIGHT TO GIVE IT DEFINITION.
AND WHAT WILL YOU BE THEN, MY DARKSOME LORD?
WHAT WILL I BE?
WHY, I WILL BE GOD, OF COURSE.

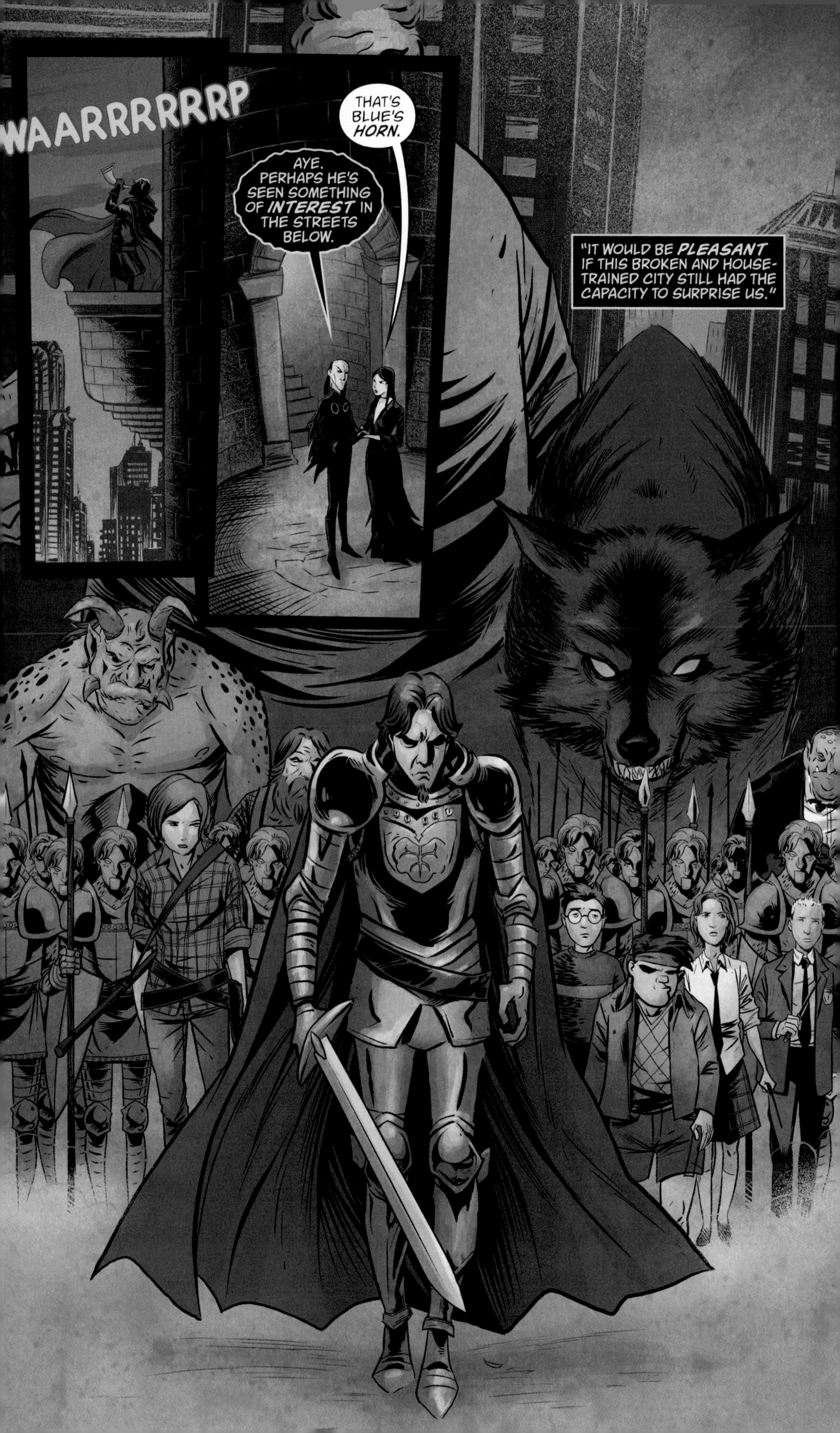
WAARRRRRRP
THAT'S BLUE'S *HORN.*
AYE. PERHAPS HE'S SEEN SOMETHING OF *INTEREST* IN THE STREETS BELOW.
"IT WOULD BE *PLEASANT* IF THIS BROKEN AND HOUSE-TRAINED CITY STILL HAD THE CAPACITY TO SURPRISE US."

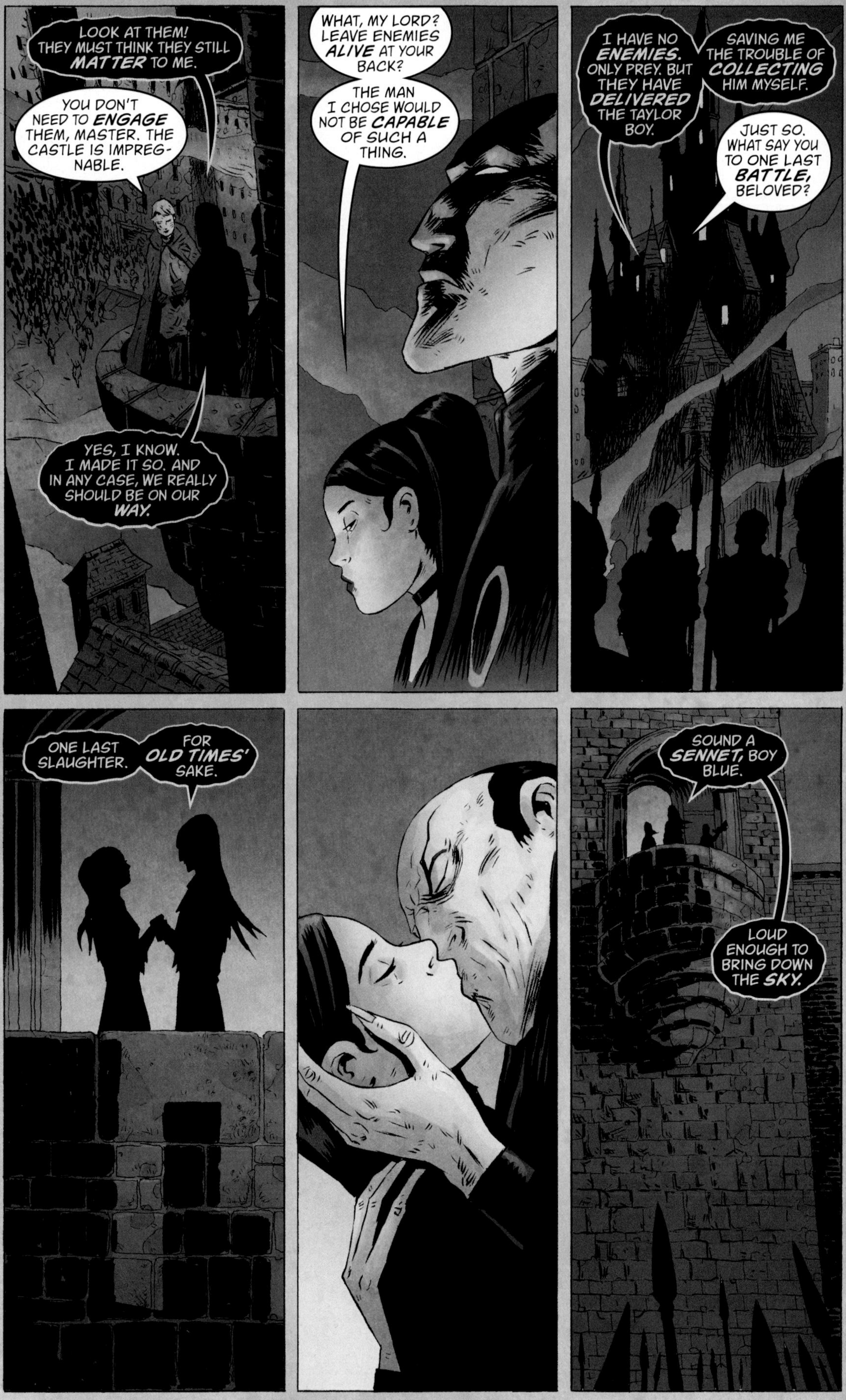
LOOK AT THEM! THEY MUST THINK THEY STILL MATTER TO ME.
YOU DON'T NEED TO ENGAGE THEM, MASTER. THE CASTLE IS IMPREG-NABLE.
YES, I KNOW. I MADE IT SO. AND IN ANY CASE, WE REALLY SHOULD BE ON OUR WAY.
WHAT, MY LORD? LEAVE ENEMIES ALIVE AT YOUR BACK?
THE MAN I CHOSE WOULD NOT BE CAPABLE OF SUCH A THING.
I HAVE NO ENEMIES. ONLY PREY. BUT THEY HAVE DELIVERED THE TAYLOR BOY.
SAVING ME THE TROUBLE OF COLLECTING HIM MYSELF.
JUST SO. WHAT SAY YOU TO ONE LAST BATTLE, BELOVED?
ONE LAST SLAUGHTER.
FOR OLD TIMES' SAKE.
SOUND A SENNET, BOY BLUE.
LOUD ENOUGH TO BRING DOWN THE SKY.

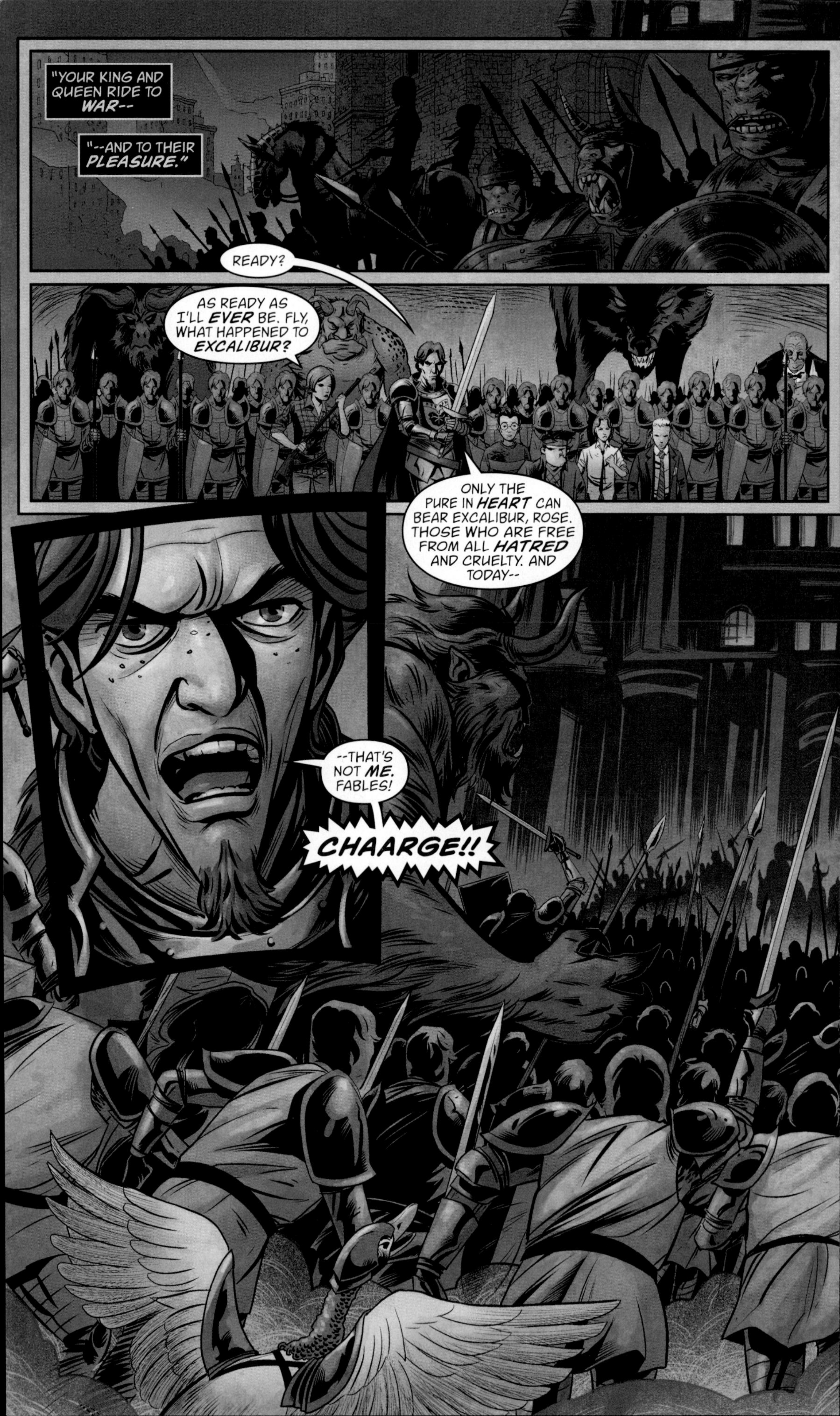
"YOUR KING AND QUEEN RIDE TO WAR--
"--AND TO THEIR PLEASURE."
READY?
AS READY AS I'LL EVER BE. FLY, WHAT HAPPENED TO EXCALIBUR?
ONLY THE PURE IN HEART CAN BEAR EXCALIBUR, ROSE. THOSE WHO ARE FREE FROM ALL HATRED AND CRUELTY. AND TODAY--
--THAT'S NOT ME. FABLES!
CHAARGE!!

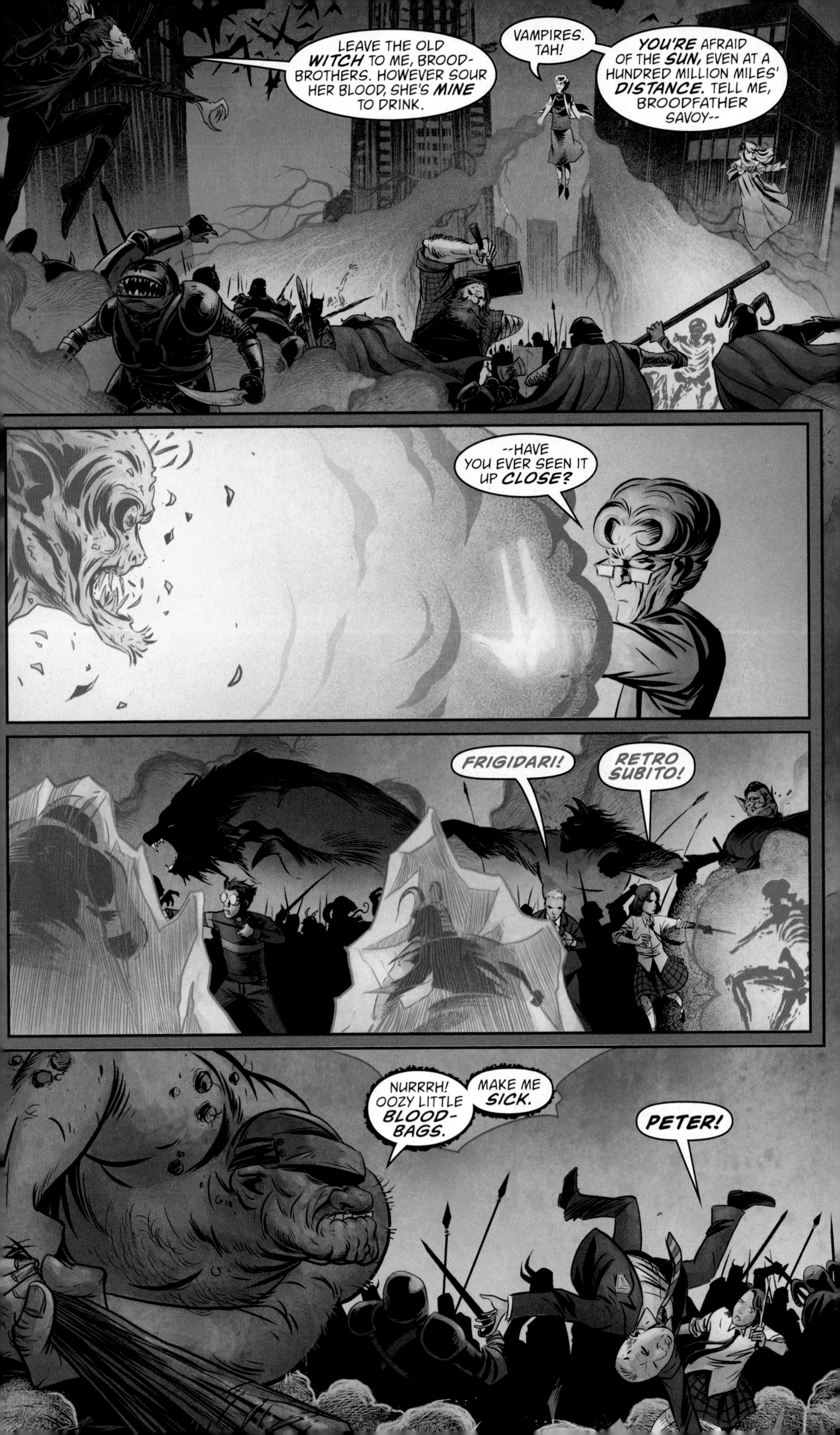
LEAVE THE OLD WITCH TO ME, BROOD-BROTHERS. HOWEVER SOUR HER BLOOD, SHE'S MINE TO DRINK.
VAMPIRES. TAH!
YOU'RE AFRAID OF THE SUN, EVEN AT A HUNDRED MILLION MILES' DISTANCE. TELL ME, BROODFATHER SAVOY--
--HAVE YOU EVER SEEN IT UP CLOSE?
FRIGIDARI!
RETRO SUBITO!
NURRRH! OOZY LITTLE BLOOD-BAGS.
MAKE ME SICK.
PETER!

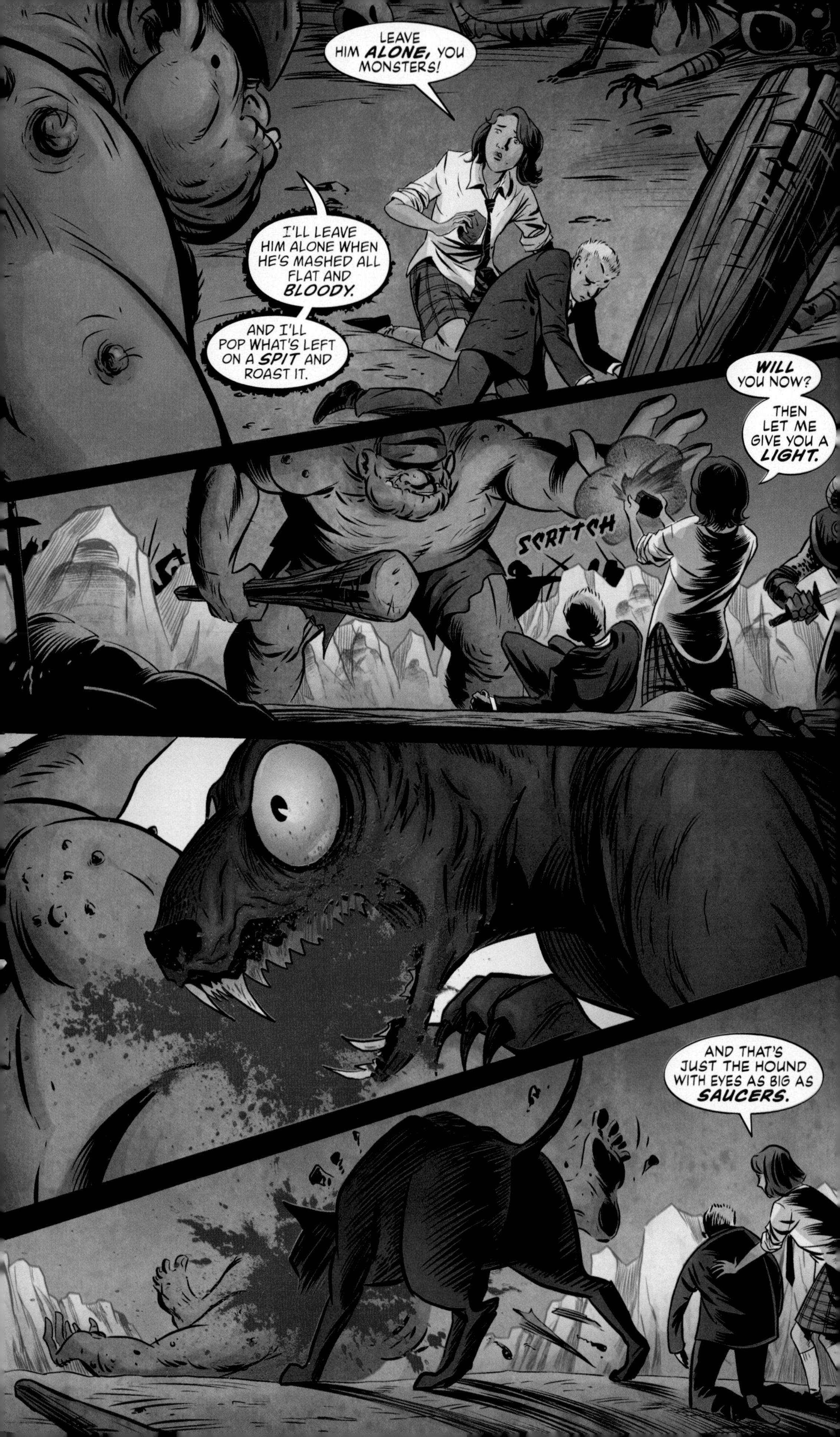
LEAVE HIM ALONE, YOU MONSTERS!
I'LL LEAVE HIM ALONE WHEN HE'S MASHED ALL FLAT AND BLOODY.
AND I'LL POP WHAT'S LEFT ON A SPIT AND ROAST IT.
WILL YOU NOW?
THEN LET ME GIVE YOU A LIGHT.
SCRTTCH
AND THAT'S JUST THE HOUND WITH EYES AS BIG AS SAUCERS.

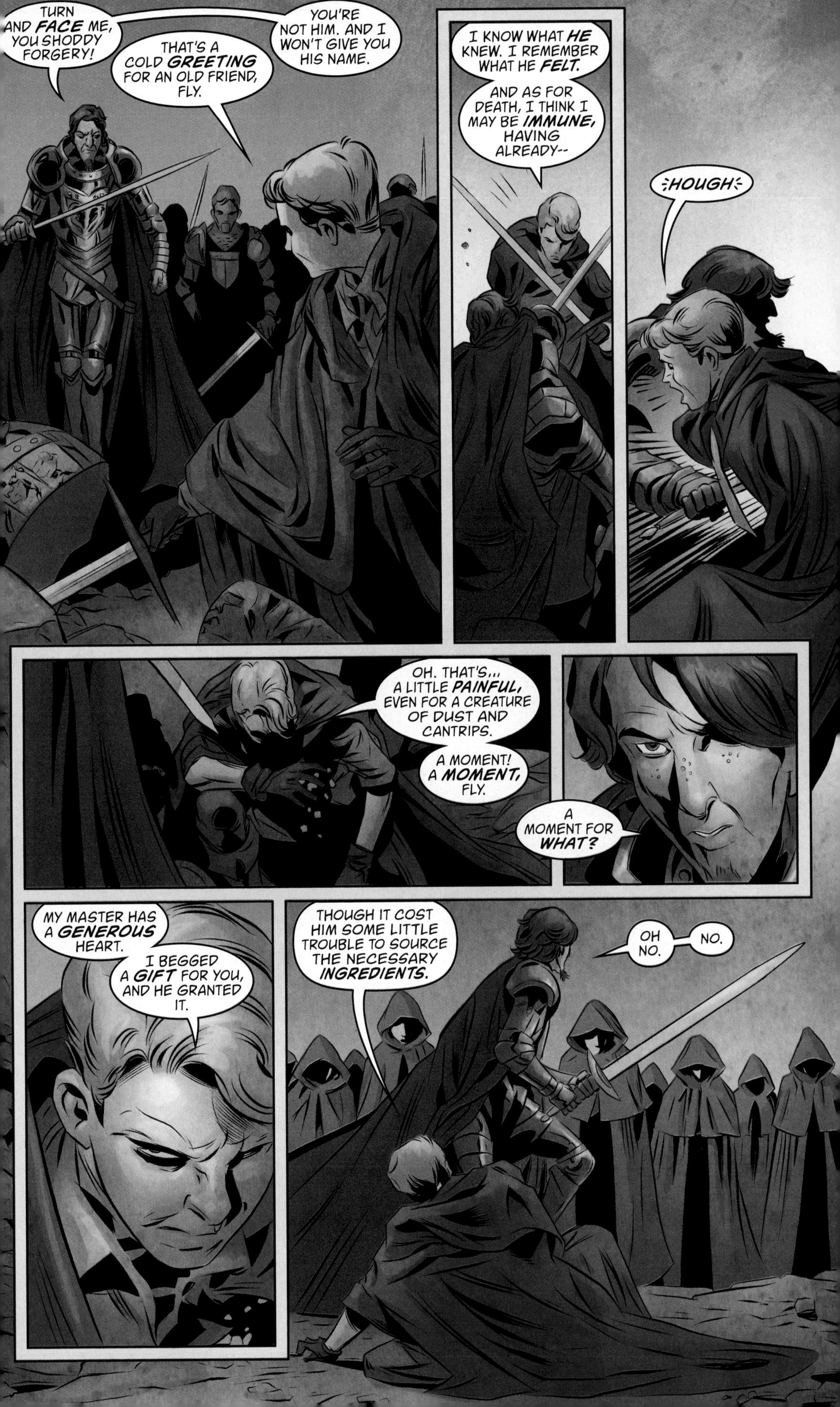
TURN AND FACE ME, YOU SHODDY FORGERY!
THAT'S A COLD GREETING FOR AN OLD FRIEND, FLY.
YOU'RE NOT HIM. AND I WON'T GIVE YOU HIS NAME.
I KNOW WHAT HE KNEW. I REMEMBER WHAT HE FELT.
AND AS FOR DEATH, I THINK I MAY BE IMMUNE, HAVING ALREADY--
HOUGH
OH. THAT'S... A LITTLE PAINFUL, EVEN FOR A CREATURE OF DUST AND CANTRIPS.
A MOMENT! A MOMENT, FLY.
A MOMENT FOR WHAT?
MY MASTER HAS A GENEROUS HEART.
I BEGGED A GIFT FOR YOU, AND HE GRANTED IT.
THOUGH IT COST HIM SOME LITTLE TROUBLE TO SOURCE THE NECESSARY INGREDIENTS.
OH NO.
NO.

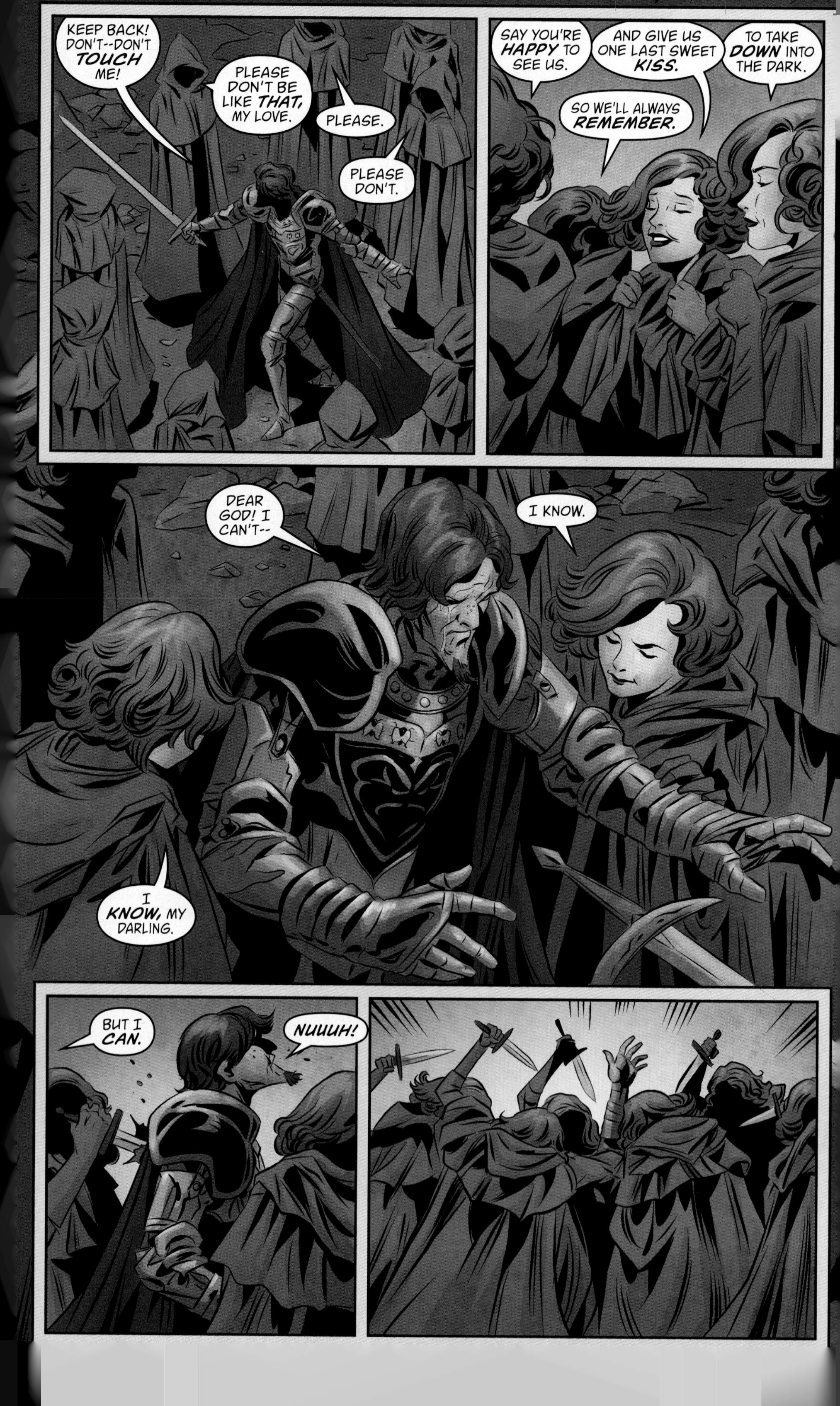
KEEP BACK! DON'T--DON'T TOUCH ME!
PLEASE DON'T BE LIKE THAT, MY LOVE.
PLEASE.
PLEASE DON'T.
SAY YOU'RE HAPPY TO SEE US.
AND GIVE US ONE LAST SWEET KISS.
TO TAKE DOWN INTO THE DARK.
SO WE'LL ALWAYS REMEMBER.
DEAR GOD! I CAN'T--
I KNOW.
I KNOW, MY DARLING.
BUT I CAN.
NUUUH!

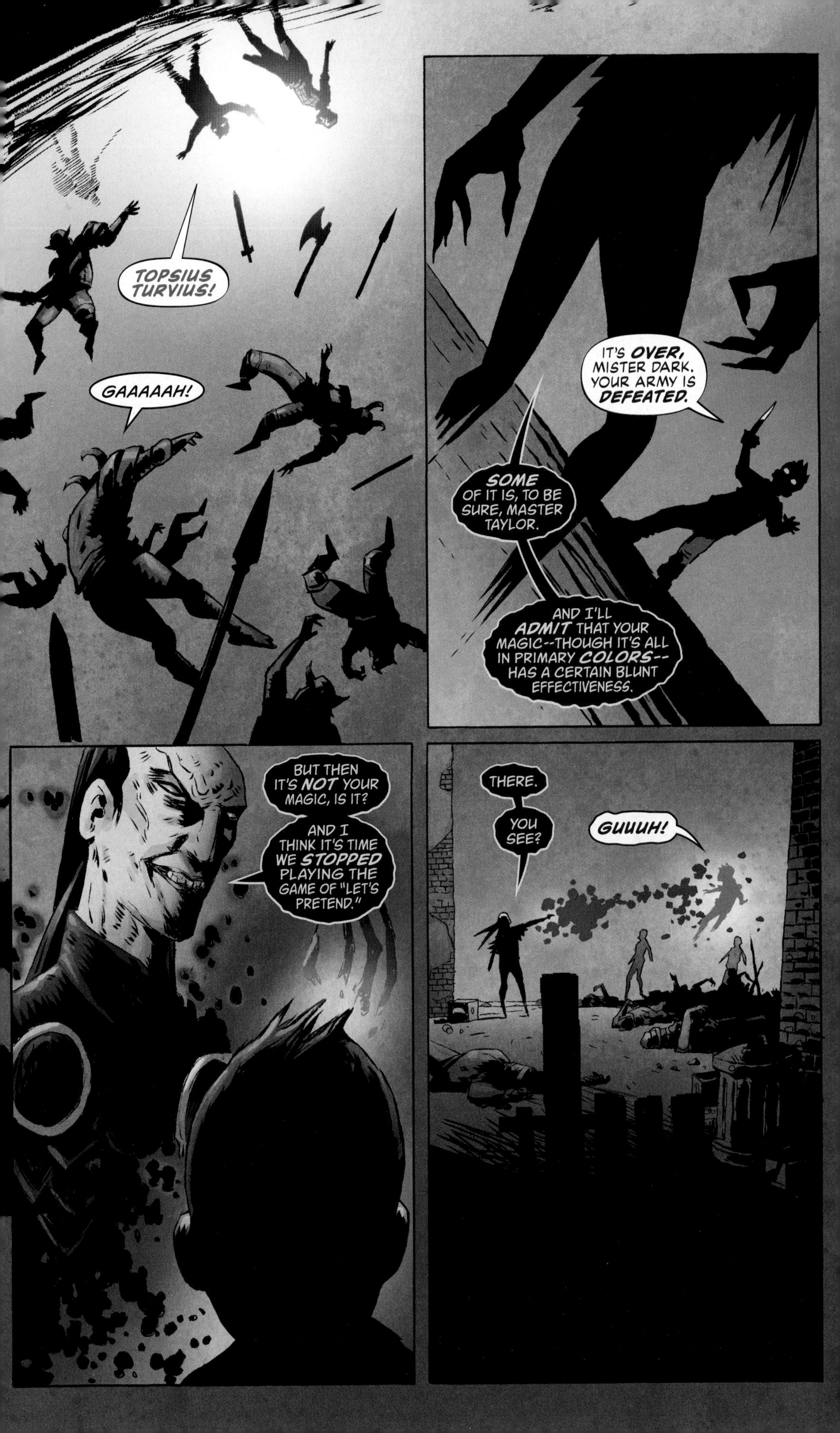
TOPSIUS TURVIUS!
GAAAAAH!
IT'S OVER, MISTER DARK. YOUR ARMY IS DEFEATED.
SOME OF IT IS, TO BE SURE, MASTER TAYLOR.
AND I'LL ADMIT THAT YOUR MAGIC--THOUGH IT'S ALL IN PRIMARY COLORS--HAS A CERTAIN BLUNT EFFECTIVENESS.
BUT THEN IT'S NOT YOUR MAGIC, IS IT?
AND I THINK IT'S TIME WE STOPPED PLAYING THE GAME OF "LET'S PRETEND."
THERE.
YOU SEE?
GUUUH!

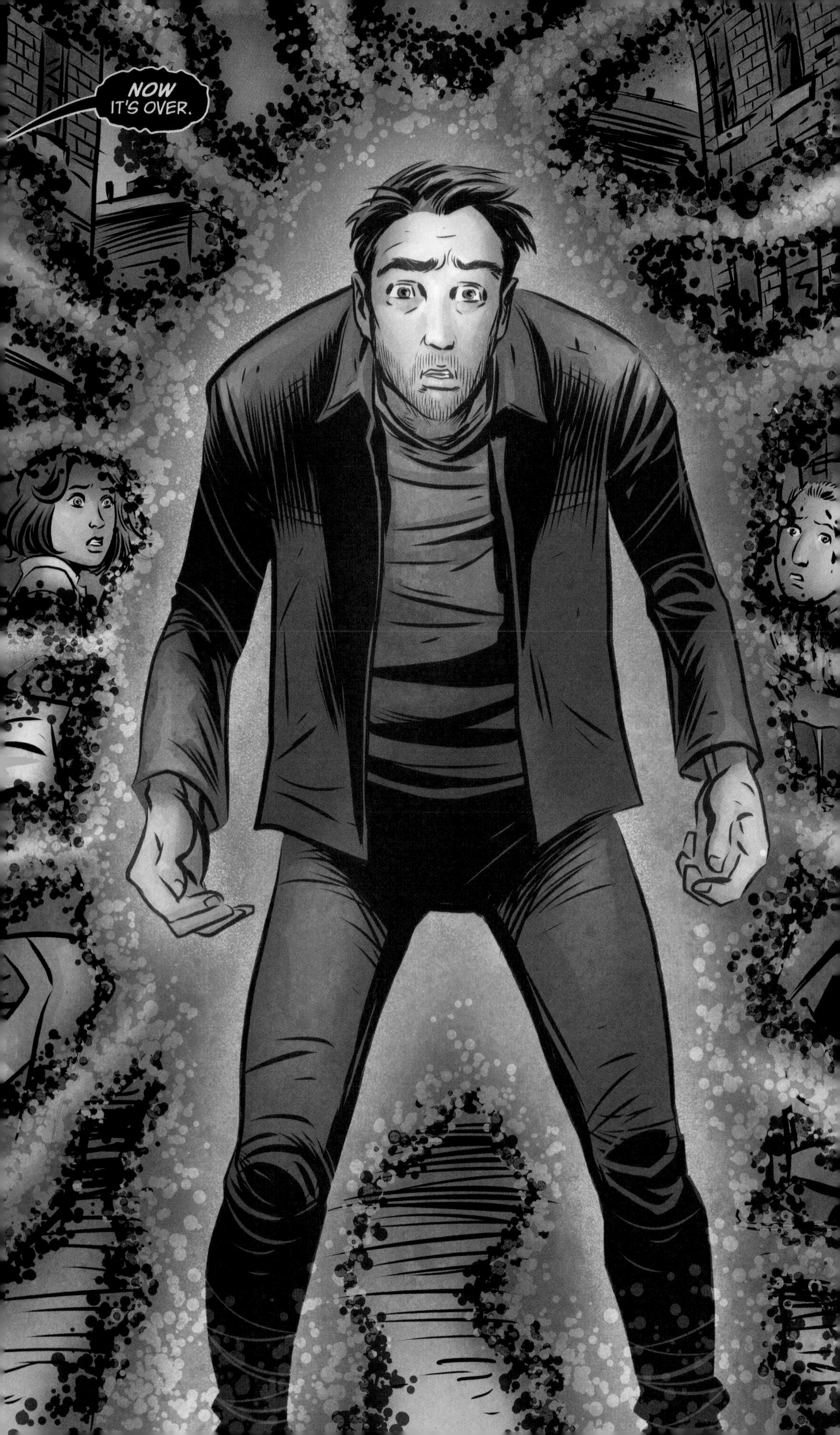
NOW IT'S OVER.

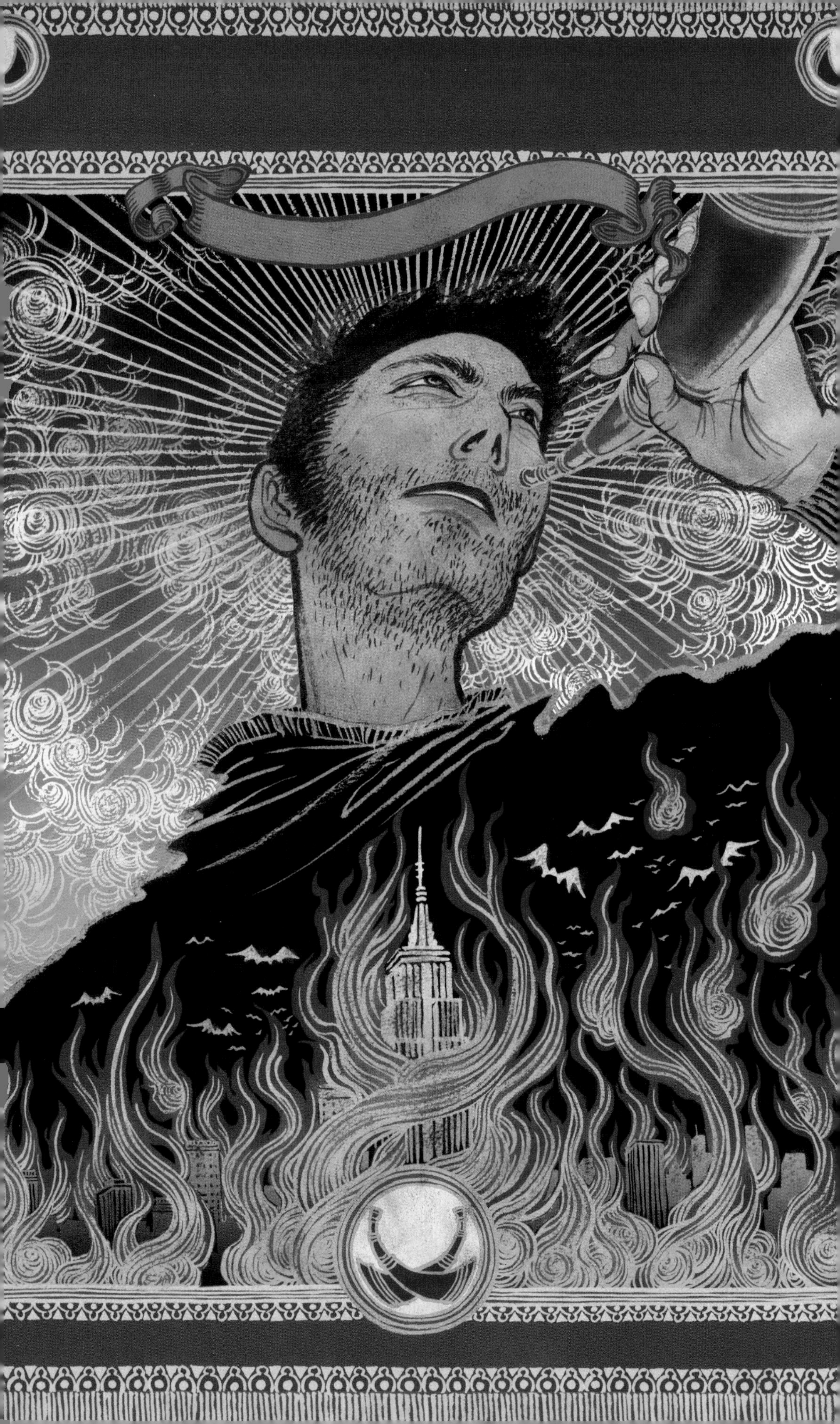

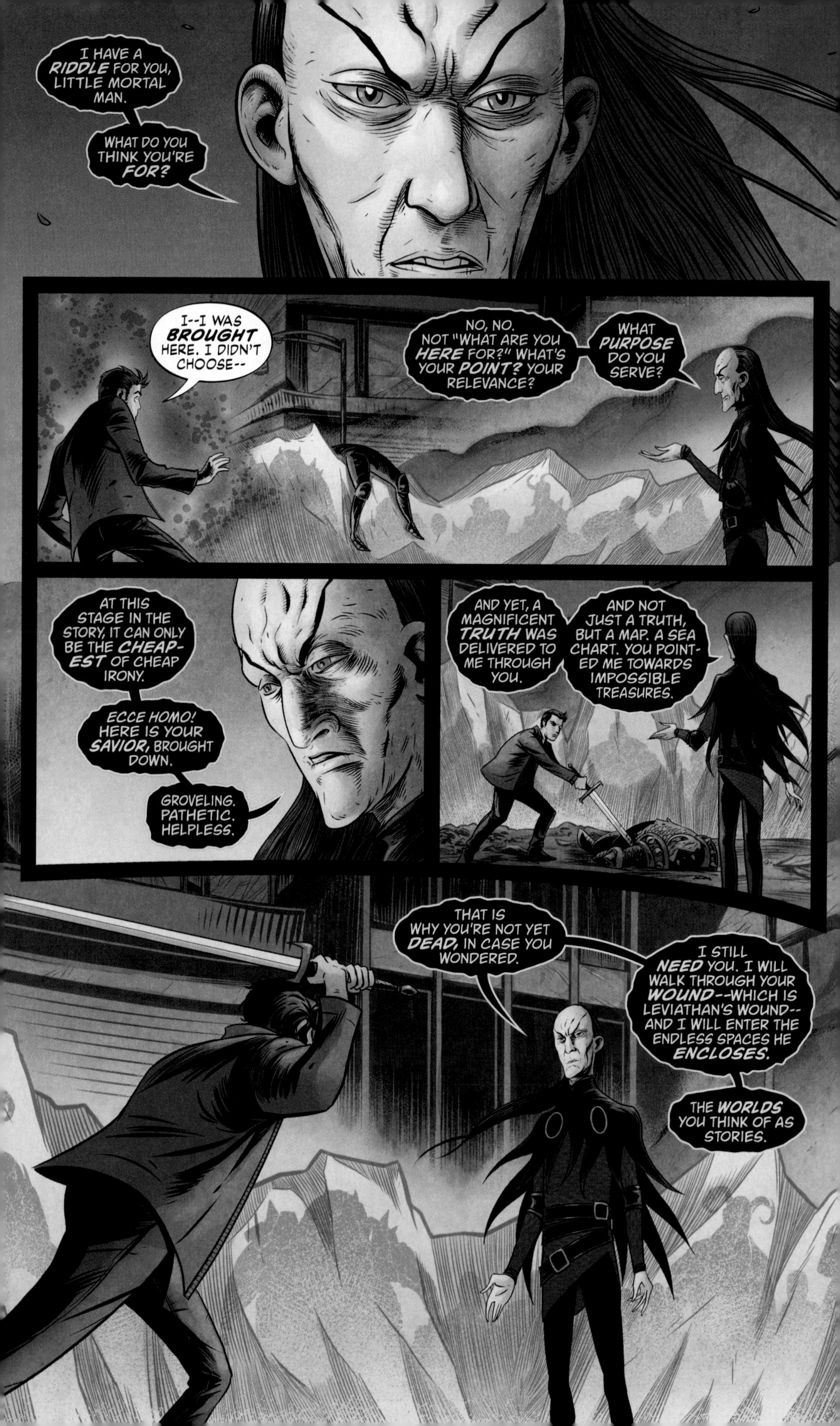
I HAVE A RIDDLE FOR YOU, LITTLE MORTAL MAN.
WHAT DO YOU THINK YOU'RE FOR?
I--I WAS BROUGHT HERE. I DIDN'T CHOOSE--
NO, NO. NOT "WHAT ARE YOU HERE FOR?" WHAT'S YOUR POINT? YOUR RELEVANCE?
WHAT PURPOSE DO YOU SERVE?
AT THIS STAGE IN THE STORY, IT CAN ONLY BE THE CHEAP-EST OF CHEAP IRONY.
ECCE HOMO! HERE IS YOUR SAVIOR, BROUGHT DOWN.
GROVELING. PATHETIC. HELPLESS.
AND YET, A MAGNIFICENT TRUTH WAS DELIVERED TO ME THROUGH YOU.
AND NOT JUST A TRUTH, BUT A MAP. A SEA CHART. YOU POINT-ED ME TOWARDS IMPOSSIBLE TREASURES.
THAT IS WHY YOU'RE NOT YET DEAD, IN CASE YOU WONDERED.
I STILL NEED YOU. I WILL WALK THROUGH YOUR WOUND--WHICH IS LEVIATHAN'S WOUND--AND I WILL ENTER THE ENDLESS SPACES HE ENCLOSES.
THE WORLDS YOU THINK OF AS STORIES.

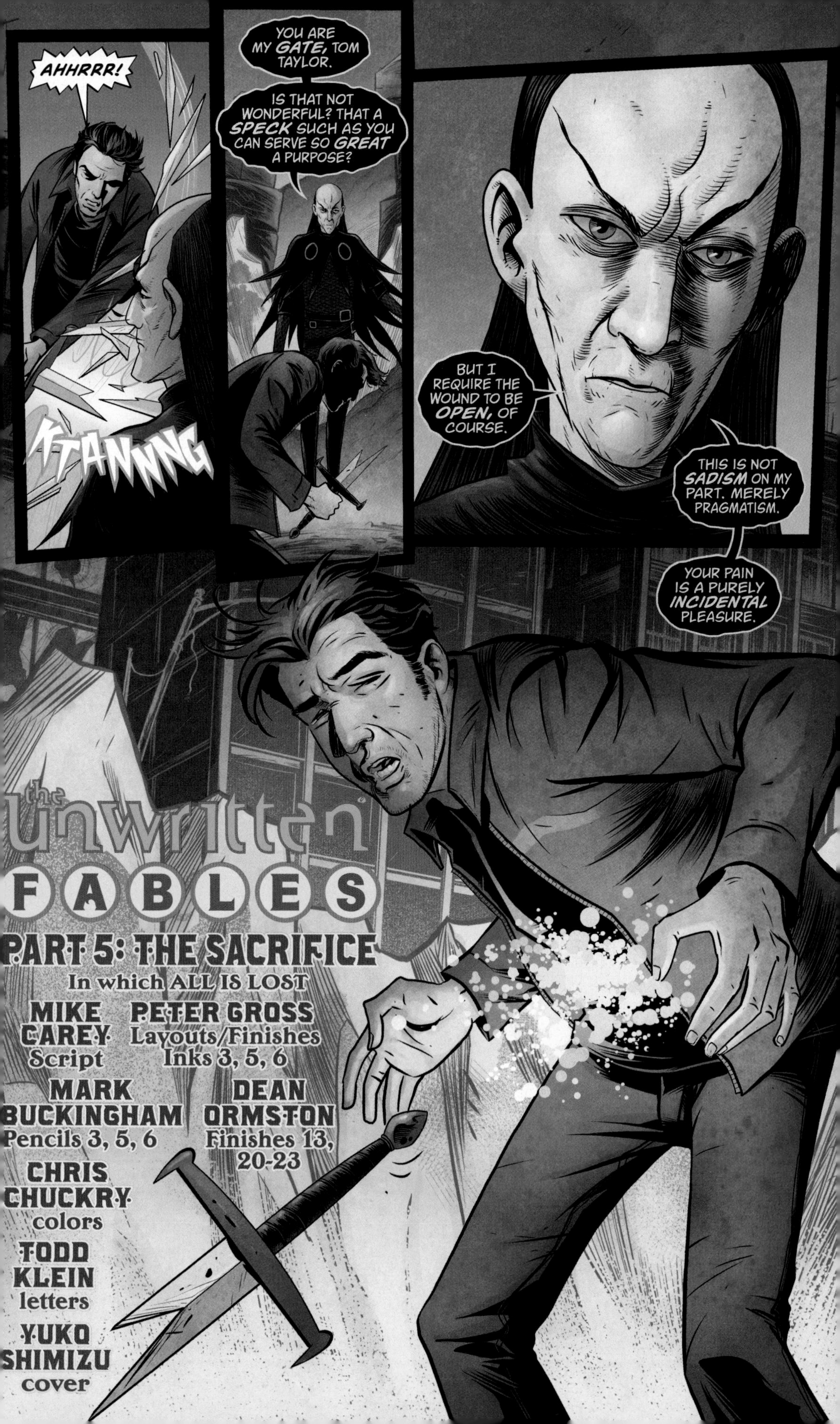
AHHRRR!
KTANNNG
YOU ARE MY GATE, TOM TAYLOR.
IS THAT NOT WONDERFUL? THAT A SPECK SUCH AS YOU CAN SERVE SO GREAT A PURPOSE?
BUT I REQUIRE THE WOUND TO BE OPEN, OF COURSE.
THIS IS NOT SADISM ON MY PART. MERELY PRAGMATISM.
YOUR PAIN IS A PURELY INCIDENTAL PLEASURE.
the unwritten
FABLES
PART 5: THE SACRIFICE
In which ALL IS LOST
MIKE CAREY Script
PETER GROSS Layouts/Finishes Inks 3, 5, 6
MARK BUCKINGHAM Pencils 3, 5, 6
DEAN ORMSTON Finishes 13, 20-23
CHRIS CHUCKRY colors
TODD KLEIN letters
YUKO SHIMIZU cover

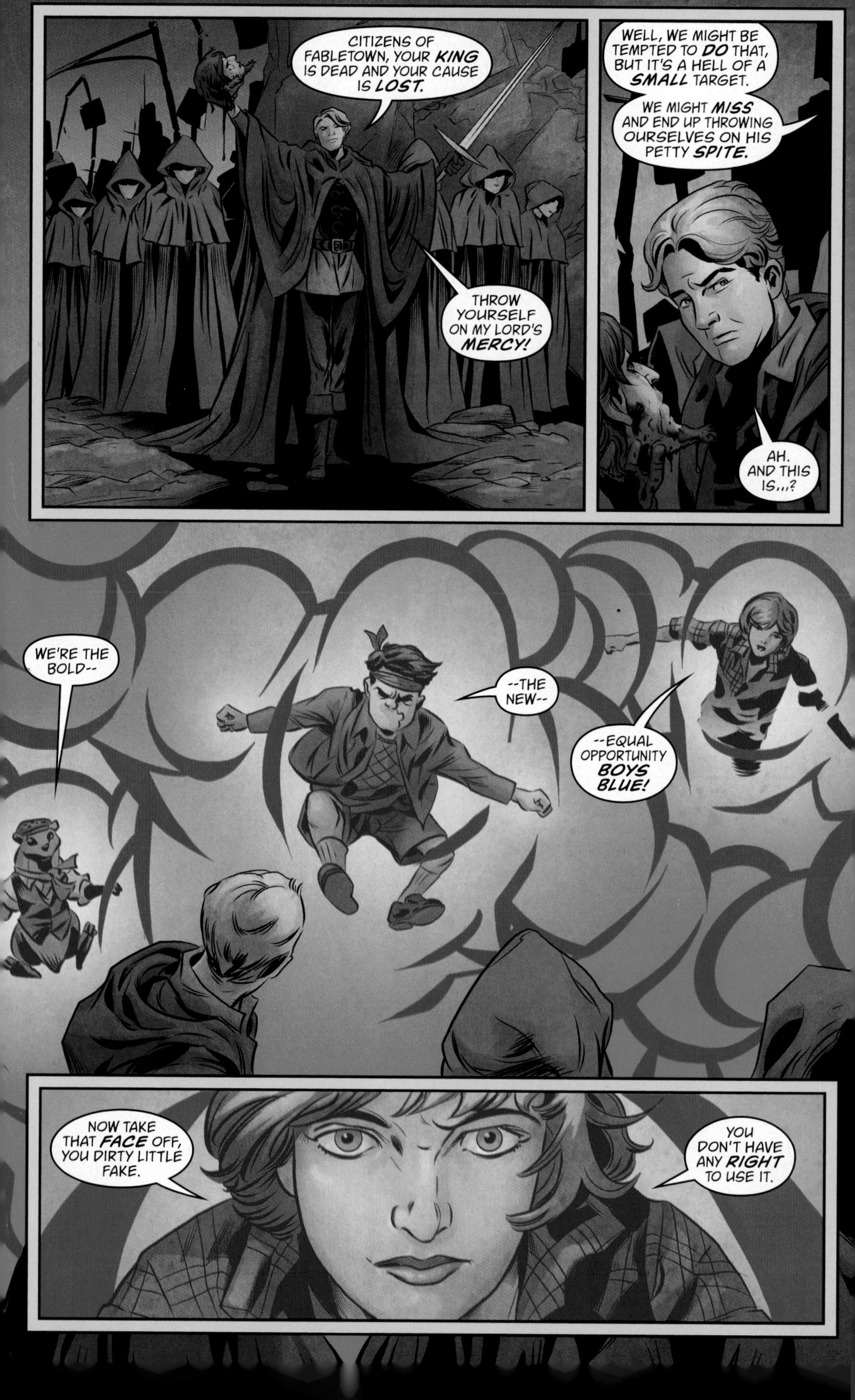

CITIZENS OF FABLETOWN, YOUR KING IS DEAD AND YOUR CAUSE IS LOST.
THROW YOURSELF ON MY LORD'S MERCY!
WELL, WE MIGHT BE TEMPTED TO DO THAT, BUT IT'S A HELL OF A SMALL TARGET.
WE MIGHT MISS AND END UP THROWING OURSELVES ON HIS PETTY SPITE.
AH. AND THIS IS...?
WE'RE THE BOLD--
--THE NEW--
--EQUAL OPPORTUNITY BOYS BLUE!
NOW TAKE THAT FACE OFF, YOU DIRTY LITTLE FAKE.
YOU DON'T HAVE ANY RIGHT TO USE IT.

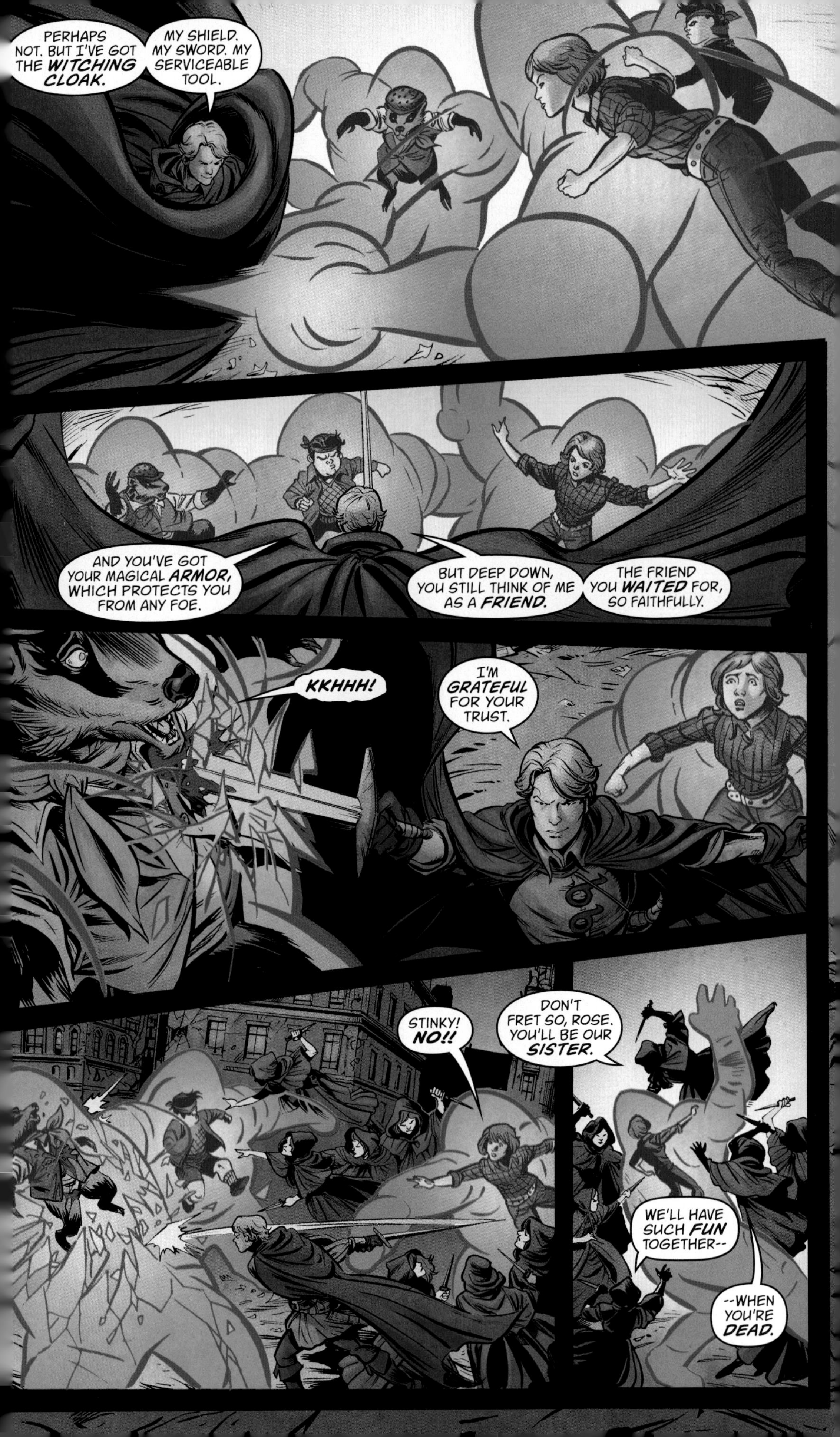
PERHAPS NOT. BUT I'VE GOT THE WITCHING CLOAK.
MY SHIELD. MY SWORD. MY SERVICEABLE TOOL.
AND YOU'VE GOT YOUR MAGICAL ARMOR, WHICH PROTECTS YOU FROM ANY FOE.
BUT DEEP DOWN, YOU STILL THINK OF ME AS A FRIEND.
THE FRIEND YOU WAITED FOR, SO FAITHFULLY.
KKHHH!
I'M GRATEFUL FOR YOUR TRUST.
STINKY! NO!!
DON'T FRET SO, ROSE. YOU'LL BE OUR SISTER.
WE'LL HAVE SUCH FUN TOGETHER--
--WHEN YOU'RE DEAD.

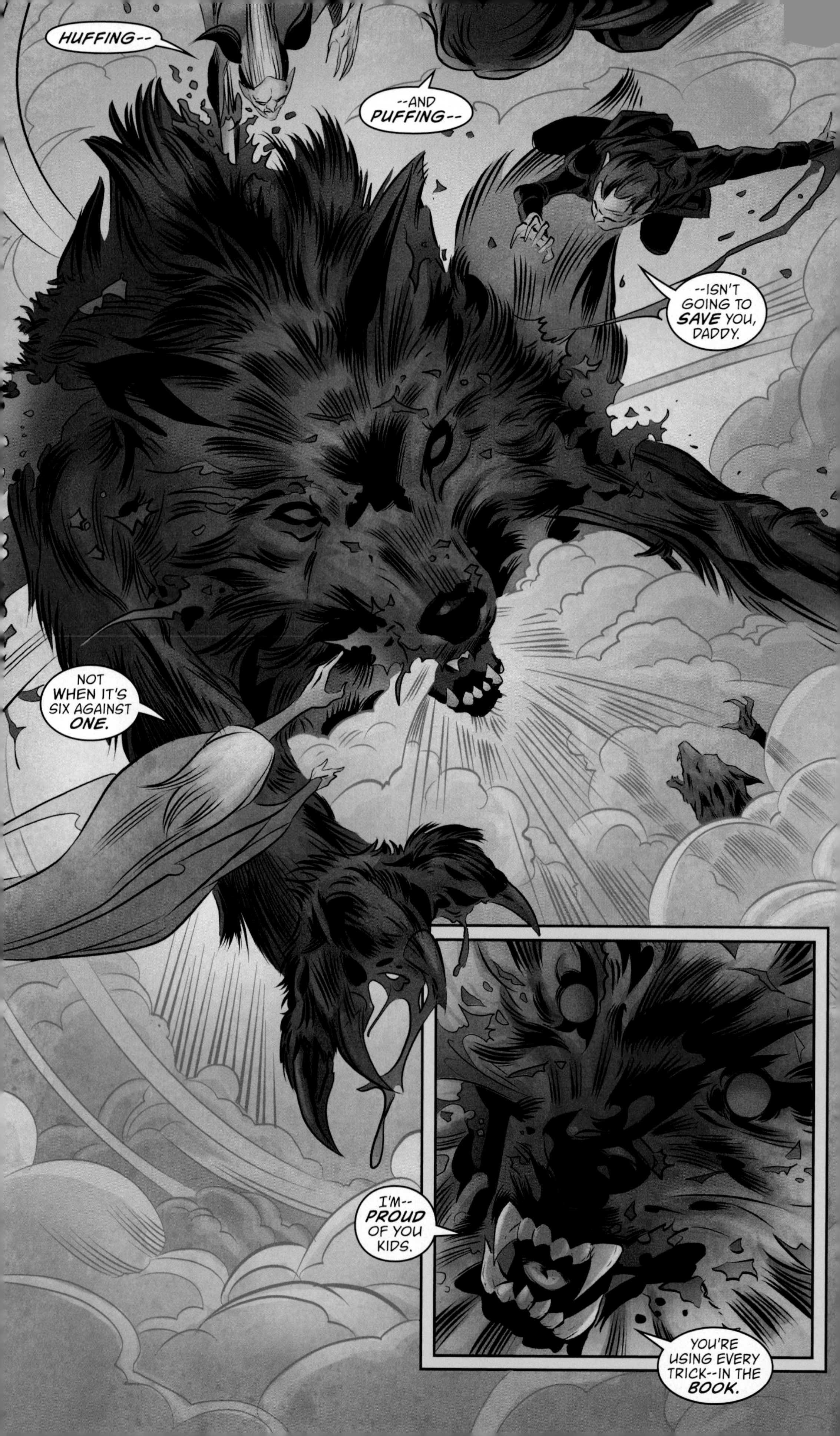
HUFFING--
--AND PUFFING--
--ISN'T GOING TO SAVE YOU, DADDY.
NOT WHEN IT'S SIX AGAINST ONE.
I'M-- PROUD OF YOU KIDS.
YOU'RE USING EVERY TRICK--IN THE BOOK.

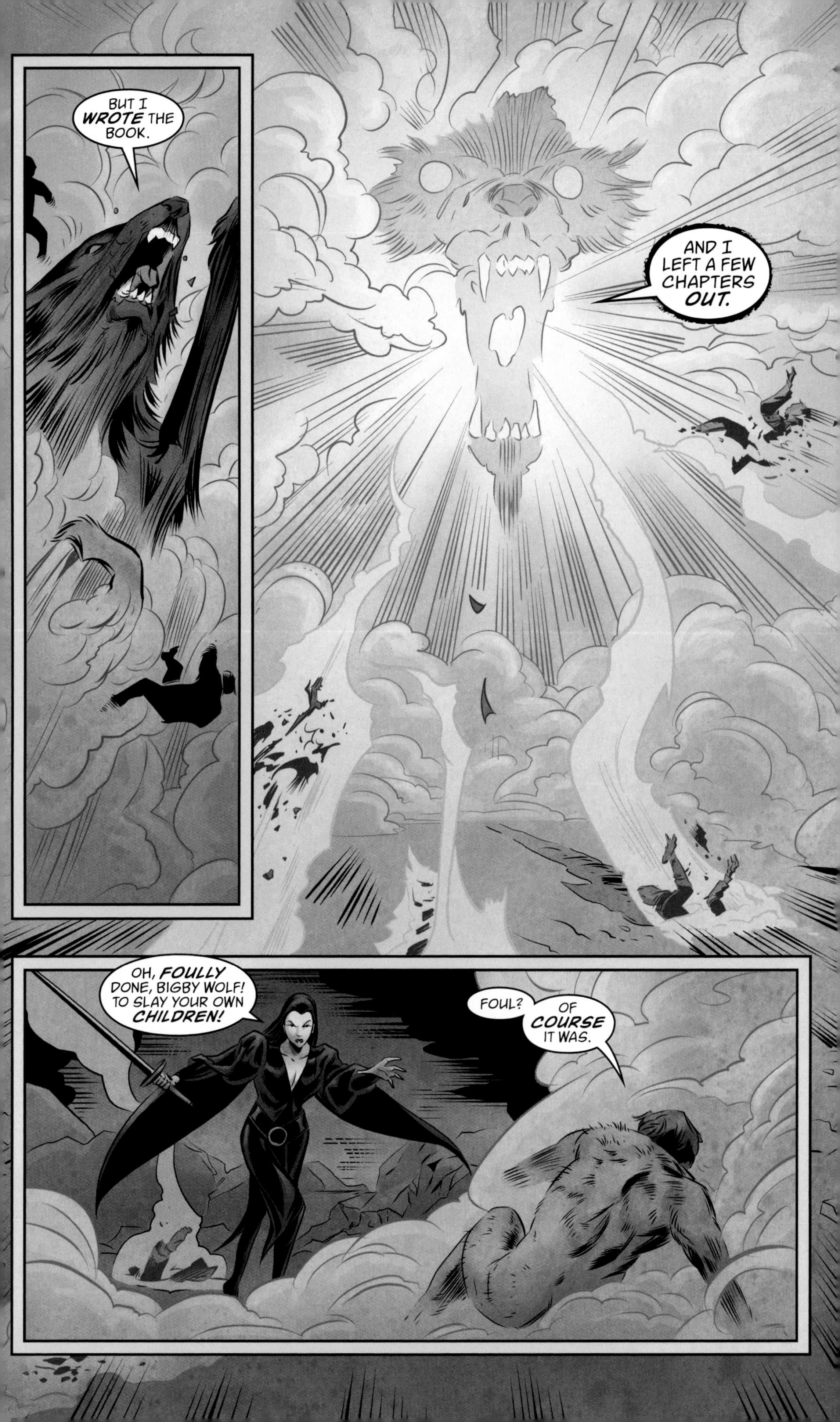
BUT I WROTE THE BOOK.
AND I LEFT A FEW CHAPTERS OUT.
OH, FOULLY DONE, BIGBY WOLF! TO SLAY YOUR OWN CHILDREN!
FOUL?
OF COURSE IT WAS.

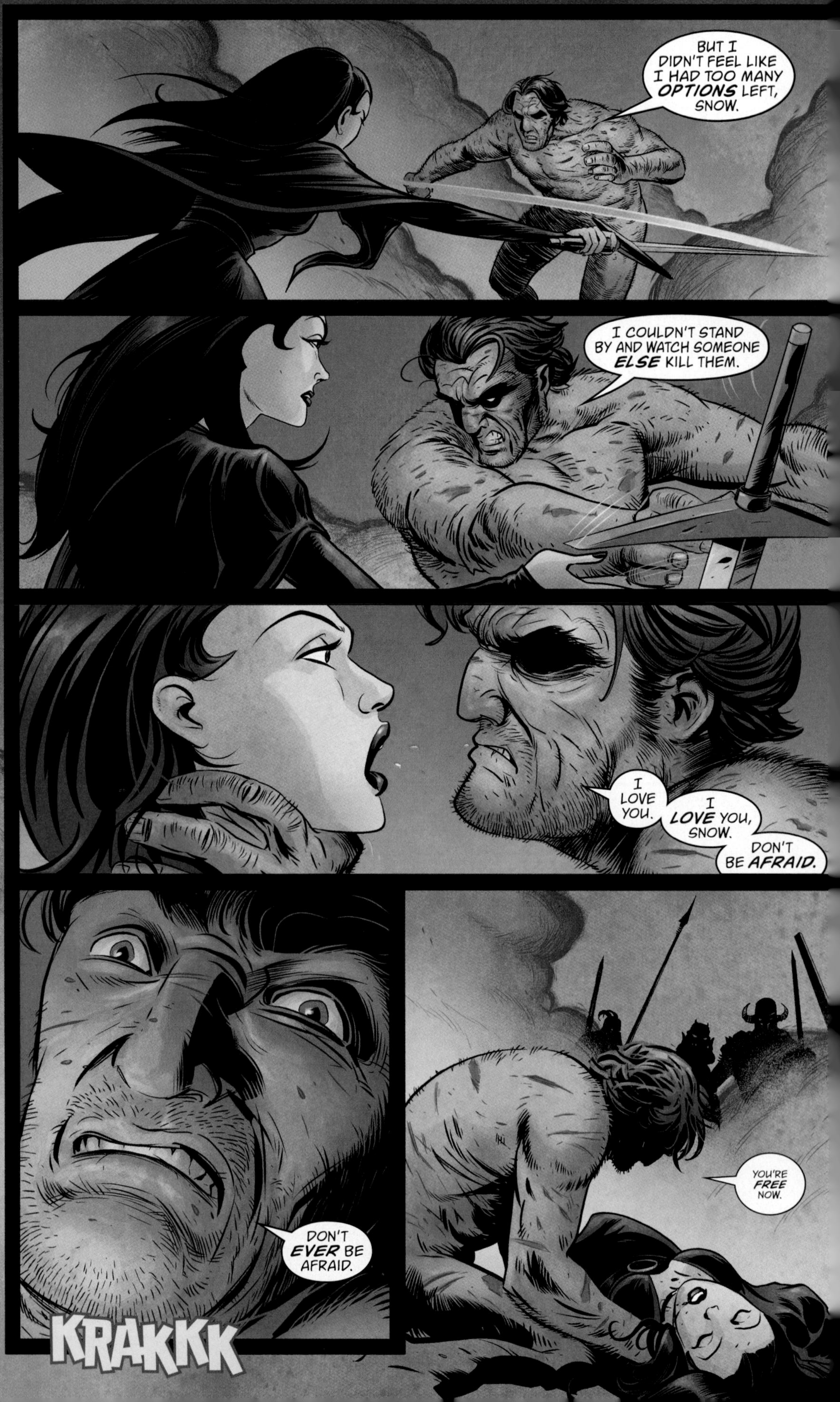
BUT I DIDN'T FEEL LIKE I HAD TOO MANY OPTIONS LEFT, SNOW.
I COULDN'T STAND BY AND WATCH SOMEONE ELSE KILL THEM.
I LOVE YOU.
I LOVE YOU, SNOW.
DON'T BE AFRAID.
DON'T EVER BE AFRAID.
KRAKKK
YOU'RE FREE NOW.

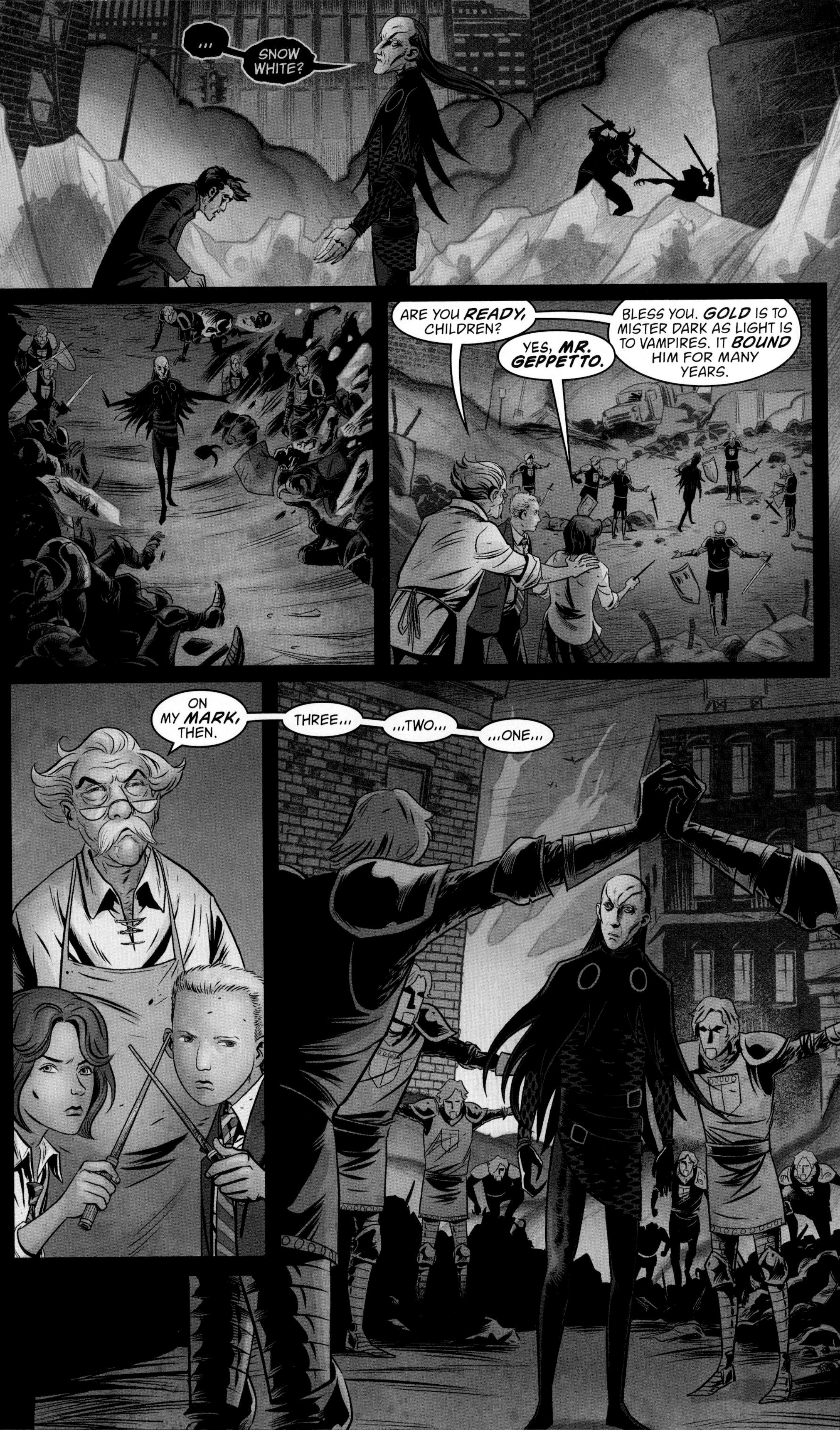
...
SNOW WHITE?
ARE YOU READY, CHILDREN?
YES, MR. GEPPETTO.
BLESS YOU. GOLD IS TO MISTER DARK AS LIGHT IS TO VAMPIRES. IT BOUND HIM FOR MANY YEARS.
ON MY MARK, THEN.
THREE...
...TWO...
...ONE...

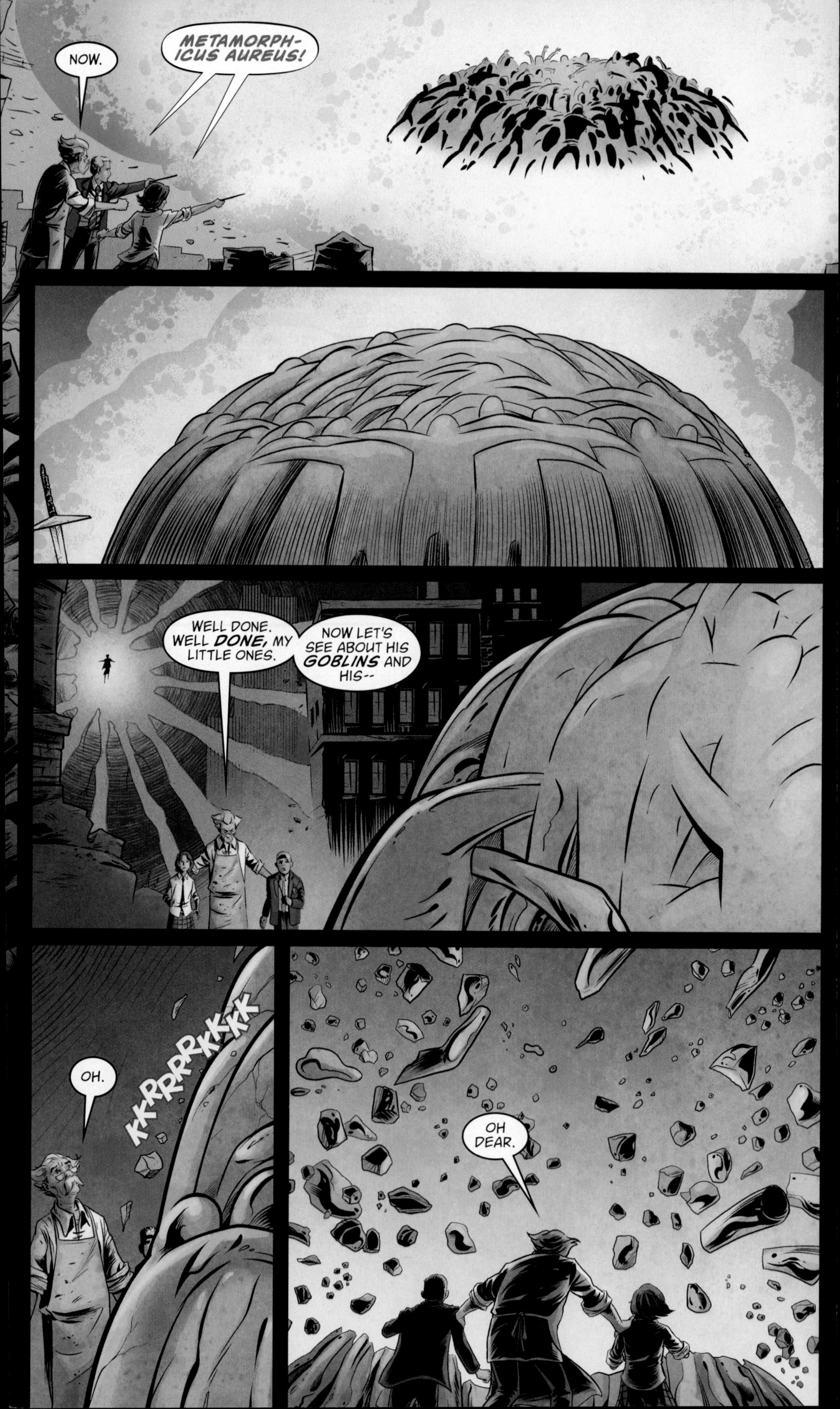
NOW.
METAMORPHICUS AUREUS!
WELL DONE. WELL DONE, MY LITTLE ONES.
NOW LET'S SEE ABOUT HIS GOBLINS AND HIS--
OH.
KKRRRRKKKKK
OH DEAR.

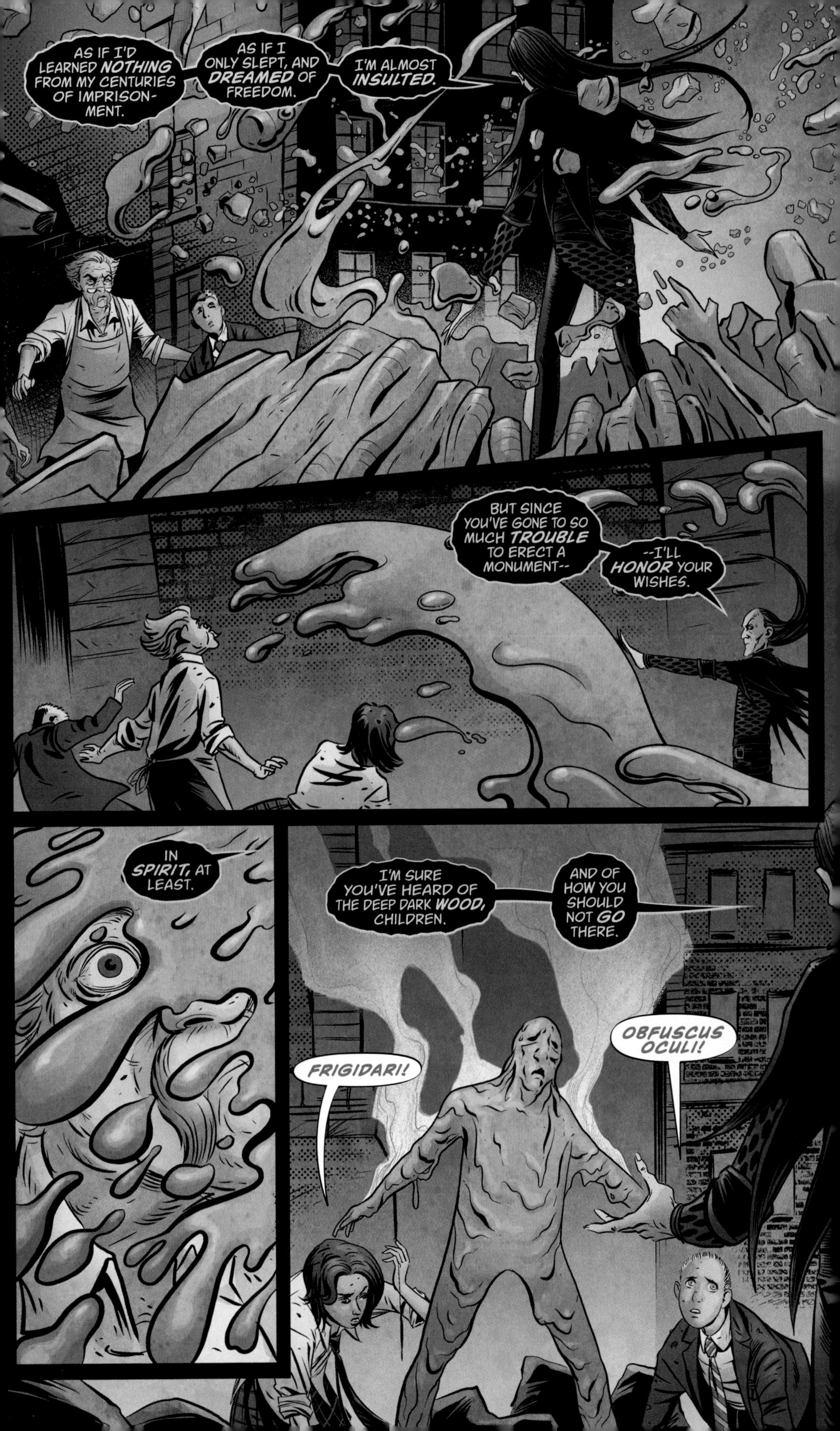

AS IF I'D LEARNED NOTHING FROM MY CENTURIES OF IMPRISON-MENT.
AS IF I ONLY SLEPT, AND DREAMED OF FREEDOM.
I'M ALMOST INSULTED.
BUT SINCE YOU'VE GONE TO SO MUCH TROUBLE TO ERECT A MONUMENT--
--I'LL HONOR YOUR WISHES.
IN SPIRIT, AT LEAST.
I'M SURE YOU'VE HEARD OF THE DEEP DARK WOOD, CHILDREN.
AND OF HOW YOU SHOULD NOT GO THERE.
FRIGIDARI!
OBFUSCUS OCULI!

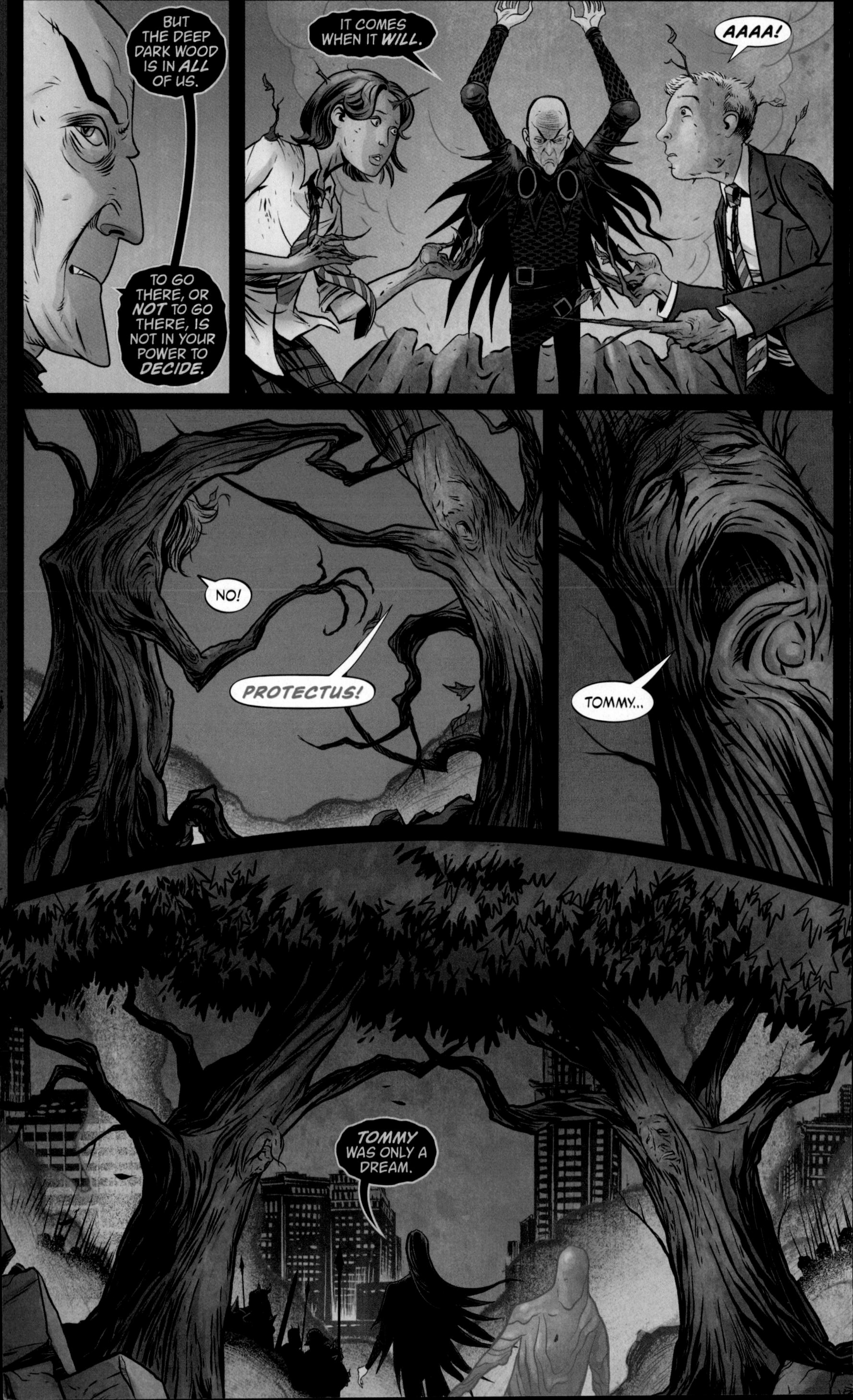
BUT THE DEEP DARK WOOD IS IN ALL OF US.
TO GO THERE, OR NOT TO GO THERE, IS NOT IN YOUR POWER TO DECIDE.
IT COMES WHEN IT WILL.
AAAA!
NO!
PROTECTUS!
TOMMY...
TOMMY WAS ONLY A DREAM.

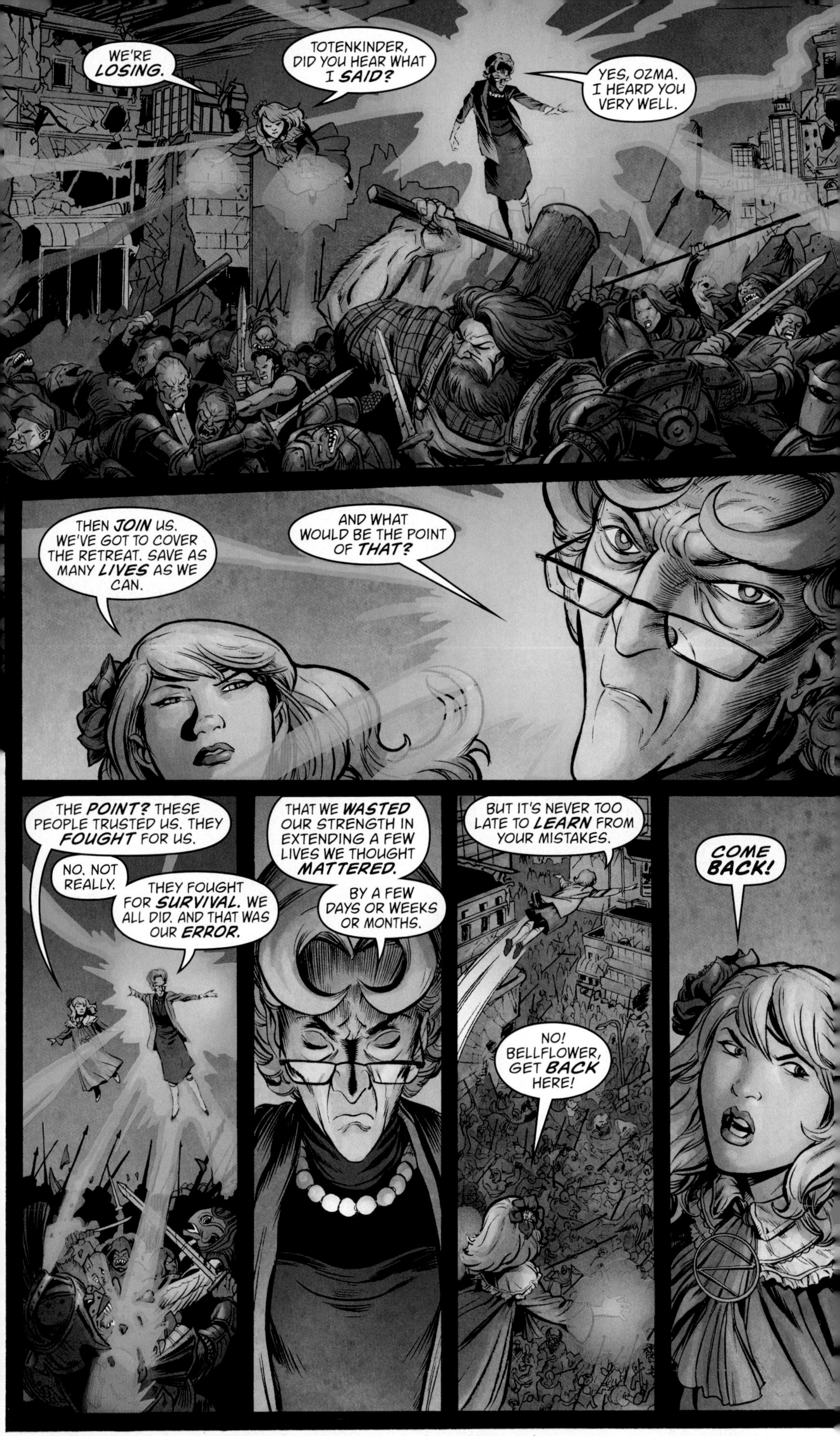
WE'RE LOSING.
TOTENKINDER, DID YOU HEAR WHAT I SAID?
YES, OZMA. I HEARD YOU VERY WELL.
THEN JOIN US. WE'VE GOT TO COVER THE RETREAT. SAVE AS MANY LIVES AS WE CAN.
AND WHAT WOULD BE THE POINT OF THAT?
THE POINT? THESE PEOPLE TRUSTED US. THEY FOUGHT FOR US.
NO. NOT REALLY.
THEY FOUGHT FOR SURVIVAL. WE ALL DID. AND THAT WAS OUR ERROR.
THAT WE WASTED OUR STRENGTH IN EXTENDING A FEW LIVES WE THOUGHT MATTERED.
BY A FEW DAYS OR WEEKS OR MONTHS.
BUT IT'S NEVER TOO LATE TO LEARN FROM YOUR MISTAKES.
NO! BELLFLOWER, GET BACK HERE!
COME BACK!

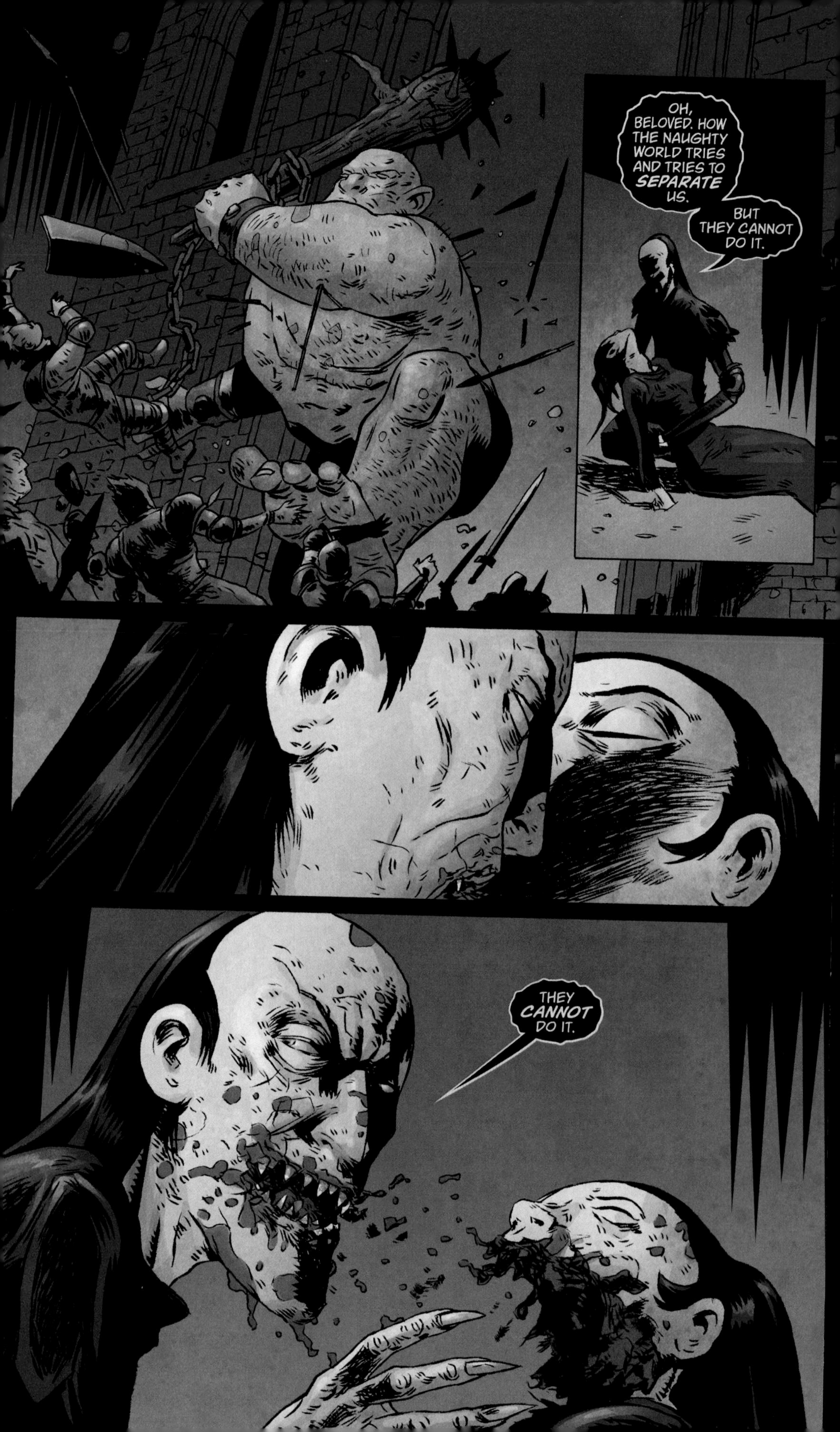
OH, BELOVED. HOW THE NAUGHTY WORLD TRIES AND TRIES TO SEPARATE US.
BUT THEY CANNOT DO IT.
THEY CANNOT DO IT.

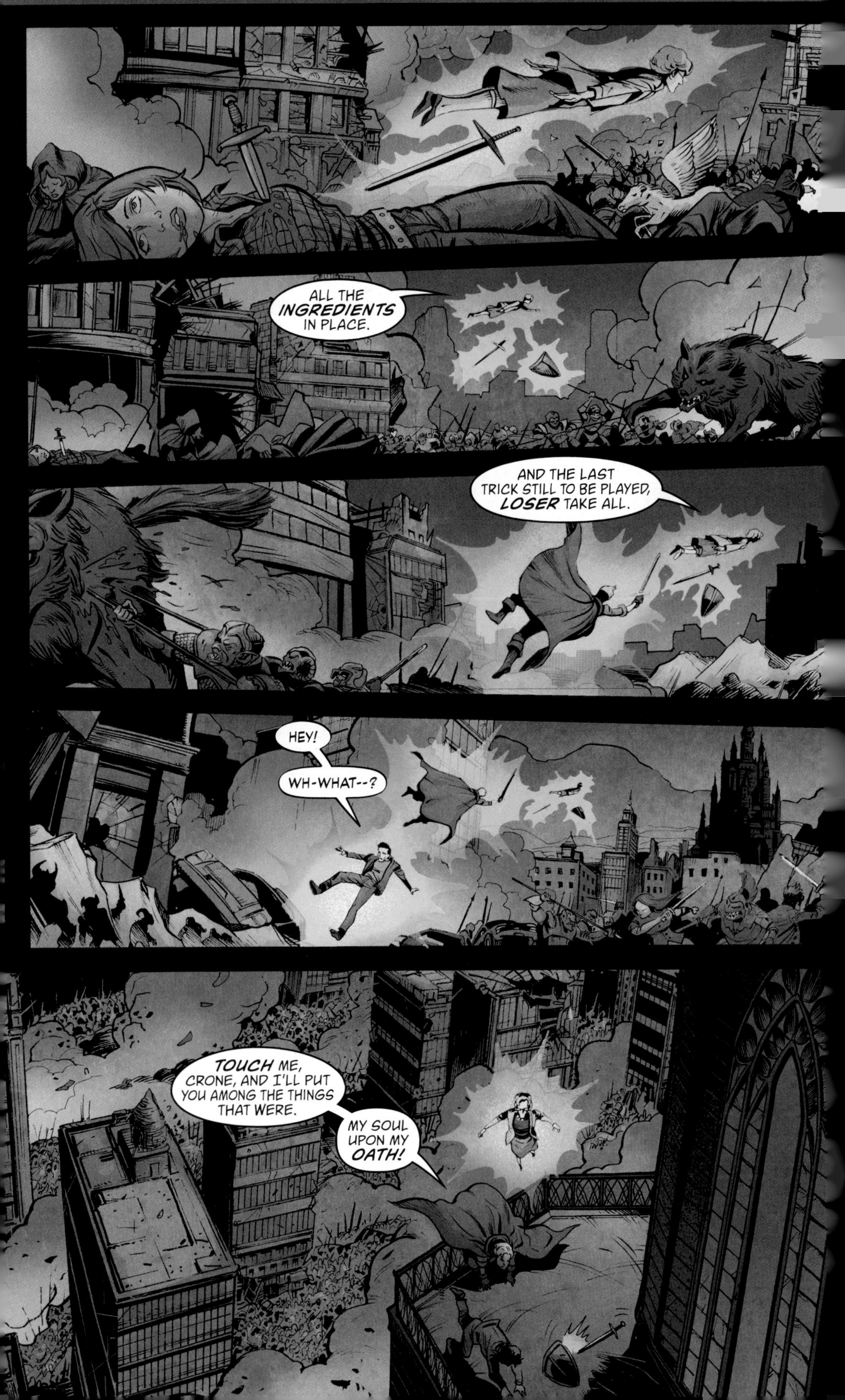
ALL THE INGREDIENTS IN PLACE.
AND THE LAST TRICK STILL TO BE PLAYED, LOSER TAKE ALL.
HEY!
WH-WHAT--?
TOUCH ME, CRONE, AND I'LL PUT YOU AMONG THE THINGS THAT WERE.
MY SOUL UPON MY OATH!

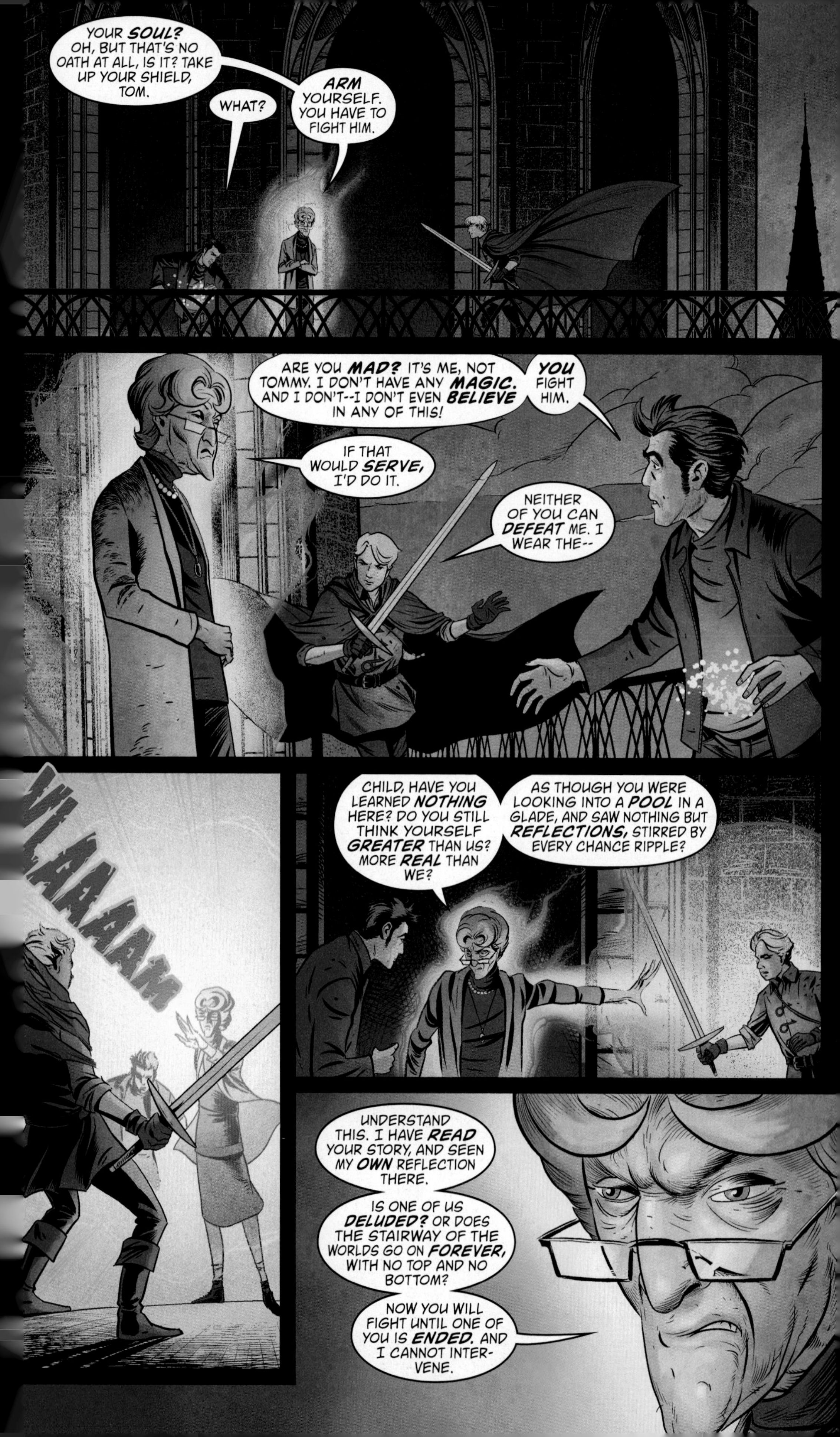
YOUR SOUL? OH, BUT THAT'S NO OATH AT ALL, IS IT? TAKE UP YOUR SHIELD, TOM.
WHAT?
ARM YOURSELF. YOU HAVE TO FIGHT HIM.
ARE YOU MAD? IT'S ME, NOT TOMMY. I DON'T HAVE ANY MAGIC. AND I DON'T--I DON'T EVEN BELIEVE IN ANY OF THIS!
YOU FIGHT HIM.
IF THAT WOULD SERVE, I'D DO IT.
NEITHER OF YOU CAN DEFEAT ME. I WEAR THE--
WLAAAAM
CHILD, HAVE YOU LEARNED NOTHING HERE? DO YOU STILL THINK YOURSELF GREATER THAN US? MORE REAL THAN WE?
AS THOUGH YOU WERE LOOKING INTO A POOL IN A GLADE, AND SAW NOTHING BUT REFLECTIONS, STIRRED BY EVERY CHANCE RIPPLE?
UNDERSTAND THIS. I HAVE READ YOUR STORY, AND SEEN MY OWN REFLECTION THERE.
IS ONE OF US DELUDED? OR DOES THE STAIRWAY OF THE WORLDS GO ON FOREVER, WITH NO TOP AND NO BOTTOM?
NOW YOU WILL FIGHT UNTIL ONE OF YOU IS ENDED. AND I CANNOT INTERVENE.

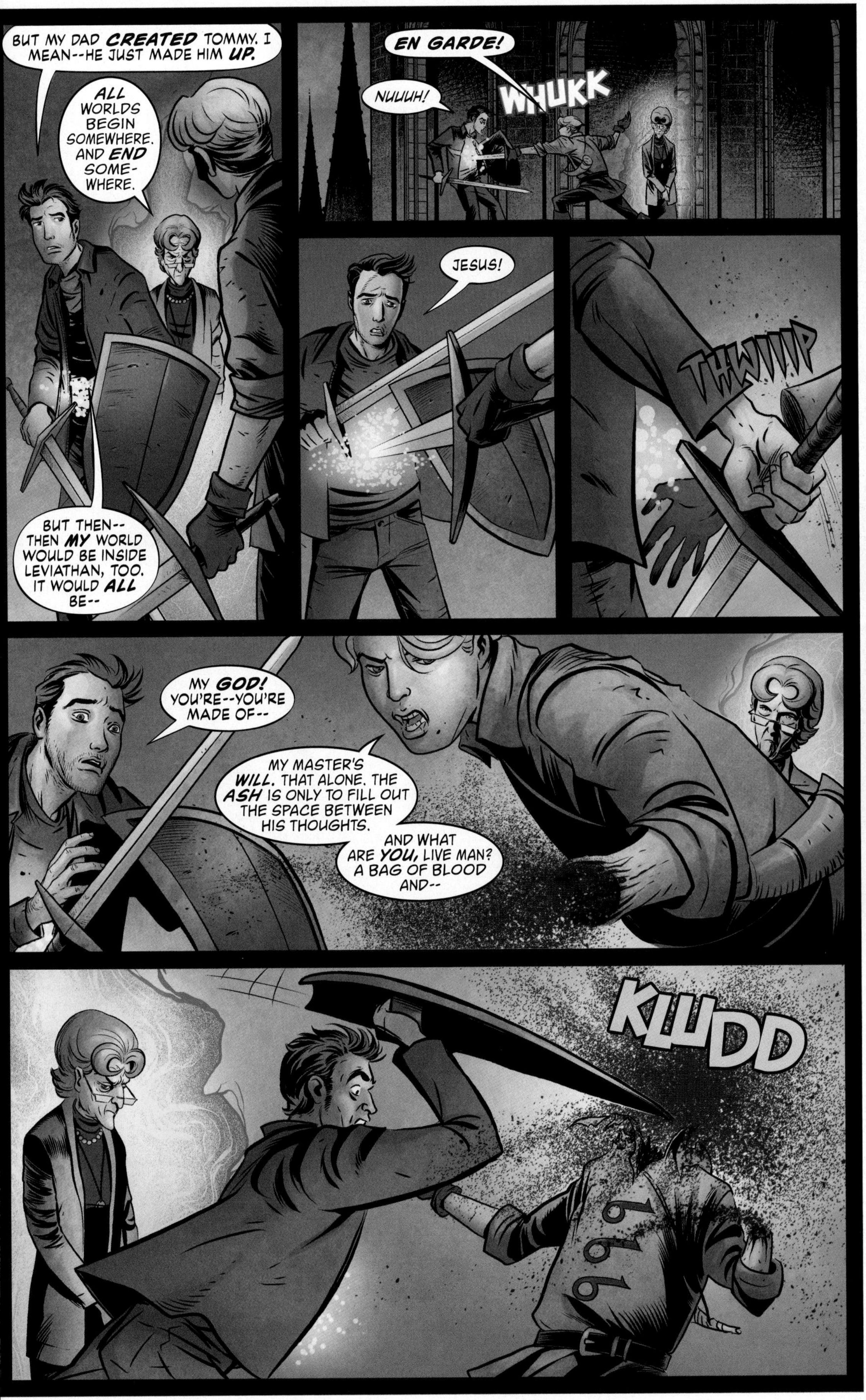
BUT MY DAD CREATED TOMMY. I MEAN--HE JUST MADE HIM UP.
ALL WORLDS BEGIN SOMEWHERE. AND END SOMEWHERE.
BUT THEN--THEN MY WORLD WOULD BE INSIDE LEVIATHAN, TOO. IT WOULD ALL BE--
EN GARDE!
NUUUH!
WHUKK
JESUS!
THWIIIP
MY GOD! YOU'RE--YOU'RE MADE OF--
MY MASTER'S WILL. THAT ALONE. THE ASH IS ONLY TO FILL OUT THE SPACE BETWEEN HIS THOUGHTS.
AND WHAT ARE YOU, LIVE MAN? A BAG OF BLOOD AND--
KLUDD

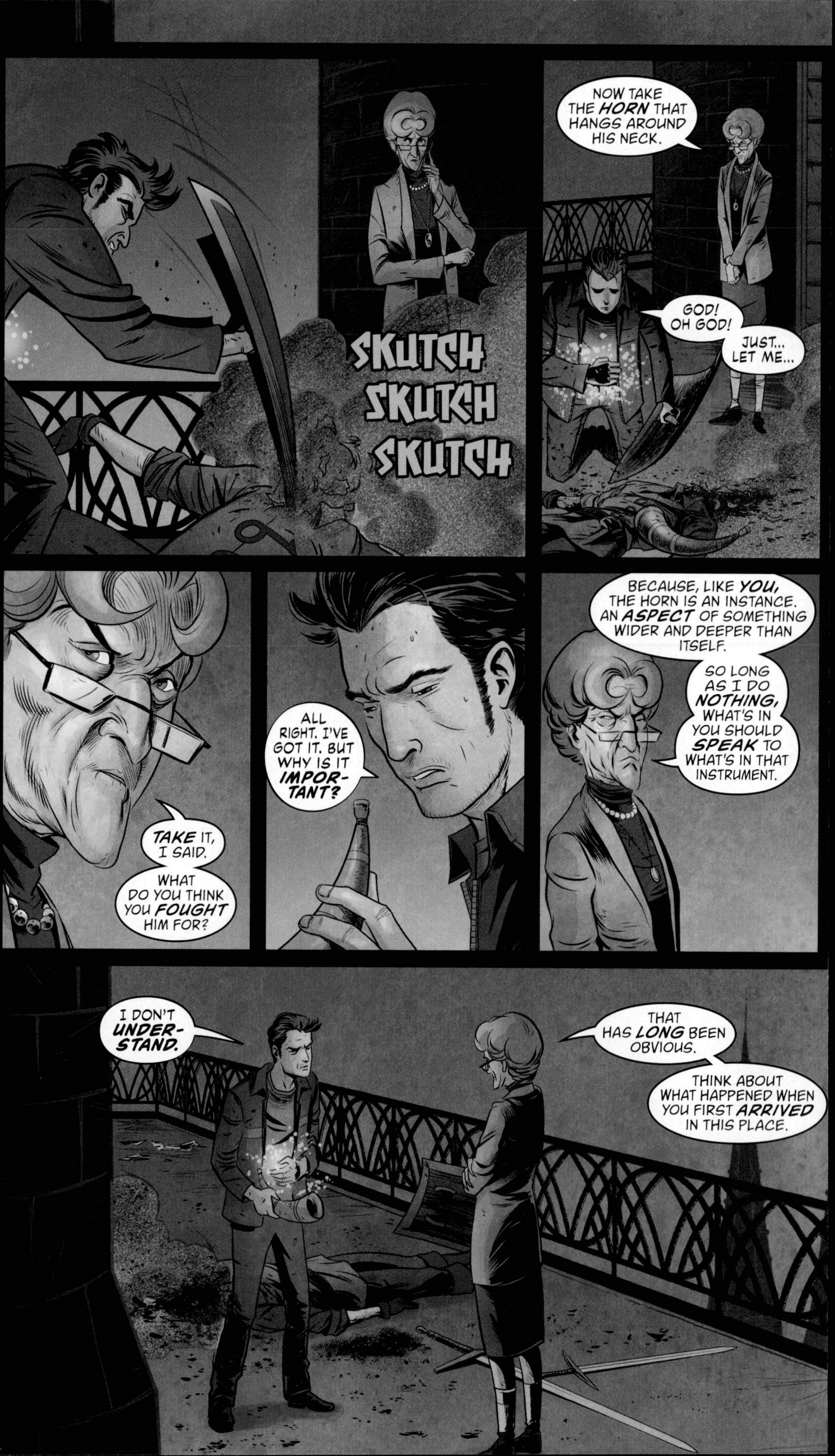

SKUTCH
SKUTCH
SKUTCH
NOW TAKE THE **HORN** THAT HANGS AROUND HIS NECK.
GOD! OH GOD!
JUST... LET ME...
TAKE IT, I SAID.
WHAT DO YOU THINK YOU **FOUGHT** HIM FOR?
ALL RIGHT. I'VE GOT IT. BUT WHY IS IT **IMPORTANT?**
BECAUSE, LIKE **YOU,** THE HORN IS AN INSTANCE. AN **ASPECT** OF SOMETHING WIDER AND DEEPER THAN ITSELF.
SO LONG AS I DO **NOTHING,** WHAT'S IN YOU SHOULD **SPEAK** TO WHAT'S IN THAT INSTRUMENT.
I DON'T **UNDERSTAND.**
THAT HAS **LONG** BEEN OBVIOUS.
THINK ABOUT WHAT HAPPENED WHEN YOU FIRST **ARRIVED** IN THIS PLACE.

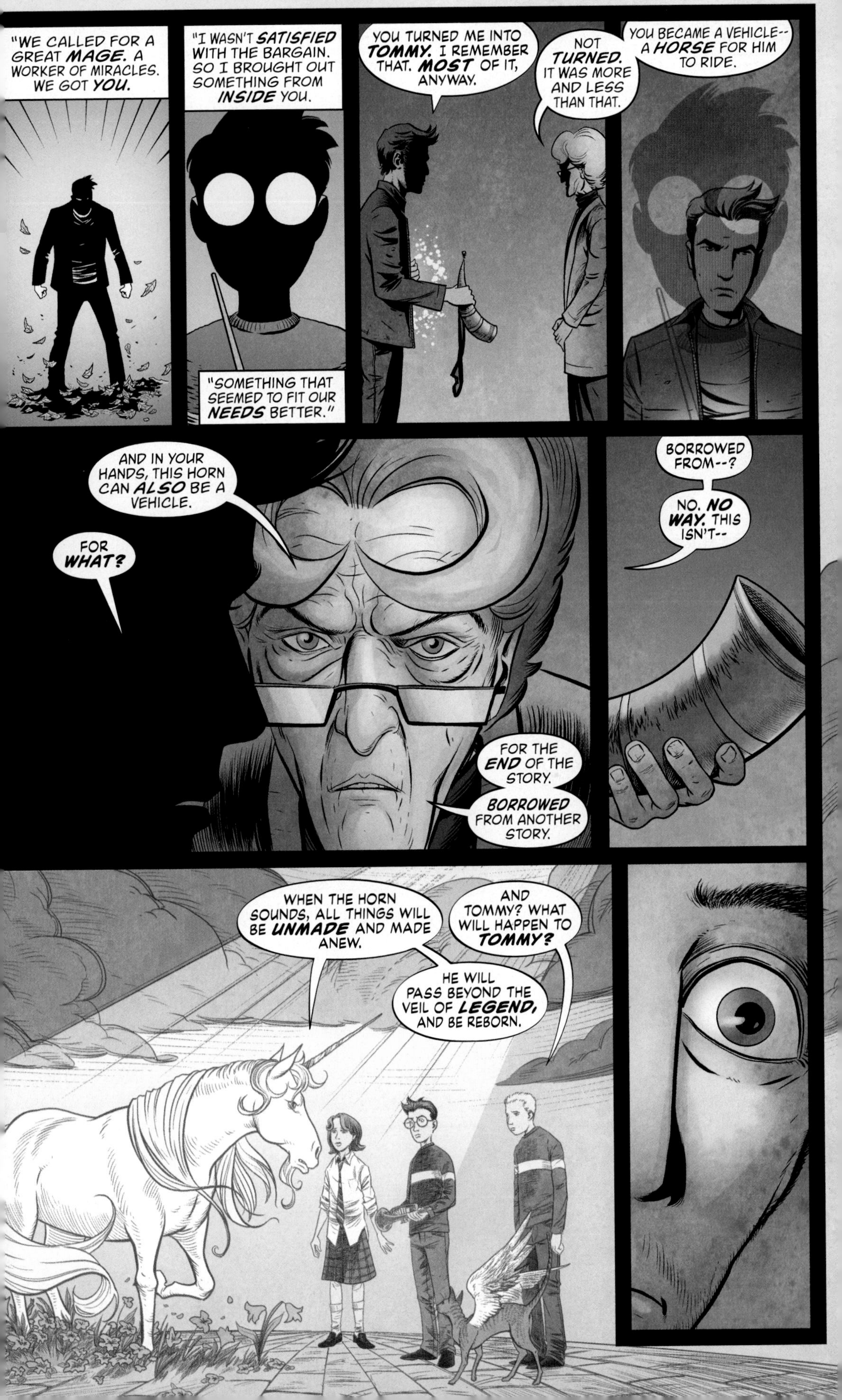
"WE CALLED FOR A GREAT MAGE. A WORKER OF MIRACLES. WE GOT YOU.
"I WASN'T SATISFIED WITH THE BARGAIN. SO I BROUGHT OUT SOMETHING FROM INSIDE YOU.
"SOMETHING THAT SEEMED TO FIT OUR NEEDS BETTER."
YOU TURNED ME INTO TOMMY. I REMEMBER THAT. MOST OF IT, ANYWAY.
NOT TURNED. IT WAS MORE AND LESS THAN THAT.
YOU BECAME A VEHICLE--A HORSE FOR HIM TO RIDE.
AND IN YOUR HANDS, THIS HORN CAN ALSO BE A VEHICLE.
FOR WHAT?
FOR THE END OF THE STORY.
BORROWED FROM ANOTHER STORY.
BORROWED FROM--?
NO. NO WAY. THIS ISN'T--
WHEN THE HORN SOUNDS, ALL THINGS WILL BE UNMADE AND MADE ANEW.
AND TOMMY? WHAT WILL HAPPEN TO TOMMY?
HE WILL PASS BEYOND THE VEIL OF LEGEND, AND BE REBORN.

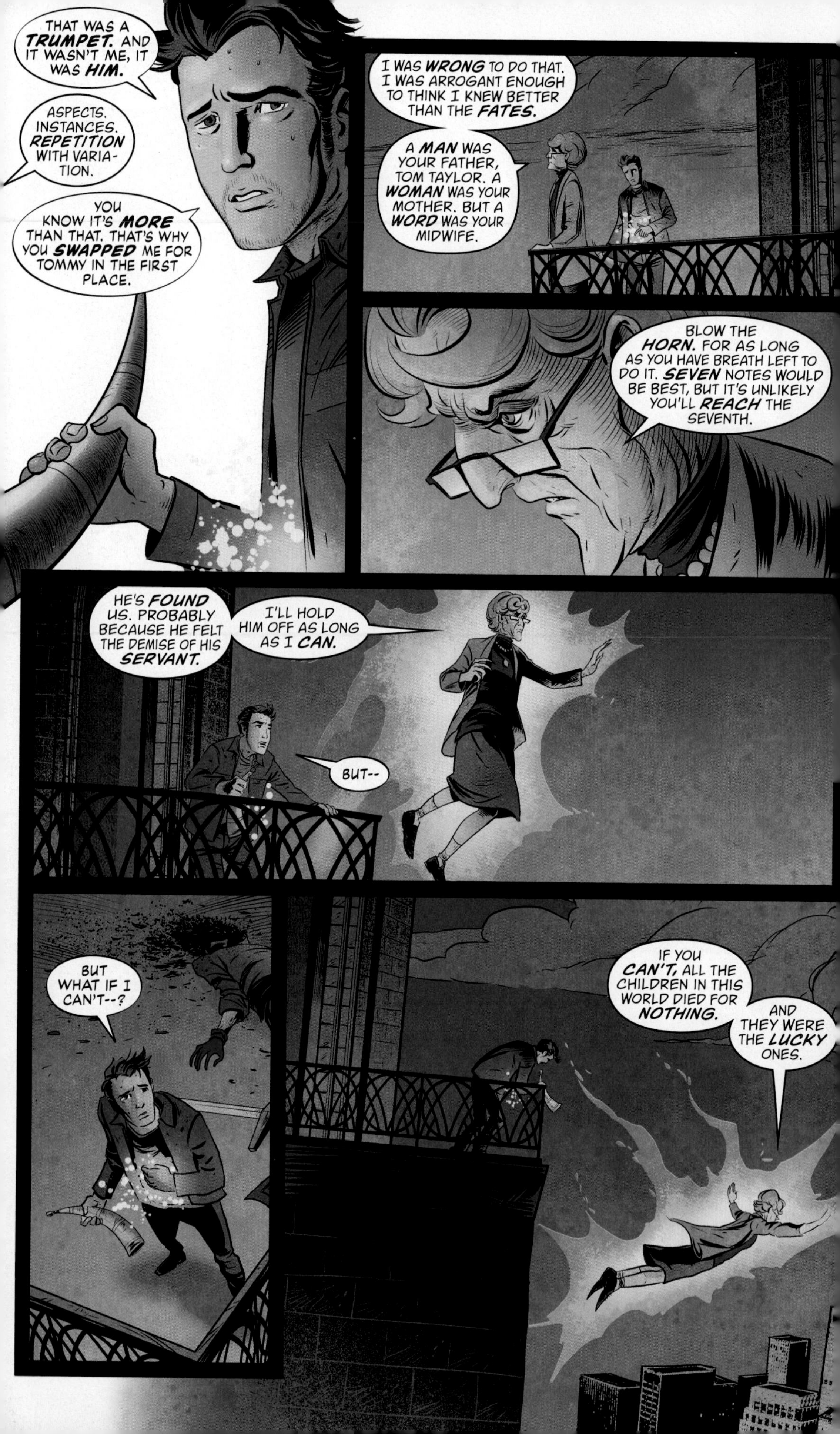
THAT WAS A TRUMPET. AND IT WASN'T ME, IT WAS HIM.
ASPECTS. INSTANCES. REPETITION WITH VARIA-TION.
YOU KNOW IT'S MORE THAN THAT. THAT'S WHY YOU SWAPPED ME FOR TOMMY IN THE FIRST PLACE.
I WAS WRONG TO DO THAT. I WAS ARROGANT ENOUGH TO THINK I KNEW BETTER THAN THE FATES.
A MAN WAS YOUR FATHER, TOM TAYLOR. A WOMAN WAS YOUR MOTHER. BUT A WORD WAS YOUR MIDWIFE.
BLOW THE HORN. FOR AS LONG AS YOU HAVE BREATH LEFT TO DO IT. SEVEN NOTES WOULD BE BEST, BUT IT'S UNLIKELY YOU'LL REACH THE SEVENTH.
HE'S FOUND US. PROBABLY BECAUSE HE FELT THE DEMISE OF HIS SERVANT.
I'LL HOLD HIM OFF AS LONG AS I CAN.
BUT--
BUT WHAT IF I CAN'T--?
IF YOU CAN'T, ALL THE CHILDREN IN THIS WORLD DIED FOR NOTHING.
AND THEY WERE THE LUCKY ONES.

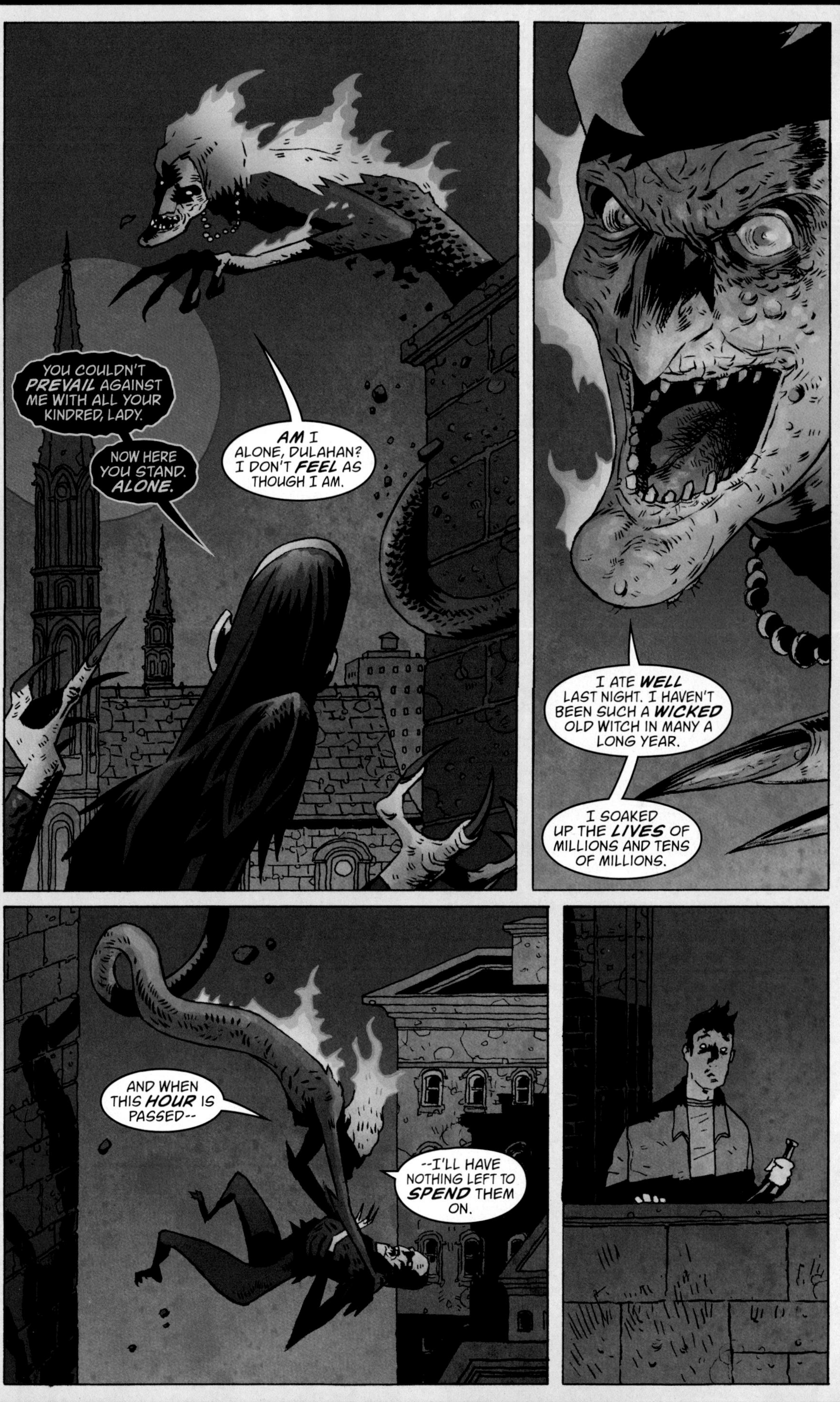
YOU COULDN'T PREVAIL AGAINST ME WITH ALL YOUR KINDRED, LADY.
NOW HERE YOU STAND. ALONE.
AM I ALONE, DULAHAN? I DON'T FEEL AS THOUGH I AM.
I ATE WELL LAST NIGHT. I HAVEN'T BEEN SUCH A WICKED OLD WITCH IN MANY A LONG YEAR.
I SOAKED UP THE LIVES OF MILLIONS AND TENS OF MILLIONS.
AND WHEN THIS HOUR IS PASSED--
--I'LL HAVE NOTHING LEFT TO SPEND THEM ON.

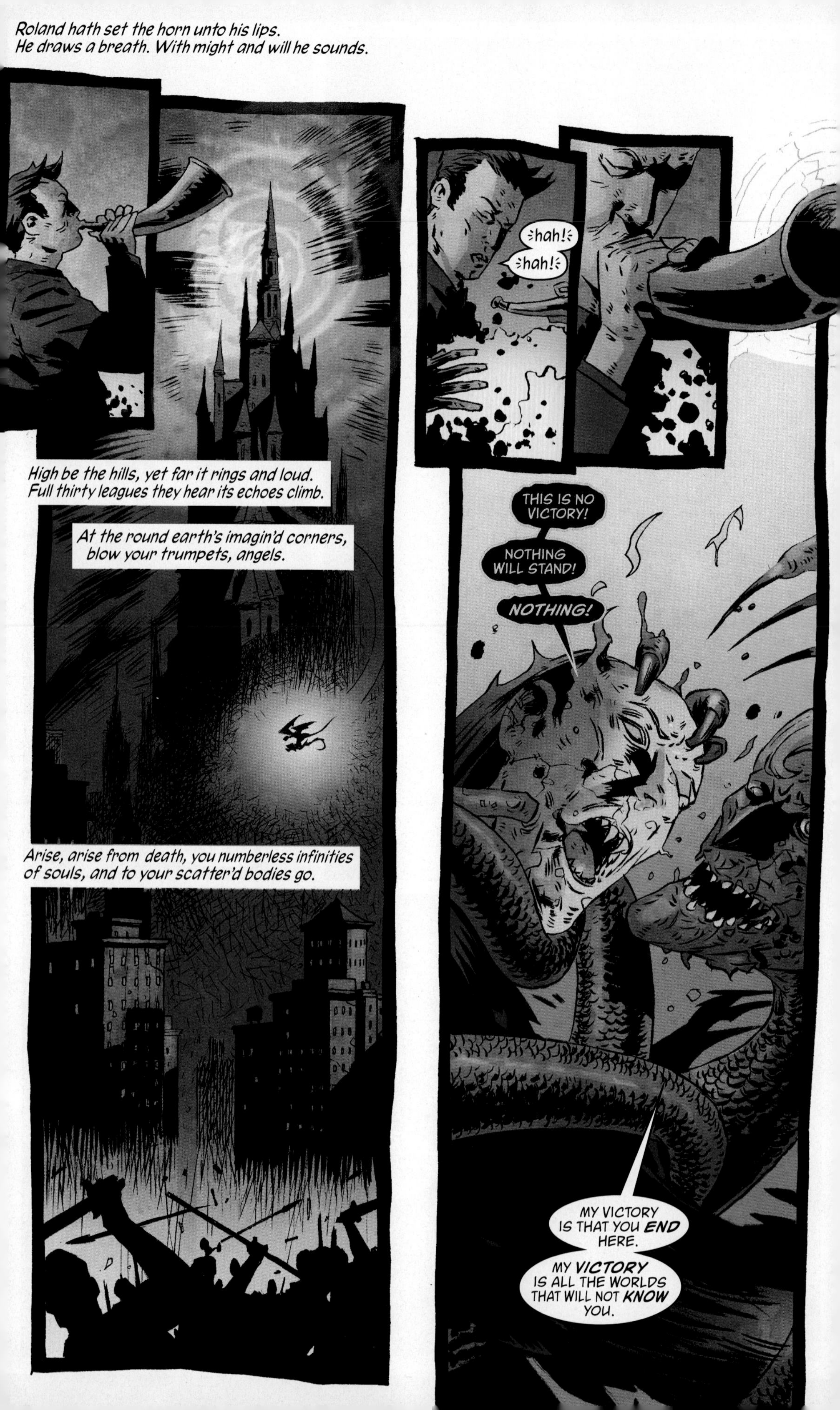

Roland hath set the horn unto his lips.
He draws a breath. With might and will he sounds.
High be the hills, yet far it rings and loud.
Full thirty leagues they hear its echoes climb.
At the round earth's imagin'd corners, blow your trumpets, angels.
Arise, arise from death, you numberless infinities of souls, and to your scatter'd bodies go.
hah!
hah!
THIS IS NO VICTORY!
NOTHING WILL STAND!
NOTHING!
MY VICTORY IS THAT YOU END HERE.
MY VICTORY IS ALL THE WORLDS THAT WILL NOT KNOW YOU.

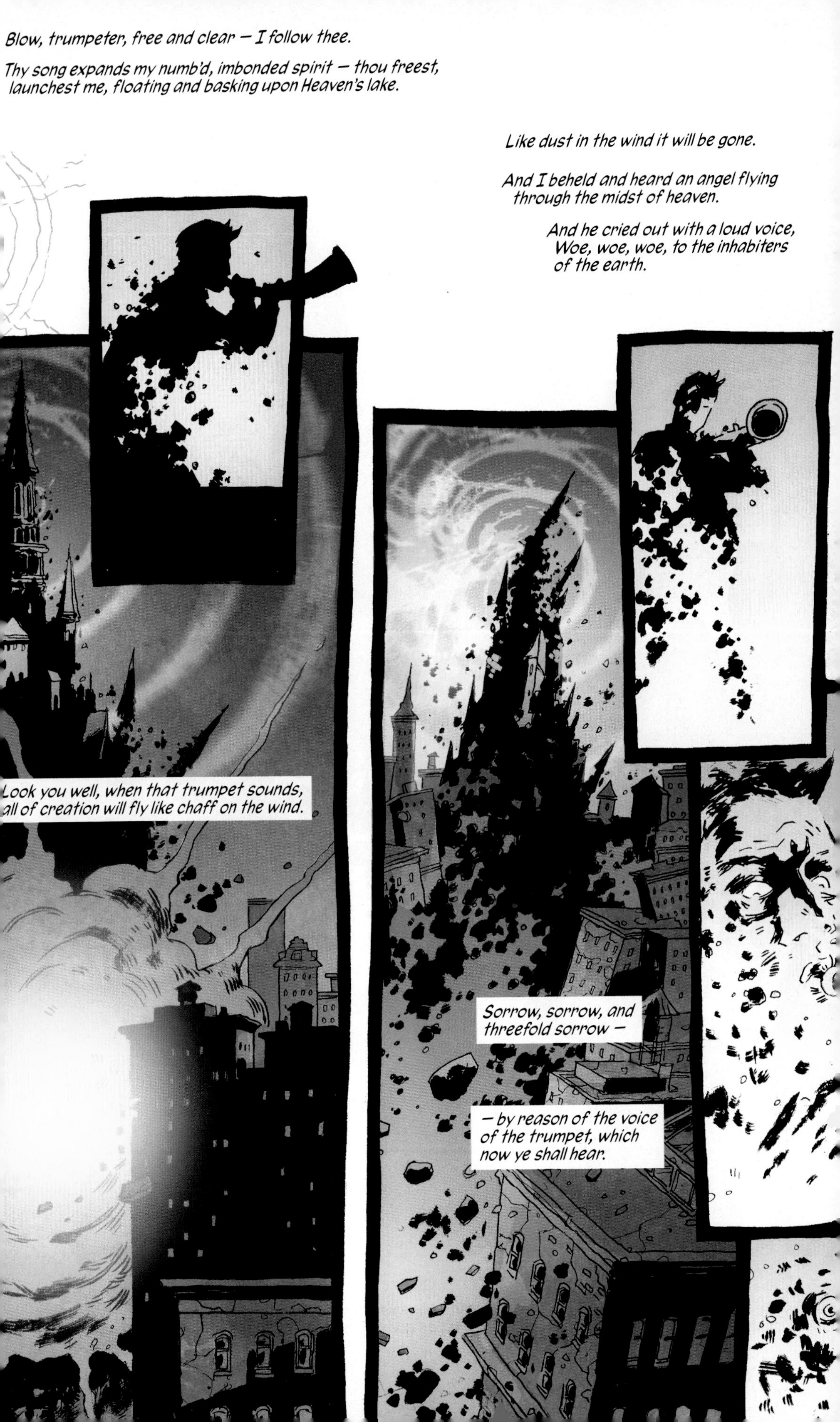
Blow, trumpeter, free and clear — I follow thee.
Thy song expands my numb'd, imbonded spirit — thou freest, launchest me, floating and basking upon Heaven's lake.
Look you well, when that trumpet sounds, all of creation will fly like chaff on the wind.
Like dust in the wind it will be gone.
And I beheld and heard an angel flying through the midst of heaven.
And he cried out with a loud voice, Woe, woe, woe, to the inhabiters of the earth.
Sorrow, sorrow, and threefold sorrow —
— by reason of the voice of the trumpet, which now ye shall hear.

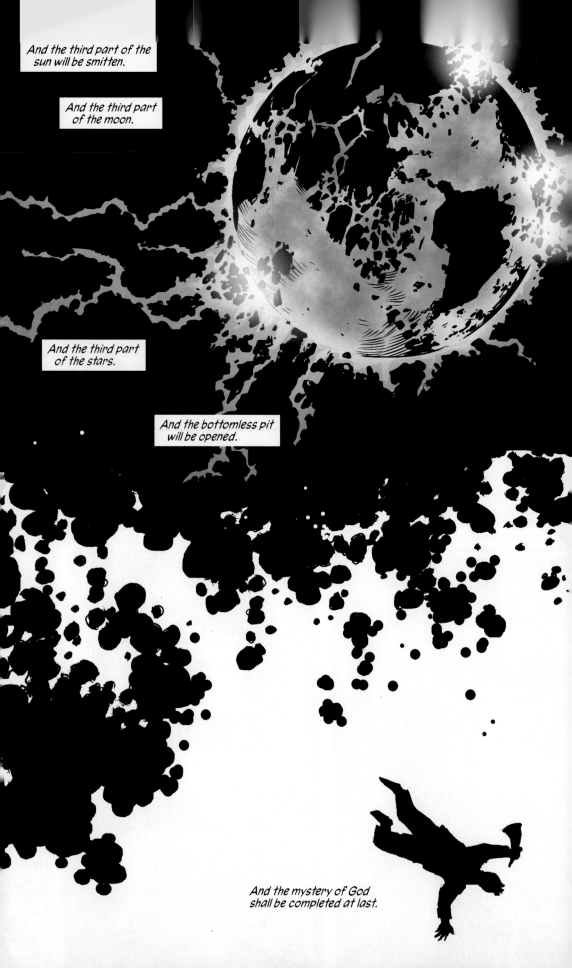

And the third part of the sun will be smitten.

And the third part of the moon.

And the third part of the stars.

And the bottomless pit will be opened.

And the mystery of God shall be completed at last.

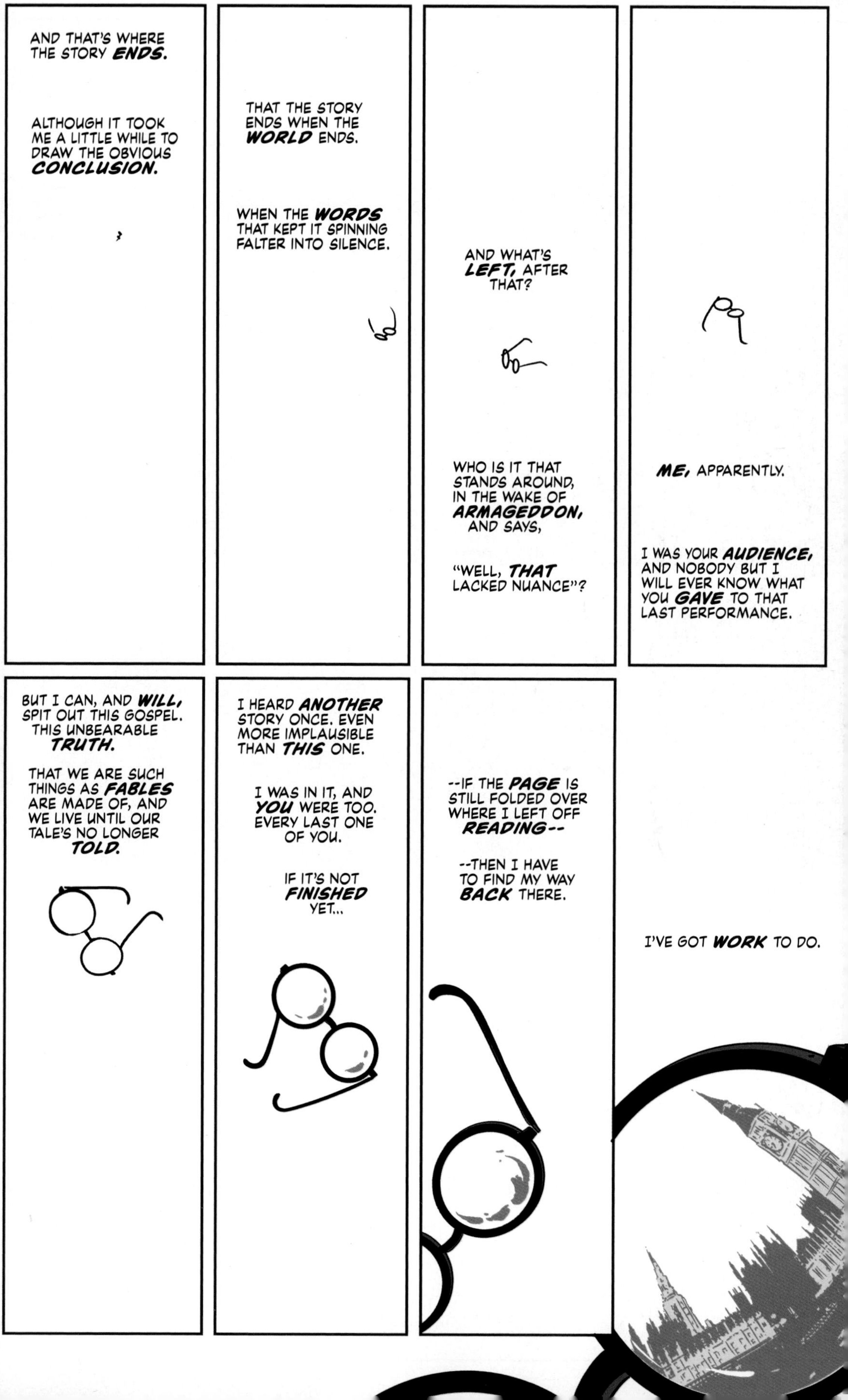

AND THAT'S WHERE THE STORY ENDS.
ALTHOUGH IT TOOK ME A LITTLE WHILE TO DRAW THE OBVIOUS CONCLUSION.
THAT THE STORY ENDS WHEN THE WORLD ENDS.
WHEN THE WORDS THAT KEPT IT SPINNING FALTER INTO SILENCE.
AND WHAT'S LEFT, AFTER THAT?
WHO IS IT THAT STANDS AROUND, IN THE WAKE OF ARMAGEDDON, AND SAYS,
"WELL, THAT LACKED NUANCE"?
ME, APPARENTLY.
I WAS YOUR AUDIENCE, AND NOBODY BUT I WILL EVER KNOW WHAT YOU GAVE TO THAT LAST PERFORMANCE.
BUT I CAN, AND WILL, SPIT OUT THIS GOSPEL. THIS UNBEARABLE TRUTH.
THAT WE ARE SUCH THINGS AS FABLES ARE MADE OF, AND WE LIVE UNTIL OUR TALE'S NO LONGER TOLD.
I HEARD ANOTHER STORY ONCE. EVEN MORE IMPLAUSIBLE THAN THIS ONE.
I WAS IN IT, AND YOU WERE TOO. EVERY LAST ONE OF YOU.
IF IT'S NOT FINISHED YET...
--IF THE PAGE IS STILL FOLDED OVER WHERE I LEFT OFF READING--
--THEN I HAVE TO FIND MY WAY BACK THERE.
I'VE GOT WORK TO DO.

Pencils for issue #54 by Mark Buckingham

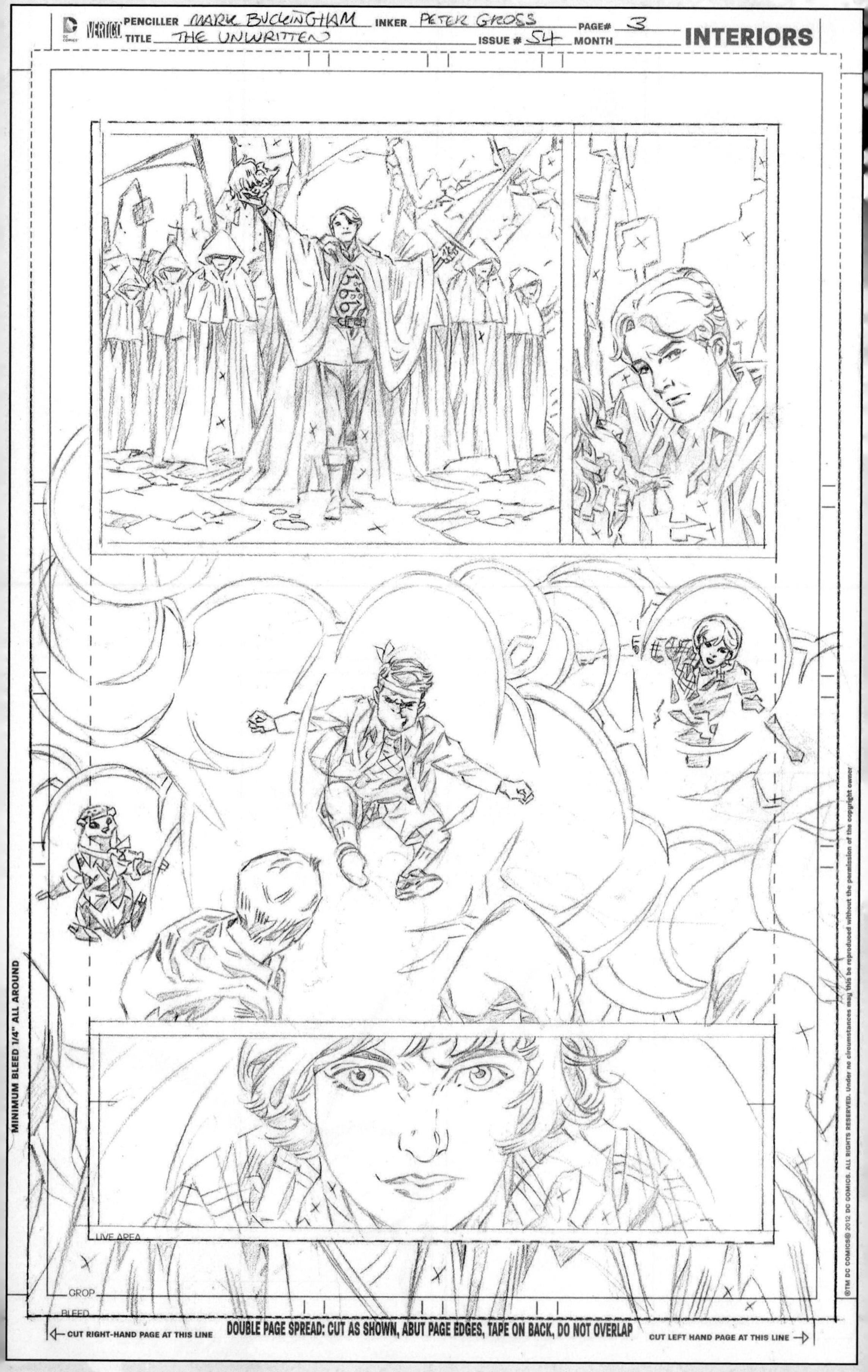
PENCILLER MARK BUCKINGHAM
INKER PETER GROSS
PAGE# 3
INTERIORS
TITLE THE UNWRITTEN
ISSUE # 54
MONTH
LIVE AREA
CROP
BLEED
MINIMUM BLEED 1/4" ALL AROUND
©TM DC COMICS© 2012 DC COMICS. ALL RIGHTS RESERVED. Under no circumstances may this be reproduced without the permission of the copyright owner
CUT RIGHT-HAND PAGE AT THIS LINE
DOUBLE PAGE SPREAD: CUT AS SHOWN, ABUT PAGE EDGES, TAPE ON BACK, DO NOT OVERLAP
CUT LEFT HAND PAGE AT THIS LINE

LIVE AREA

Cover sketches by Yuko Shimizu

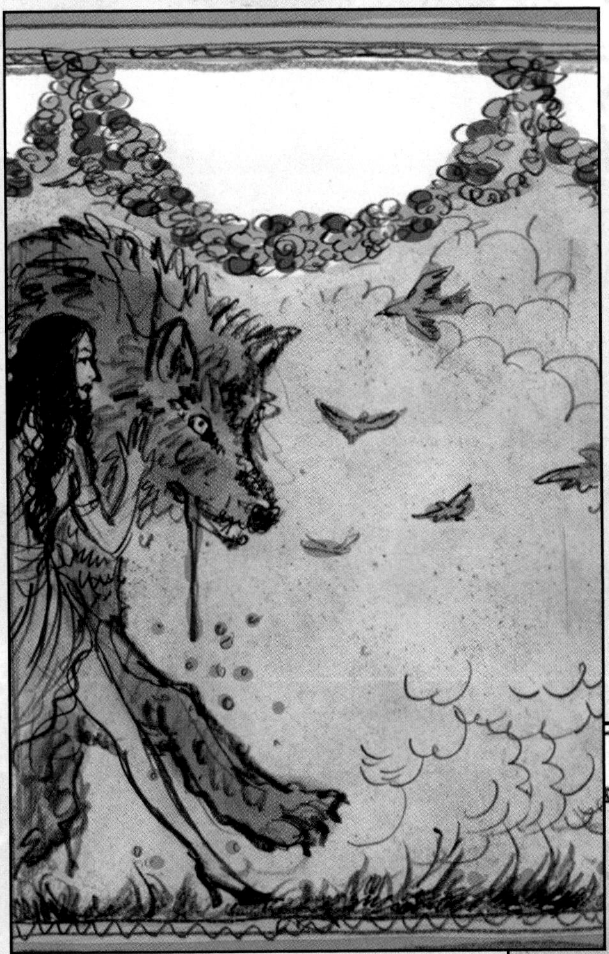

Sketch for cover issue #50

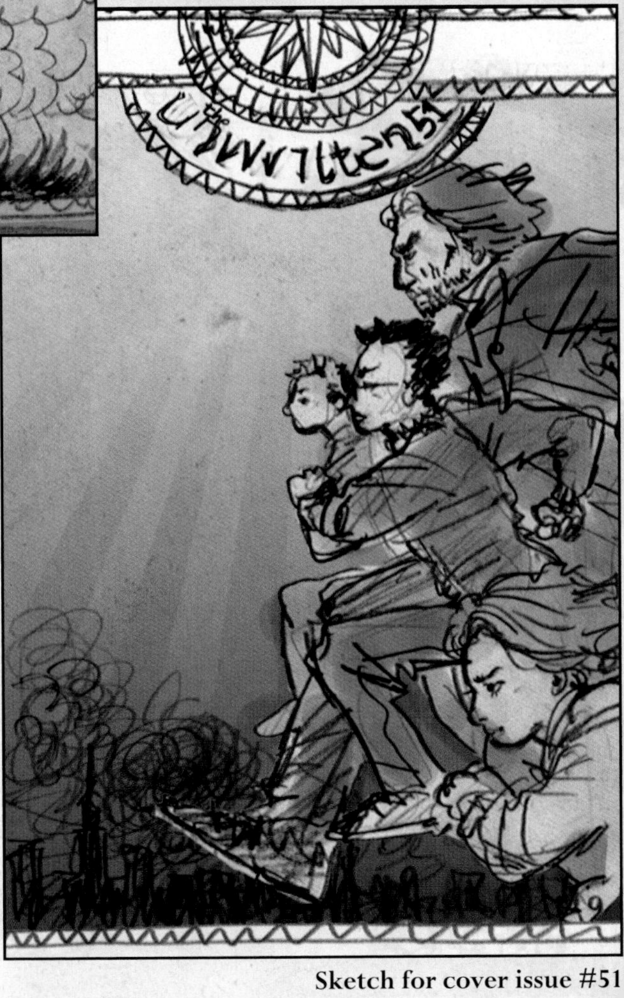

Sketch for cover issue #51

Sketch for cover issue #52

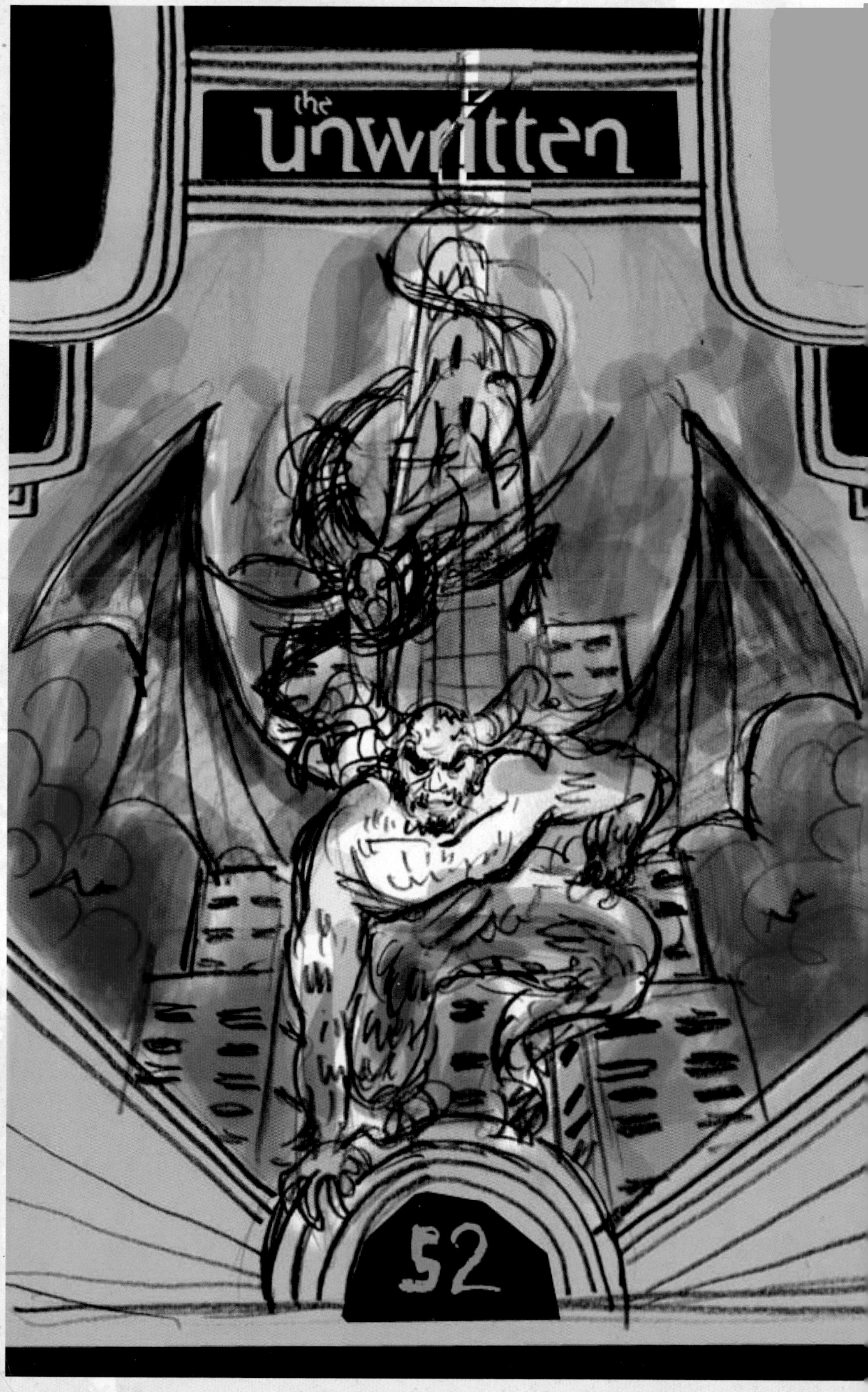
the
Unwritten
52

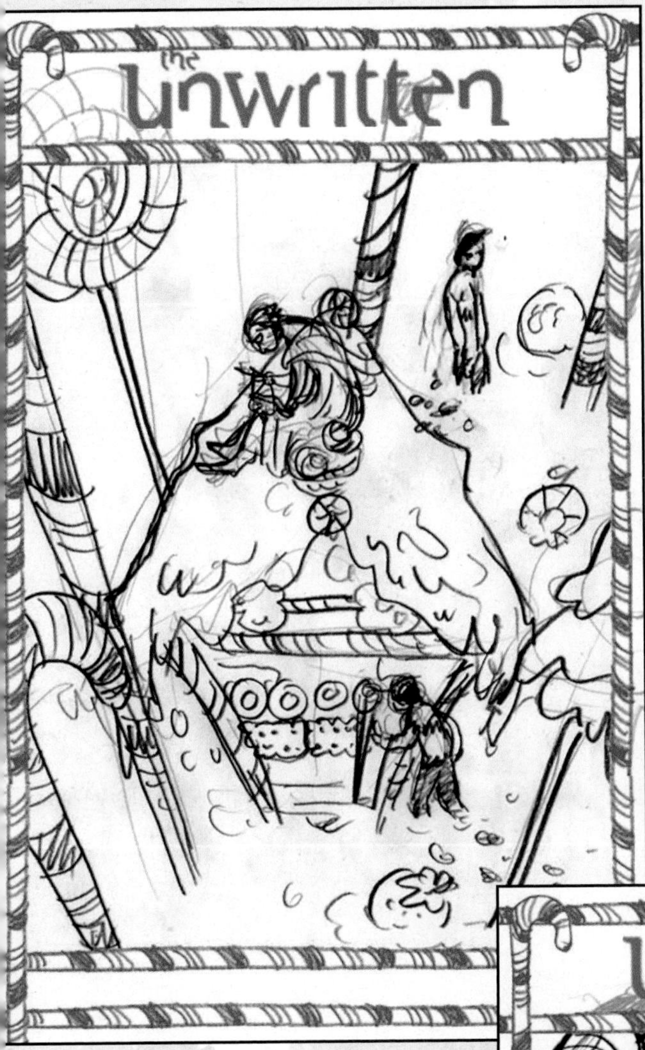
the Unwritten

Sketches for cover issue #53

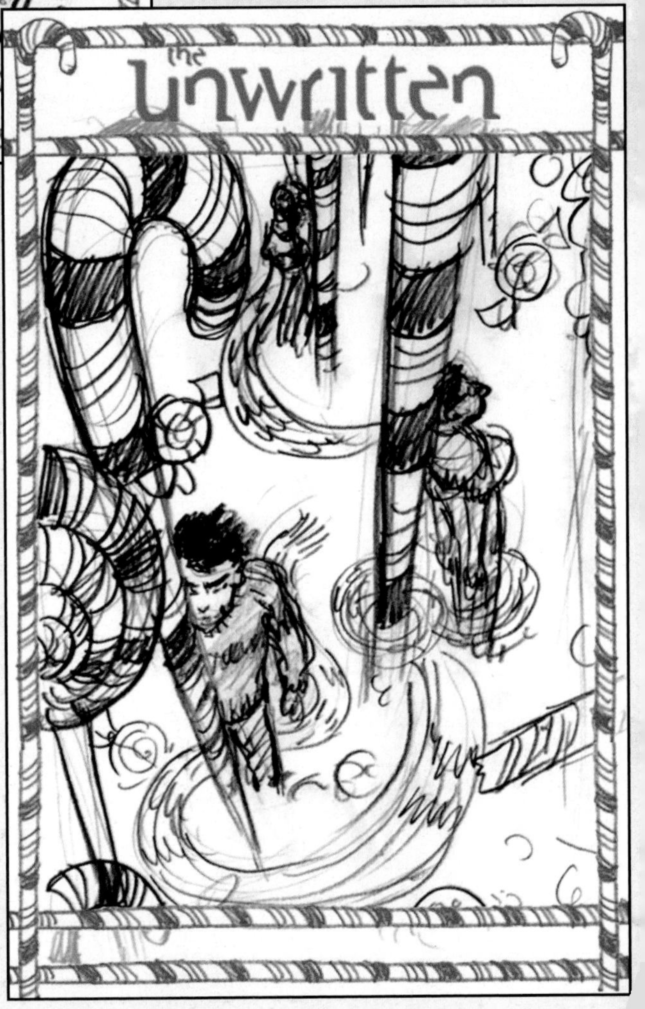
the Unwritten

Sketch for cover issue #

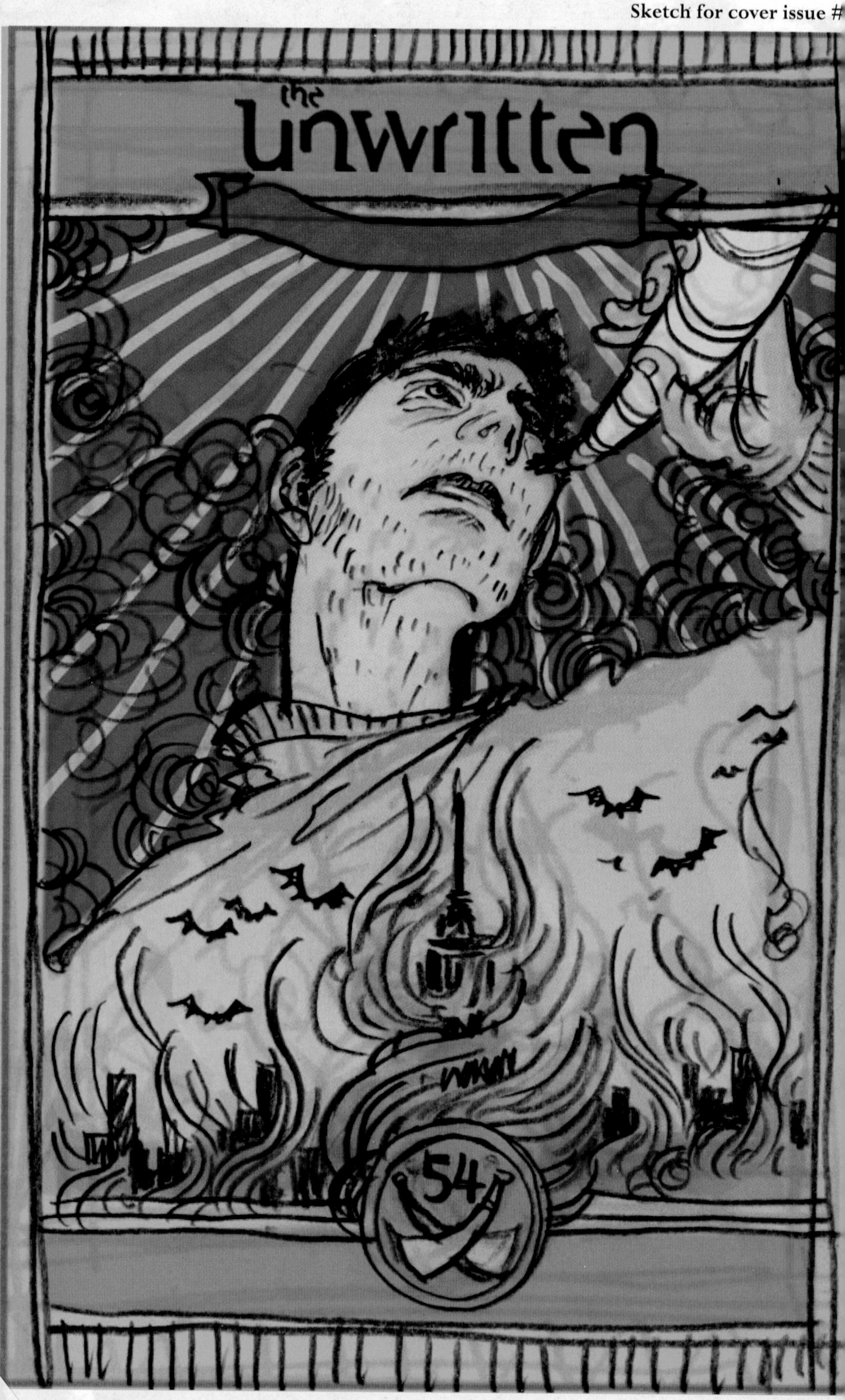

the
unwritten
54